This ambitious study, by a leading Spanish social scientist, analyses the mutual relationships between politics and the economy. Focusing on the experiences of Southern and Eastern Europe, it examines the complex interdependence between democracies, economic growth, social redistribution, and political culture. Are democratization processes the product of previous experiences of development, or of economic crisis? Can political regimes influence economic development and the distribution of material resources? In a context of economic constraints, to what extent are social democratic governments able to present a distinct identity in their policies? And can democratic governments, once established, increase support for democratic principles?

Professor Maravall explores these and other crucial questions utilizing a wealth of evidence from official statistics to public opinion polls. His appendices also provide chronologies of the most influential studies on these topics, offering valuable background information and ideas for further reading.

OXFORD STUDIES IN DEMOCRATIZATION

Series editor: Laurence Whitehead

• • • • • • • • •

REGIMES, POLITICS, AND MARKETS

OXFORD STUDIES IN DEMOCRATIZATION

Series editor: Laurence Whitehead

. . . .

Oxford Studies in Democratization is a series for scholars
and students of comparative politics and related disciplines.
Volumes will concentrate on the comparative study of the
democratization processes that accompanied the decline and
termination of the cold war. The geographical focus of the
series will primarily be Latin America, the Caribbean,
Southern and Eastern Europe, and relevant experiences in
Africa and Asia.

OTHER BOOKS IN THE SERIES

The New Politics of Inequality in Latin America:
Rethinking Participation and Representation
Douglas A. Chalmers

Human Rights and Democratization in Latin America:
Uruguay and Chile
Alexandra Barahona de Brito

Citizenship Rights and Social Movements:
A Comparative and Statistical Analysis
Joe Foweraker and Todd Landman

Democracy Between Consolidation and
Crisis in Southern Europe
Leonardo Morlino

The Bases of Party Competition in Eastern Europe:
Social and Ideological Cleavages in Post Communist States
Geoffrey Evans and Stephen Whitefield

The International Dimensions of Democratization:
Europe and the Americas
Laurence Whitehead

Regimes, Politics, and Markets

Democratization and Economic Change in Southern and Eastern Europe

....

JOSÉ MARÍA MARAVALL

Translated by
JUSTIN BYRNE

OXFORD UNIVERSITY PRESS
1997

Oxford University Press, Great Clarendon Street, Oxford OX2 6DP

Oxford New York

Athens Auckland Bangkok Bogota Bombay
Buenos Aires Calcutta Cape Town Dar es Salaam
Delhi Florence Hong Kong Istanbul Karachi
Kuala Lumpur Madras Madrid Melbourne
Mexico City Nairobi Paris Singapore
Taipei Tokyo Toronto
and associated companies in
Berlin Ibadan

Oxford is a trade mark of Oxford University Press

Published in the United States
by Oxford University Press Inc., New York

© José María Maravall 1997

British Library Cataloguing in Publication Data
Data available

Library of Congress Cataloging in Publication Data
Data available
ISBN 0-19-828083-1

1 3 5 7 9 10 8 6 4 2

Typeset by Graphicraft Typesetters Ltd., Hong Kong
Printed in Great Britain
on acid-free paper by
Bookcraft (Bath) Ltd
Midsomer Norton, Somerset

．．．．．．．．．．．．．．．．

Preface

．．．．．．．．．．．．．．．．

This book analyses the mutual influences between politics and the economy. More specifically, it studies the relationships between democracies, economic growth, social redistribution, and political culture. Do democracies promote economic development or, on the contrary, are dictatorships more efficient? Are democratization processes the product of previous experiences of development, or of economic crises? Are democracies able to redistribute resources better and more equitably than dictatorships? And, finally, can democracies increase the number of democrats? These are the principal questions which this book will explore from a comparative perspective, examining above all the experiences of Southern and Eastern Europe.

The book may be considered as an exercise in 'thinkful wishing'. It defends the thesis that democratization processes took place in the context of economic difficulties which were to a large extent attributed to the political institutions of the dictatorships, even if these difficulties came after a long period of economic growth. It also argues that the new democracies had more incentives and information to face the economic crises than the authoritarian regimes, whilst the capacity of the governments depended on the nature and extent of their mandates, the degree of consensus, and the nature of political learning within their societies. And, that despite the tendency for the macroeconomic policies of the different governments to converge, inspired by the intellectual maps of their political leaders, social democratic and conservative governments continued to be distinguished by their redistributive outcomes, fundamentally due to the differences in their fiscal and social policies. Finally, the book maintains that democrats usually preceded democracy, the legitimacy of which was to a large extent autonomous of economic results, whilst citizens' opinion of their regimes, and of politics in general, was mainly determined by the actions of politicians, the social conditions of life, and the performance of the institutions.

Democracy is not just a means to an end; *même défoncée*, to use

Paul Eluard's words, it is an end in itself. However, to what extent can democracy also be defended in instrumental terms? And, more particularly, must we accept the existence of what Kohli has called the 'cruel choice' between development and democracy, or that democratization implies a conservative formula with respect to the redistribution of material resources and life chances?[1] The 'thinkful wishing' behind this book is that these questions may be answered in the negative. It might be suggested, of course, that this standpoint introduces a valorative bias into the reasoning and discussion of the empirical evidence. Yet we know that 'neutral' positions do not exist, that biases may serve as a source of intellectual interpretations, and that the potentially distorting effects of ideological preferences are reduced when the arguments, and the evidence on which they are based, are subjected to open debate and personal reflexivity.[2] What matters is not ideological neutrality or valorative ascesis, but intellectual honesty, the coherence of the arguments, and the strength of the evidence presented.

The decision to study the cases of Southern and Eastern Europe largely reflects the adoption of Mill's 'method of agreement' in order to explain similar processes in very different societies.[3] Thus, when comparing the evolution of the economies of Portugal, Greece, and Spain, Hungary, Poland, and the Czech Republic during the dictatorship, the transition, and democracy in Chapters 2 and 3, I am looking for common characteristics which may be explained by political factors despite the differences in the nature of the previous regimes and their economic systems. And, when analysing the policies of the social democratic and conservative governments in France, Greece, and Spain in Chapter 4, I am interested in discovering the extent to which similar ideologies gave rise to comparable

---

[1] Atul Kohli, 'Democracy and Development', in John P. Lewis and Valeriana Kallab (eds.), *Development Strategies Reconsidered* (Washington DC, Overseas Development Council, 1986), 156.

[2] More than fifty years ago Otto Neurath argued that '"wishful thinking" is often accused of distorting argument. I think that this criticism of "wishful thinking" may be reasonable, but one should not overlook that there is no "neutral" position from which we may judge. And further, love and hate are often good teachers; people may select certain problems and pile up scientifically sound arguments,—let us speak of "thinkful" wishing in such cases. People full of "thinkful" wishing may present the same scientific material as people of other habits but may combine it differently. In this way a sociologist may support scientifically some decisions without becoming unscientific.' See his 'Foundations of the Social Sciences' in the *International Encyclopedia of Unified Science*, ii, no. 1 (Chicago, University of Chicago Press, 1944), 43.

[3] John Stuart Mill, *A System of Logic* (London, Longman, 1930), 253–66.

programmes, despite the differences in these countries' democratic experiences and levels of economic development. At the same time, I have limited the number of cases studied in an attempt to control the variables and avoid additional variations in the economic and political pre-conditions. This type of analysis contrasts with the cross-sectional approach developed in Chapter 1.

This book has been influenced by my personal involvement in democratic and social democratic politics in Spain over many years. I have also discussed arguments and information presented in this book with politicians and political scientists in the Southern and Eastern European countries studied here, in visits that were sometimes academic, sometimes political. Thus, participation was intimately related to observation. In the more strictly academic world, many of the arguments have been presented in my courses at the Instituto Juan March, the Universidad Complutense of Madrid, as well as at Columbia University when I taught as the Edward Larocque Tinker Visiting Professor. Parts of the book have also been discussed in a series of lectures I gave in the Jean Monnet Chair at the European University Institute in Florence, and in the Minda de Gunzburg Center for European Studies of Harvard University. I would like to thank Grzegorz Ekiert, Timothy Colton, Yves Mény, Gösta Esping-Andersen, Colin Crouch, and Alessandro Pizzorno for their comments and observations on these occasions. I have also used parts of the text in articles published in the *Journal of Democracy*, the *Rivista Italiana di Scienza Politica*, and *Claves*.

Norbert Lechner, Edward Malefakis, Juan Linz, Nikiforos Diamandouros, Larry Diamond, José Ramón Montero, Lena Kolarska-Bobinska, Joaquín Arango, László Bruszt, Richard Gunther, János Simon, and Marta Lagos have given helpful comments or information relating to various parts of the book. Conversations with Javier Pradera, Joaquín Almunia, and Adam Przeworski over the years have provided a major intellectual stimulus in the writing of this book. In crucial moments I have benefited from the support and encouragement of José Luis Yuste. The intellectual atmosphere of the Instituto Juan March has made this an ideal place in which to work on this study. The research was largely possible thanks to Project AME91-0257 of the Spanish Comisión Interministerial de Ciencia y Tecnología. I am in debt to Mark Ungar, Carlos Maravall, and Pilar Gangas for their help with the statistical analysis in Chapters 1, 3, 4, and 5. Justin Byrne has made an excellent job of the English version of the book. I would also like to thank the three anonymous referees of the Oxford University Press for their many thorough and highly stimulating comments.

Finally, the book is dedicated to Chus, Miguel, and Carlos. Their company was a privileged experience of affection, fun, intelligence, and complicity. It made the book possible and everything worthwhile.

....

Contents

....

List of Tables

List of Figures

Les routes même défoncées
Paul Eluard

....

1

....

Economies and Political Regimes

In this chapter I will analyse some aspects of the relationship between the economy and politics in the new democracies. I am going to study this relationship from two perspectives in order to determine, first, whether politics affects economic performance, and secondly, whether this in turn has political consequences. I will begin by examining the effects economies have on regimes, in order to discover if economic development fosters democratization, if, conversely, it stabilizes dictatorships, or whether it is the economic failure of dictatorships which leads to democracy. Secondly, I will study the effects of regimes on the economy, to see if it is possible to differentiate between the efficiency of dictatorships and democracies, and if so, how these differences might be explained.

We live in a period of exceptional experimentation in democracy and political institutions. The number of democracies doubled during the fifteen years after the 'revolution of the carnations' in Portugal in April 1974. Competitive elections were held in Portugal, Greece, and Spain; in Argentina, Bolivia, Brazil, Chile, Uruguay, Paraguay, Peru, and the Philippines; in South Korea; in Pakistan; in Turkey; in the countries of Central and Eastern Europe; and in the federations of the former Soviet Union. Yet in the majority of these countries the emergence of new democracies coincided with deep economic crises which were particularly acute in countries such as Brazil, Argentina, Peru, Hungary, Poland, or Yugoslavia. This combination of political and economic transformations poses an enormous challenge to the social sciences. What can they tell us about the viability of different institutions, the cultural characteristics which influence the consolidation or 'quality' of democracies, or the relationships between the economy and politics, between efficiency and legitimacy? To what extent can they help us to interpret scenarios, to identify and evaluate different alternatives, to take decisions? The challenge is all the greater since democracies are now established very rapidly. Whilst in Britain democratization took two centuries, the slowest contemporary processes (for example in Brazil or Poland) have lasted ten years, whilst the fastest (as in the cases of Czechoslovakia, Romania, Argentina, or Greece) have taken just a few days. Democratization no longer consists of a slow and gradual evolution, during which the participants can negotiate the rules of the game and establish systems of mutual guarantees. The time-scale in Robert Dahl's analysis of the establishment of democratic regimes has been drastically reduced: the sequences have become shorter, and competitive pluralism no longer precedes mass participation.[1] It is possible, therefore, that the accumulated knowledge of the social sciences, the comparison of experiences, and the availability of models, may compensate for the brevity of the time available to construct viable democracies.

This chapter presents a very general analysis of the relationship between the economy and politics in democratization processes, examining the two sides of this relationship, in other words, the dual direction of causality. What effect do economies have on regimes? And what effect do regimes have on economies?

1.1. The Economic Conditions of Democratization

Let us begin with the first side of the problem: the economy as a cause of democracy. The question can be put as follows: is political change generated by economic development or by economic crisis? Is it due to economic success or failure? As is often the case in the social sciences, both explanations have coexisted somewhat paradoxically. Two mutually exclusive causes have been put forward to explain democratization. That is, both development and crisis have been used to explain the same result, namely the collapse of dictatorships and the establishment of democratic regimes.

Perhaps the most long-standing thesis is that which presents development as a cause of democracy. This thesis has been supported by extensive empirical evidence, mainly drawn from comparative quantitative studies. Following Seymour Martin Lipset's seminal work,[2] some thirty studies of this type have been carried out covering a wide range of different countries. On the basis of

---

[1] Robert A. Dahl, *Polyarchy* (New Haven, Yale University Press, 1971), ch. 3.

[2] Seymour Martin Lipset, 'Some Social Requisites of Democracy: Economic Development and Political Legitimacy', *American Political Science Review*, 53/1 (1959), 69–105.

the statistical analysis of a small number of variables, their empirical generalizations have repeatedly concluded that economic growth facilitates democratization. However, this thesis contains a number of weak points derived from the logic of the argument and the evidence on which it is based.

The relationship between economic development and political democracy has frequently been understood in functional terms. Democracy 'requires' a certain level of economic development whilst, in turn, there comes a point when economic development 'requires' democratic institutions. This vision has been shared by various traditions within the social sciences. In this way, a Marxist would reason that the development of the forces of production has political consequences, and that, as Lenin affirmed in *State and Revolution*, democracy constitutes the best 'shell' for capitalism. Meanwhile, a functionalist would argue that societies are systems of interrelated, functionally integrated institutions which must always maintain a necessary 'degree of fit'. In this way, political change would consist of an adjustment to a prior economic change. Thus, the logic of this type of explanation leads to the conclusion that there are certain specific requisites for democracy, that only when these are met will democracy be possible (that is, will it appear and survive), but also that when these requisites are satisfied democracy will result.

Let us examine the reasoning according to which democracy is generated by economic development in a little more detail. The relationship between the economy and politics is presented in terms of probability. The most important empirical studies of democratizations do not defend the existence of a mechanical, deterministic relationship between economic development and democracy. Rather, they merely affirm that if the former takes place, the probability of the latter occurring increases.[3] No law of destiny guarantees that a developed country will be democratic,

---

[3] The following are just some examples of this type of argument from the last few decades. In 1959 Lipset maintained that 'democracy is related to the state of economic development. . . . And the factors subsumed under economic development carry with it the political correlate of democracy.' More than thirty years later he reasserted the same thesis: 'The available data on economic levels and democratization suggests . . . that the correlation between them is more pronounced in the early 1980s than in the late 1950s.' Seymour Martin Lipset, 'Some Social Requisites of Democracy', 75 and 80; Seymour Martin Lipset, Kyoung-Ryung Seong, and John C. Torres, 'A Comparative Analysis of the Social Requisites of Democracy', *International Social Science Journal*, 136 (1993), 157.

Bollen and Jackman suggest that 'the level of economic development has a pronounced effect on political democracy, even when other non-economic factors

or a poor country a dictatorship. If the causality is weak, this is because it reflects the considerable room for manœuvre societies enjoy in the face of the determinism of the structural conditions. Economic development would only favour democracy, and exceptions would always exist: Germany in the 1930s, for example, or conversely, India or Costa Rica. Thus, economic development would not be a sufficient cause of democracy,[4] nor would the relationship exclude the possibility of involutions of political regimes taking place despite economic development. Nor, moreover, would the relationship be linear, whether over time or among countries with different levels of development. The probabilities of democratization would increase during certain phases of economic development and decline in others,[5] and they would not augment before a certain minimum threshold is reached, nor after a maximum has been surpassed. These economic 'thresholds' of democracy correspond to what Samuel P. Huntington has labelled 'the transition zone': on entering this, the prospects for democratization multiply. Huntington developed this argument in relation to countries at an intermediate level of development, precisely those that have accounted for two-thirds of all the democratizations which have taken place since 1974. After a period of growth, these countries entered this 'transition zone'; as a result, in three out of four cases they had established democratic regimes fifteen years later. In Huntington's words: 'In considerable measure, the wave of democratizations that began in 1974 was the product of the economic growth of the previous two decades.'[6] According to this thesis, sooner

are considered.' Kenneth A. Bollen and Robert W. Jackman, 'Economic and Non-economic Determinants of Political Democracy', *Research in Political Sociology*, 1 (1985), 38.

   In a study covering 125 countries between 1960 and 1985, Helliwell indicated that 'countries at higher income levels are more likely to have democratic forms of government.' John F. Helliwell, 'Empirical Linkages between Democracy and Economic Growth', *Working Paper no. 4066* (Cambridge, Mass., National Bureau of Economic Research, 1992), 21.

   [4] In 1971 Dahl emphasized the probabilistic character of the relationship, a point which has subsequently been noted by most authors. See for instance, Lipset, Seong, and Torres, 'A Comparative Analysis', 156, 158, 170.

   [5] Lipset originally argued that the relationship was linear. Subsequently, Robert W. Jackman suggested that it was curvilinear in 'On the Relation of Economic Development to Democratic Performance', *American Journal of Political Science*, 17 (1973), 611–21. Finally, Lipset, Seong, and Torres have described it as N-shaped, with probability declining after an initial period of development and then rising again in a later phase.

   [6] Samuel P. Huntington, *The Third Wave: Democratization in the Late Twentieth Century* (Norman, University of Oklahoma Press, 1991), 61.

or later developmental dictatorships usually discover that the aspirations of their societies are not only confined to the sphere of consumption, but also encompass liberties and political rights.

The causal effect of economic development on political democratization would operate indirectly, through a variety of intermediate variables. In this way, as an economy develops it also becomes more complex, and hence more difficult to manage under authoritarian institutions. As Dahl argues, the long-term performance of an advanced economy will be less productive under coercion than if based on voluntary compliance: that is, authoritarian diktats will be less efficient than collective negotiation.[7] Moreover, the social order will also become more plural, and in consequence resources will become less concentrated, coercion less viable, and demands for political pluralism more intense. Thus, social groups and organizations will acquire greater autonomy from the state, the number of intermediate associations will multiply, civil society will become stronger, a new equilibrium will be achieved in the relationship between this and the state, and new patterns of negotiation will replace the relations of imposition. Social polarization will be reduced; the improvement of living standards will no longer be a zero-sum game, in which one group may only benefit at the expense of another; and the middle classes will also become a more important force in the stratification system. The development of communications and education will strengthen society's collective capacity to exercise the rights of citizenship. And these economic and social conditions will eventually influence values, fostering tolerance, trust, and feelings of personal efficacy, which, in turn, are seen as the cultural foundations of democracy.[8]

Some of these intermediate variables, however, may not only depend on the level of economic development. Social reforms, for example, may distribute resources in very different ways. Poor countries are not inevitably characterized by the concentration of resources, the submissiveness of their societies, and extensive illiteracy. Factors other than the increased resources brought by development may enable these conditions to be altered. Hence it is possible for democracy to become established in these countries

---

[7] Dahl, *Polyarchy*, 77.

[8] Besides Dahl, see Alex Inkeles and Larry Diamond, 'Personal Development and National Development: A Cross-National Perspective', in Alexander Szalai and Frank M. Andrews (eds.), *The Quality of Life* (London, Sage, 1990); Larry Diamond, 'Economic Development and Democracy Reconsidered', in Gary Marks and Larry Diamond (eds.), *Reexamining Democracy* (Newbury Park, Calif., Sage, 1992), 117–19.

if material needs and social inequality are reduced. In this way, social policies and education acquire a specific value; a functionalist would consider them to be functional alternatives to economic development. As a result, development would not be a necessary cause of democratization. These empirical studies do recognize this possibility:[9] in fact, this is the basis of many of the hopes of survival that a democracy may hold in a poor country.

There is a further reason why the economy affects dictatorships. The more dictatorships claim legitimacy on the grounds of performance rather than ideology, the more vulnerable they become to economic crises. This vulnerability not only affects governments but also the regimes themselves. For, as Huntington has argued, under authoritarianism the 'legitimacy of the rulers' (based on performance) overlaps with 'procedural legitimacy' (based on the rules of the game). When the former collapses, so too does the latter. In democracies, in contrast, the two are more clearly differentiated, hence it is possible to change the government whilst preserving the regime. A double legitimacy crisis of this type preceded the transitions in Southern and Eastern Europe, in Argentina, Uruguay, Peru, Brazil, and the Philippines. After examining 23 governments in East and South-East Asia, Latin America, and Africa, Stephen Haggard and Robert Kaufman have shown that 'authoritarian regimes tended to rely more heavily than democratic ones on purely instrumental appeals and were thus particularly vulnerable to "legitimation crises" when economic conditions turned sour.'[10] Appeals of this kind can only be made as long as economic growth continues: when it stops, the crisis will also be political.

Thus, democracy appears to be an 'unintended consequence' of economic development, the result of a contradictory combination of economic success and political obsolescence. By developing their economies, dictatorships sow the seeds of their own destruction. In Dahl's words 'the more they [dictatorships] succeed in transforming the economy (and with it, inevitably, society), the more they are threatened with political failure'.[11]

These are the main arguments defended by a long tradition of

---

[9] In this sense Helliwell writes that 'schooling goes some distance in explaining the variations in democracy not captured by differences in GDP per capita', Helliwell, 'Empirical Linkages', 8.

[10] Stephen Haggard and Robert R. Kaufman (eds.), *The Politics of Economic Adjustment* (Princeton, Princeton University Press, 1992), 330.

[11] Dahl, *Polyarchy*, 78.

comparative quantitative research. Nearly all of the 30-odd studies produced over the last three decades have reached similar conclusions.[12] Accordingly, these should probably be taken as the frame of reference for any analysis of the economic conditions for democratization.[13] In this way, when the experiences of Spain, Portugal, Greece, Hungary, Poland, or the Czech Republic are examined, we need to verify whether democratization was preceded by high rates of economic growth and took place when these countries had reached certain 'thresholds' of development; whether the political institutions of the dictatorships found it increasingly difficult to manage their economies (in Eastern Europe because these were both communist economies and political dictatorships); whether economic change generated more plural social orders and stronger and more autonomous civil societies; whether the material and cultural evolution of these societies reduced polarization and fuelled the extension of democratic values; and whether the problems of economic performance provoked a crisis of legitimacy for de-ideologized dictatorships.

Taking these comparative studies and their quantitative generalizations as the frame of reference does not imply that we are unaware of their many theoretical and empirical problems. The use of very aggregate data has often led to oversimplified classifications of complex national experiences. Stereotypes have been used abundantly; thus, many authors have argued that all economically developed countries now have democratic regimes, with the sole exceptions of Singapore and the Gulf States, and that economic development seems to have facilitated democratization processes such as those of Southern Europe, Chile, or South Korea. However, this interpretation substantially misrepresents the political processes in these countries. Thus, in Chapter 2, I will challenge such interpretations of political change in Southern Europe. As for South Korea, this explanation overlooks the fact that for the Park Chung Hee government economic growth (averaging 7% per annum between 1967 and 1987) was an instrument for the maintenance of authoritarian rule, and that the democratization process which eventually brought 26 years of dictatorship to an end was largely due to the growing strength of the opposition, the

---

[12] A chronological list of these studies is given in Appendix 1.

[13] For an example of comparative historical research that takes these empirical generalizations as its frame of reference, see Dietrich Rueschemeyer, Evelyne H. Stephens, and John D. Stephens, *Capitalist Development and Democracy* (Cambridge, Mass., Polity Press, 1992), ch. 2.

political incompetence of President Chun Doo Hwan, and a radically different international situation. As for Chile, the country had a long history of democracy before Pinochet's *coup d'état* in 1973, and in the mid-1980s it had yet to recover the level of economic development it had enjoyed in 1970.

Many of the comparative quantitative studies whose conclusion is that they have demonstrated an acceptable causality[14] merely show a weak and rough statistical correlation, and the accuracy of their measurements is often spurious. The definition of indicators and the selection of countries and chronological periods have always proved problematic.[15] The dependent and independent variables are not always well specified: for example, it is sometimes unclear whether the explanation refers to the emergence or the persistence of democracies, or whether the independent variable is the level of development or the rate of growth. The direction of causality can also be confusing: it is not always clear whether development promotes democracy or vice versa. A typical problem of functionalist logic is also recurrent: the use of teleological reasoning, in which democracy is not explained by its causes, but by its consequences (that is, by its functions). And this long tradition of research has produced only limited knowledge on the complex relationship between economies and political regimes and its role in the genesis of democracies; the same results would appear to be derived from distinct causes, and the same causes would appear to produce different results.

Let us consider the way in which a single result, democratization, is attributed to antithetical causes. Whilst many quantitative studies suggest that economic development promotes democratization, there is also a considerable body of statistical evidence that suggests that the latter more frequently occurs when economies are in crisis. If that is the case, transitions would be a result of the failure of the dictatorships' economic management, rather than the 'unintended consequences' of their economic success. Fernando Limongi and Adam Przeworski concluded from their analysis of the Latin American dictatorships between 1945 and 1988 that the likelihood of democratization taking place was twice as high if the economy had been in crisis the previous year than if it had been

[14] Although almost half the variance remains unexplained.

[15] For example, Phillips Cutright mixed measurements of democracy with measurements of political stability in 'National Political Development: Measurement and Analysis', *American Sociological Review*, 28 (1963), 253–64. Similarly, Jackman mixed measurements of democracy with measurements of electoral participation in the study mentioned in n. 5.

expanding.[16] The democratizations from communist regimes or military dictatorships during the 1980s occurred in the context of falling GDPs in real terms, fiscal crises of the states, and overwhelming foreign debt burdens. These difficulties or crises were neither a necessary nor a sufficient cause of the collapse of the dictatorships. But they did generally undermine the dictatorships' claims to legitimacy on the grounds of their greater economic efficiency. Hence they shattered the cornerstone of what might be called the 'authoritarian pact': the promise of economic prosperity in return for political acquiescence. In this way, democratization would be the result of a combination of both economic and political failure.

Table 1.1 provides some additional information on this point.[17] It covers the period from 1951 to 1988 and contains data on the collapse of 46 democracies (from 94 regimes of this type) and 43 dictatorships (from a total of 107). This evidence shows that below a level of development of US$2,000 per capita, 31 of the 38 democracies and 24 of the 67 dictatorships collapsed; between US$2,000 and $4,000 13 of the 23 democracies and 11 of the 21 dictatorships fell; above US$4,000 2 of the 33 democracies and 8 of the 19 dictatorships came to an end. If we take into account both the level of development and the annual growth rate (throughout the regime's existence, although never before 1951), it can be seen that the crises of dictatorships were slightly more frequent when these levels and rates were high. Above all, however, the data show that, although both democracies and dictatorships proved vulnerable at low levels of per capita income, democracies were weaker in these circumstances and when growth rates were negative or

[16] Fernando Limongi and Adam Przeworski, 'Democracy and Development in South America, 1946–1988', *Working Paper 1994/55* (Madrid, Center for Advanced Study in the Social Sciences, Instituto Juan March de Estudios e Investigaciones, 1994), 6–8.

[17] Table 1.1 has been compiled from information provided by Adam Przeworski. From data referring to 139 countries and 238 regimes between 1950 and 1990, Przeworski argues that economic development does not promote democratization, and that democracies are vulnerable at low levels of development and negative growth rates. However, with regard to growth rates, aggregate data for long periods does not allow us to identify clearly the combination of economic development and acute crises that I consider lethal for many dictatorships. Furthermore, his data on levels of development show that, when these surpass a certain threshold, democracies prove immune to crises (i.e. negative growth rates). Przeworski's argument is particularly pertinent in the case of poor democracies facing economic crises. See Adam Przeworski and Fernando Limongi, 'Modernization: Theories and Facts', *Working Paper no. 4* (Chicago Center on Democracy, University of Chicago, 1994).

TABLE 1.1. *Economic conditions of regime crises, 1951–1988*

A. Level of development of regimes which collapsed (in US $, 1985)	Dictatorships		Democracies	
	%	no.	%	no.
Less than 1,000	7	3	24	11
Between 1,000 and 2,000	49	21	44	20
Between 2,000 and 3,000	9	4	15	7
Between 3,000 and 4,000	16	7	13	6
Between 4,000 and 5,000	14	6	4	2[b]
More than 5,000	5	2[a]	—	—
TOTAL	100	43	100	46
Average per capita income	2,468		1,778	
B. Growth rates of regimes which collapsed				
Negative	14	6[c]	17	8[d]
Stagnation (±1%)	14	6	31	14
Positive	72	31[e]	52	24[f]
TOTAL	100	43	100	46
Average annual growth rate	2.9		1.2	

[a] The two cases were Spain in 1977 and South Korea in 1988.

[b] The two cases were Uruguay in 1973 and Argentina in 1976.

[c] The two most extreme cases were Argentina in 1963 (–3.6%) and Bolivia in 1982 (–4.2%).

[d] The two most notable cases were Bolivia in 1980 (–5.7%) and Haiti in 1961 (–5.2%).

[e] The cases with the highest rates were South Korea in 1988 (16.4%), Portugal in 1976 (9.3%), Spain in 1977 (8.2%), Ecuador in 1989 (7.6%), Pakistan in 1962 (7.5%), Greece in 1974 (7.2%), and Thailand in 1979 (7.1%).

[f] The cases with the highest rates were Greece in 1967 (8.2%), Brazil in 1964 (8.2%), Thailand in 1976 (6.2%), Panama in 1968 (5.8%), Argentina in 1966 (5.5%), and Bolivia in 1968 (5.1%).

stagnant. In contrast, at higher income levels, the democracies were more stable than the dictatorships. Thus, these data suggest that economic development reinforces democracies more than dictatorships. They also raise a number of questions: for example, a large proportion of the dictatorships in Huntington's 'transition zone' were able to survive, whilst a notable number of democratizations occurred outside that zone. But the data have limitations: they only refer to cases of regime crisis; they compare regimes with very different lifespans; the growth rates refer to averages over sometimes very long periods, which cannot reflect those cases in which the change of regime was influenced by a sharp economic downturn after a prolonged period of growth. Hence the table reflects the highly inconclusive nature of the relationship between economies and regimes. This relationship only involves 'favourable' or 'unfavourable' conditions; the probabilities vary very little; and other factors may play a decisive role in bringing about democratization. As a result, political actors possess considerable autonomy. But what seems evident is that the promotion of democracy requires support for its economic development, not the 'modernization' of dictatorships.

These apparently contradictory relationships between economy and democracy may be due to an analytical confusion. We have already seen that two contradictory causes (development and crisis) appear to have the same effect. Yet to what extent is this true? The contradiction may simply be due to the fact that we are studying different processes, which are not well reflected in the dependent and independent variables. Suppose, for example, that the breakdown of a dictatorship is the result of economic collapse; this breakdown would probably imply a traumatic rupture with the past and be followed by a period of profound political and economic instability, which might or might not lead to democracy, and, in any event, if democratization were to occur, the new regime would be hard-pressed to survive. Imagine, on the contrary, a transition coming in the wake of a long period of growth followed by a sharp economic crisis which would invalidate the exchange of material prosperity and political acquiescence. Sectors of the population would blame the interruption of economic development on the political regime; social movements created during the period of expansion would intensify the pressure for political change; and democratization would be the consequence of longer-term, and more gradual, transformations than in the first example. Provided that the economic crisis does not continue indefinitely, the prospects of the new regime becoming consolidated might be greater.

This debate over which economic conditions favour democratic transitions is not solely of academic interest. It may shed light on the dilemmas faced by new democratic governments. If democracies tend to be born in the context of economic crises (as was indeed the case throughout the 1980s), then these governments will be unable to concentrate on political problems. Rather, they will encounter a twofold problem: how to overcome the crisis and promote economic development, and how to consolidate the newly established institutions. That is, they will not be in a position to follow the traditional advice of political scientists: to avoid taking on economic and political reforms simultaneously, overloading agendas, and overlapping conflicts. The economic reforms required to surmount the crises inevitably lead, at least temporarily, to a deterioration in the living conditions of a very large part of the population. If this deterioration continues, the legitimacy of the new regime may be considerably weakened, unless the provision of political goods and social protection in case of need compensates for hardship. Moreover, these economic difficulties may erode the state's capacity (i.e. its resources), and undermine both public order and the reform process itself. Indeed, these problems have been experienced by many of the recent democracies.

What has been the nature of the economic crisis and the policy responses to it? During the two decades after 1960, the GDP of the Latin American countries grew at an average annual rate of 5.2%; in Eastern European countries, the net material product increased on average by 6.0% in the same period. In contrast, during the five years after 1980, there was zero growth in Latin America, and growth of less than 1% in Hungary, Poland, and Yugoslavia (the only communist countries for which the IMF had data). During the 1980s, the per capita GDP in Latin America fell by an average of 9.4%; the annual inflation rate rose from 55% in 1980 to 1,260% in 1990 (and topped more than 7,400% in countries such as Peru and Nicaragua), while the per capita debt rose to $1,556 in Argentina, $1,539 in Chile, and $769 in Brazil. In Eastern Europe, the per capita debt in Hungary reached $1,656 (the highest of any country in the world), $1,113 in Poland, and $444 in Czechoslovakia. The communist economies started to collapse as a result of their lack of competitiveness, state bankruptcy, the burden of price and production subsidies, the high degree of monopolization, the enormous imbalances in the consumer markets, and the low and ever-decreasing productivity of their economies.

The causes of the crisis are well known: the escalation of oil prices in 1974 and 1979; the changes in the international financial markets; the adoption of stiffer monetary policies by the industrialized creditor countries; the enormous increase in the cost of debts following the rise in interest rates after 1982; the fall in the price of exports from these debtor countries; and the radical change in capital flows. All this provoked a serious deterioration of the states' solvency, balance of payments deficits, the stagnation or decline of the GDP in real terms, and very high inflation rates.

The consequences were the exhaustion of the protectionist strategies and populist policies which had led to an inefficient expansion of the states, excessive economic regulation, uncontrolled expenditure, and massive public debt. Both in Latin America and in Eastern Europe, states faced major fiscal crises; authoritarian regimes were often also bankrupt regimes. Although the new democratic governments in Southern Europe faced far less dramatic economic conditions, the difficulties were also serious in terms of the stagnation of the GDP (with growth rates of less than 1%), rising inflation (over 20%), the public deficit, labour costs, and employment (above all in Spain, where 1,950,000 jobs disappeared between 1975 and 1985, whilst unemployment went up from 4.5 to 21.9%). Table 1.2 shows some of the differences in the economic conditions of a number of democratizations which took place from the mid-1970s onwards.

The economic crisis gradually led to a change in the paradigm of economic policies. Thus, it was increasingly accepted that markets were efficient instruments for the allocation of economic resources; that price systems were required in order to reflect shortages and distribute resources, and that open foreign trade would bring competition and new technologies. Accordingly, the reform blueprint consisted of ten main points:[18] tighter fiscal discipline; new public expenditure priorities; tax reform, consisting of widening the tax-base rather than raising rates; positive, and market-determined, interest rates; trade liberalization and the creation of an export-oriented economy; market-determined exchange rates; the removal of restrictions on direct foreign capital investment; the privatization of publicly owned companies; the deregulation of economic activities; and the establishment of guaranteed property rights. These were the basic elements of the stabilization policies and structural economic reforms introduced in Southern Europe, Latin America, and Eastern Europe. The reforms enacted in Poland, Bulgaria, Romania, the former Czechoslovakia, and Hungary shared such orientations; the differences had to do with the lesser or greater scope of the reforms, the pace at which they were introduced, and the extent to which they were accompanied by social policies.

Inevitably, these reforms have harsh effects. Stabilization, structural economic reform, and the reduction of subsidies restrict consumption and demand, lead to the closure of inefficient companies, higher unemployment, and lower real wages. Some economists believe that these costs are in fact indicators of the reforms'

---

[18] John Williamson (ed.), *Latin American Adjustment* (Washington, DC: Institute of International Economics, 1990), 8–17.

TABLE 1.2. *Economic conditions at the beginning of the transition*

	Portugal (1974)	Greece (1974)	Spain (1976)	Argentina (1983)	Uruguay (1984)	Brazil (1985)	Chile (1989)	Poland (1989)	Hungary (1989)
GDP per capita[a]	3,352	3,478	5,568	3,509	3,524	3,282	—	1,520	2,210
Growth during preceding 3 years	29.2	24.5	—	-13.4	-18.4	1.0	26.4	11.1	4.8
Total public expenditure[b]	—	—	25.9	20.0	22.7	24.2	29.3	38.7	56.2
Tax revenue[bd]	32.4	26.3	27.1	16.8	21.4	15.5	22.9	35.1	49.4
Tax on personal incomes[cd]	5.1	10.9	16.7	0.2	2.6	0.9	3.5	—	0.6
Public deficit[b]	—	4.0	0.3	13.7	5.6	11.5	—	—	—
Inflation the previous year (%)	19	21	17	349	61	235	21	66	15
Debt per capita[b]	134	331	—	1,556	1,117	769	1,539	1,113	1,656

Source: World Bank, *World Tables* (1989–90).

[a] In purchasing power parities: $US in 1980.
[b] As a percentage of GDP.
[c] As a percentage of total income.
[d] Data for Greece from 1981; Portugal and Spain, 1986; Argentina, Brazil, and Chile, 1987; Hungary and Poland, 1988.

success; at times this argument has been echoed somewhat masochistically by politicians. In this way, unemployment becomes a sign of economic efficiency. On a number of occasions, the Czech prime minister Vaclav Klaus had to argue that the country's low unemployment rate was not a sign that his economic policy had failed, and described full employment as 'irrational'.[19] However, this does not merely imply that blood, sweat, and tears are required from society, although that is certainly the case. The high costs of reforms are necessary and inevitable, but they alone do not guarantee the success of the reform programme, and they may well prove difficult for a new democracy to assimilate.

Yet are democracies incapable of facing these difficulties and surviving? Rather than the effects of economic development on democratization, let us now consider the second side of the relationship between economies and political regimes: namely the impact democracies have on development.

1.2. Democracy and Economic Efficiency

Because of the high costs of such reforms, it has often been argued that democracies would find it very difficult to implement them, and that if they tried to do so, they would be unlikely to survive. In other words, these arguments questioned the democracies' capacity to implement efficient policies at times of crisis, as well as the possibility that they could conserve sufficient political legitimacy in these circumstances.

The different interpretations of the relationship between the economy and political regimes can crudely be summed up in the following four theses:

(a) markets require democratic political regimes;
(b) markets require authoritarian regimes;
(c) democracies require markets; and
(d) democracies require central planning and public property.

It is possible, in turn, to distinguish three sequences of economic and political reforms.[20] In the first sequence, economic reforms

---

[19] When a journalist commented on the low level of unemployment in the Czech Republic, Klaus responded defensively, 'that is true, but it will rise'. See his two interviews in *El País*, 22 July 1991 and 9 May 1993.

[20] Peter Gourevitch, 'Democracy and Economic Policy: Elective Affinities and Circumstantial Conjunctures', *World Development*, 21/8 (1993), 1, 271–80; Stephen Haggard and Robert R. Kaufman, 'Economic Adjustment and the Prospects for Democracy', in Haggard and Kaufman (eds.), *Politics of Economic Adjustment*, 319–50.

precede political ones. The examples cited are Chile, Southern Europe, South Korea, and Taiwan. In the second, economic and political reforms take place simultaneously. The examples used are the former Soviet Union, Mexico, or Nigeria. In the third sequence, political reform precedes economic reform. This would be the case of Eastern Europe, Argentina, Brazil, Peru, Bolivia, or Uruguay. The examples are not always fortunate: to take just one case, in Mexico economic reforms in the 1980s were radical, while political reforms were very limited. But scepticism regarding the capacity of democratic regimes leads to the defence of the first sequence (the temporal priority of economic reforms). At times, these doubts also inspire a preference for authoritarian regimes which introduce market-orientated reforms, as opposed to hesitant democracies. This not only implies support for the first sequence, but also for the second thesis mentioned above, namely that markets require authoritarian regimes. The following statement by the Malaysian prime minister Mahathir Bin Mohammed is a good example of these pro-authoritarian arguments:

In the former Soviet Union and Eastern European countries, democracy was introduced along with the free market. The result is chaos and increased misery. Not only have the countries broken up, mainly through bloody civil wars, but there is actual recession and more hardship for the people than when the Communists ruled. One may ask whether democracy is the means or the end. Democracy at all costs is not much different from Communist authoritarianism, from the barrel of a gun.

In contrast,

in a number of East Asian countries, while democracy is still eschewed, the free market has been accepted and brought prosperity. Perhaps it is the authoritarian stability which enabled this to happen. Should we enforce democracy on people who may not be able to handle it and destroy stability?[21]

Scepticism regarding the economic efficiency of democracies has usually been based on two arguments. The first is that democracies are more vulnerable to pressure to increase immediate consumption at the expense of investment and growth. This would be the result of a collective action problem discussed by Mancur Olson, namely, that although in the long term different social groups would benefit from co-operative sacrifices, in the short term each would be interested in turning economic policy into a distributive game.[22]

[21] Speech to the *Europe–East Asia Economic Forum*, Hong Kong, 14 Oct. 1992.
[22] Mancur Olson, *The Rise and Decline of Nations* (New Haven, Yale University Press, 1982), 41–7.

Trade unions, in competition with each other, would lead demands for consumption; the more democratic the governments, the weaker they would be; it would be impossible for a party to win elections with a programme entailing immediate sacrifices, even when promising a better future in return. This would result in an inefficient distribution of the national income, cuts in investment programmes in favour of current consumption, less freedom of action for business, and lower growth rates. The second argument is linked to the first. The state is seen as the only potentially universalistic actor, as against other actors who behave sub-optimally. Thus, only if the state is sufficiently autonomous and insulated from particularist pressures will it be possible to promote the economic conditions required for growth.[23]

The new democracies would be particularly weak in terms of their ability to implement unpopular austerity and adjustment programmes. This weakness would be all the greater if the transition were brought about by a process of negotiation and compromise rather than by the defeat of a dictatorship. Unless it were able to improve the population's material conditions of life, the new regime would find it difficult to survive, its legitimacy would be fragile in society, while supporters of authoritarianism would maintain their power largely untouched. Moreover, the advent of new democratic regimes is usually accompanied by a multiplication of expectations. When these come up against the reality of economic restrictions, the likely result will be intense conflicts, governmental paralysis, and, eventually, populist policies. The evidence does indeed show that the vast majority of new democracies established in the 1980s experienced this multiplication of expectations. For many people, the new regimes promised not only political rights but also better material conditions. There is a wealth of information showing that this was the case in Spain. In the case of Chile, when the dictatorship ended a large majority of the population thought that democracy would promote more rapid economic development, control inflation more effectively, cut unemployment, solve the external debt problem, and reduce inequalities. The same was true in Eastern Europe. When asked what they associated democracy with, from 67% of the Czechoslovaks to 91% of the

[23] These arguments can be found in the introduction to Walter Galenson (ed.), *Labor and Economic Development* (New York, Wiley, 1959); Samuel P. Huntington, *Political Order in Changing Societies* (New Haven, Yale University Press, 1968), 32–59, 190–208; Samuel P. Huntington and Jorge I. Domínguez, 'Political Development', in Fred I. Greenstein and Nelson W. Polsby (eds.), *Handbook of Political Science*, iii (Reading, Mass., Addison-Wesley, 1975), 33–43.

Romanians said with improved economic conditions; and 45% of the former to 88% of the latter replied that they associated it with more jobs and less unemployment; and between 58% in Czechoslovakia and 80% in Bulgaria answered that they associated it with greater equality.[24]

For the sceptical vision of democracy, this evidence shows the vulnerability of the new regime's legitimacy, and confirms that stabilization plans and structural reforms are extremely difficult to implement. Given that economic austerity generates different types of political risks, authoritarian regimes would find it easier than democracies to adopt 'orthodox' economic policies. Hence this argument leads to the more or less explicit acceptance of the second of the theses mentioned above, namely that markets require authoritarian regimes. On the basis of the Latin American experience, James Malloy has written that 'present economic policy belies the prodemocratic rhetoric because, among other things, it demands decision-making centres able to impose policies resisted by almost all segments of society. This is a task that prior cycles show is beyond the capacity of other democratic regimes in Latin America.'[25]

Dictatorships, in contrast, would enjoy a number of advantages which would allow them to manage their economies more efficiently. The absence of electoral cycles and the lesser dependence of governments on popular support would increase the state's autonomy and its capacity to impose unpopular economic policies; their greater indifference to interest group pressures would reduce fiscal and budgetary problems and facilitate increased savings and investment; and the more limited rotation among holders of political office would make it easier for them to adopt a longer-term perspective when designing and executing reforms. In this sense, Haggard writes that

Institutions can overcome these collective-action dilemmas by restraining the self-interested behaviour of groups through sanctions; collective-action problems can be resolved by command. Since authoritarian political

[24] Antonio Alaminos, *Chile: Transición Política y Sociedad* (Madrid, Centro de Investigaciones Sociológicas, 1991), 134–7; László Bruszt and János Simon, *Political Culture, Political and Economical Orientations in Central and Eastern Europe during the Transition to Democracy* (unpublished manuscript, Hungarian Academy of Sciences, Budapest, 1991), 26, 33, 34.

[25] James M. Malloy, 'The Politics of Transition in Latin America', in James M. Malloy and Mitchell A. Seligson (eds.), *Authoritarians and Democrats: Regime Transitions in Latin America* (Pittsburgh, Pittsburgh University Press, 1987), 249.

arrangements give political elites autonomy from distributionist pressures, they increase the government's ability to extract resources, provide public goods, and impose the short-term costs associated with efficient economic adjustment.[26]

In so far as a state dominates civil society, restricting its rights and liberties, governments will have a greater capacity to carry out their decisions. The only requisite for an efficient economic policy would then be that the correct decisions are made. Hence the international institutions should use all their influence to this end. This is the essence of the political economy of authoritarianism: strong governments which follow the advice of the international financial institutions, i.e. domestic ruthlessness and external submissiveness. Nevertheless, whilst this might resolve the question of which regime would be more capable of implementing an economic policy, it tells us nothing about which regime has more incentives to adopt the most appropriate policy. There is no reason to believe that this capacity in itself necessarily leads to an efficient policy rather than to predatory behaviour. Why should a dictator enjoying autonomy from social pressure serve interests other than his own? Dictatorships possess greater independence from organized interests, but the power they exercise is also more arbitrary and discretional.

The argument that authoritarian regimes are more efficient has been backed up by a large body of empirical research. Most of the comparative quantitative studies carried out between the mid-1960s and the mid-1980s came to the conclusion that dictatorships promoted greater economic development than democracies.[27] Evidence for the supposedly greater capacity of authoritarian regimes to implement tough economic policies has mainly come from Latin America and East Asia. In their study of eight Latin American countries (Chile, Mexico, Costa Rica, Colombia, Venezuela, Brazil, Peru, and Argentina), Robert Kaufman and Barbara Stallings found that these countries achieved better results in terms of inflation, public deficit, and wages when under authoritarian regimes, whilst the economic performance of newly established democracies was poorer than that of consolidated democratic regimes.[28] Equally, in

---

[26] Stephen Haggard, *Pathways from the Periphery: The Politics of Growth in the Newly Industrializing Countries* (Ithaca, NY, Cornell University Press, 1990), 262.

[27] A chronological list of these studies is given in Appendix 2.

[28] Robert Kaufman and Barbara Stallings, 'Debt and Democracy in the 1980s: The Latin American Experience', in Barbara Stallings and Robert Kaufman (eds.), *Debt and Democracy in Latin America* (Boulder, Colo., Westview Press, 1989), 201–23. The problem with Kaufman's and Stallings's empirical evidence is that

the case of East Asia, none of the six countries with the greatest
rise in GDP over a period of 25 years (China, Indonesia, South Korea, Taiwan, Singapore, and Hong Kong) had democratic regimes
(although elections had been held and a political liberalization
was already under way in some); in none was power transferred
from one party to another during this period. These results are
usually compared with the case of India, where growth was little
over one-third of that of China during the 1980s, or that of Sri
Lanka, which grew little more than half as much as Taiwan in the
same period. Proponents of this argument also frequently cite the
cases of Franco's Spain and Pinochet's Chile, and somewhat paradoxically, in the former Soviet Union these cases were used as
arguments against Mikhail Gorbachev's political reforms.

Finally, the thesis that authoritarian regimes are more efficient
is usually rounded off with another argument already examined,
namely that developmental dictatorships eventually lead to democracy as an unintended result of the 'pluralist' impact their economic reforms have on society. Thus, the sequence of changes which
prioritizes economic over political reforms would be more favourable for both development and democracy. Andranik Migranian, a
political scientist and adviser to Boris Yeltsin, has written in this
sense that

it is necessary and inevitable for Russia to go through an authoritarian
phase of political development on its road to a market economy and a
democratic political system. . . . The absence of a parliament and of parties and opposition movements capable of using the massive discontent
against the president and the government, the control of the most important mass media, and a monolithic executive power create, for the president and the government, privileged possibilities to control the rise in
social tension in a less painful way and without serious unrest.[29]

It is obvious that democracy is not merely of 'instrumental' value,
that it has an 'intrinsic' value related to rights and liberties, and
that this is not only dependent on its capacity to promote relatively
greater economic development. Yet the impact of democracy on development is also much more complex than the pro-authoritarian
theses suggest. This complexity can be examined both from empirical and theoretical perspectives.

Let us begin by examining the empirical evidence. Experience

neither the data on growth rates and balance of payments, nor the experience of
Uruguay and Mexico, appear to fit in comfortably with their interpretation.

[29] Andranik Migranian, 'La Democracia Delegada', *El País*, 21 Oct. 1993, 15
and 16.

does not suggest that authoritarian regimes have a special capacity to survive economic crises, but quite the opposite. In fact, as the crisis deepened after 1982 the authoritarian regimes proved particularly politically vulnerable. Transitions to democracy multiplied during the 1980s whilst authoritarian involutions generally failed (albeit with exceptions such as Haiti, Pakistan, or Peru). Authoritarian regimes were also particularly sensitive to interest group pressures and many dictatorships were scarcely distinguished by the rigour of their economic policies. Fiscal crises and overwhelming foreign debt burdens were more often the result of the 'developmentalism' of dictatorships (the military regimes in Latin America and the communist regimes in Eastern Europe) than the 'populism' of the democracies. This was very much the experience of Argentina, Peru, and Brazil, Nicaragua, the Philippines, Haiti, Myanmar (Burma), the Central African Republic, Uganda, Zambia, or Zaire. Eastern Europe and the former Soviet Union are further examples of the same phenomena, not only because they were command economies but also because their regimes were dictatorships.

It is also true that when dictatorships were able to generate economic development, this did in fact eventually lead to unintended processes of liberalization and then to democracy. This was the case in Spain, South Korea from the early 1980s, and Taiwan after 1987 under Chiang Ching-kuo. Moreover, above a certain level of economic development, countries did tend to have democratic regimes. Thus, whilst approximately half of all governments were democracies in the 1980s, this was true of only two-fifths of the under-developed countries. In other words, democracies were concentrated in countries with developed economies, although they were not unusual (and still less impossible) in the rest. Economic growth could favour the viability of democracies, but democracies also facilitated development. After all, the only developed country in Asia was Japan. This case, along with that of Italy, undermines the thesis of the greater economic efficiency of dictatorships, since in neither country did the establishment of new democratic regimes prove an obstacle to post-war economic growth.

Towards the end of the 1980s, empirical comparative studies began to substantiate these impressions. The majority of these studies suggested that authoritarian regimes performed no better than democracies in a period of profound economic crisis.[30] Joan

---

[30] These studies are also listed in Appendix 2. The shift towards the conclusion that democracies achieve better economic results is perceptible in those studies published after 1985.

Nelson's analysis of the experience of thirteen countries and nineteen governments during the 1980s has shown that the dictatorships were more likely to fail: half either postponed introducing necessary reforms or proved incapable of implementing them successfully.[31] The economic record of the democracies varied, but the governments led by Arias and Monge in Costa Rica, Betancur in Colombia, Aquino in the Philippines, and Seaga in Jamaica performed better than those of Marcos in the Philippines, Rawlings in Ghana, Kaunda in Zambia, or Babangida in Nigeria. The democracies achieved better economic results in culturally cohesive societies, whilst the dictatorships performed comparatively better in those countries with greater ethnic, racial, or religious divisions. There were also significant regional differences, since democracies achieved relatively better results in Latin America and Africa, whilst in Asia their economic performance differed little from that of the dictatorships. Karen Remmer has also shown that new democracies managed their economies better in terms of the evolution of their GDPs and the control of the deficit.[32] Her study of 10 Latin American countries in the period from 1982 to 1989 (with a total of 29 years of dictatorship and 48 years of democracy between them), shows that whilst the democracies grew an average of 1.6% annually, the dictatorships averaged a mere 0.3%. Similarly, the democracies had an average annual public deficit of 3.6%, compared to the 9.9% of the dictatorships, even though in terms of unemployment (9% in the democracies compared to 8.9% in the dictatorships) both types of regimes achieved very similar results. On the other hand, John Helliwell concluded from his study of 98 countries between 1960 and 1985 that, even though 'the aggregate data do not support any significant linkage between the level of democracy and subsequent economic growth, . . . there appear to be important but relatively unstudied indirect linkages between democracy and economic growth flowing through education'.[33] In so far as the democracies devoted more attention and resources to education than the dictatorships, they laid the ground for future economic development.

---

[31] Joan Nelson, 'The Politics of Stabilization', in Richard E. Feinberg and Valeriana Kallab (eds.), *Adjustment Crisis in the Third World* (New Brunswick, Transaction Books, 1984), 99–118; Joan Nelson (ed.), *Economic Crisis and Policy Choice: The Politics of Adjustment in the Third World* (Princeton, Princeton University Press, 1990), Conclusions.

[32] Karen Remmer, 'Democracy and Economic Crisis: The Latin American Experience', *World Politics*, 42/3 (1990), 325–6.

[33] Helliwell, 'Empirical Linkages', 19 and 24.

TABLE 1.3. *Effects of democracy on growth, inflation, and the public deficit*

	Growth of GDP (1980–7)	Inflation (1980–90)	Public Deficit (1990)
Constant	−3.287*	49.452*	−1.811
	(1.115)	(23.507)	(1.602)
Index of Democracy (1980)	.052*	−.288	−.010
	(.016)	(.346)	(.023)
R²	.111	.009	.003
Signif. F	.002	.407	.664
No. of observations	81	80	63

* Statistically significant at 5% or less.

Note: Standard errors in parenthesis.

In view of the various political experiences considered here and the evidence presented by the many studies published over the decades, the most reasonable conclusion is that generalizations about the economic impact of political regimes are unconvincing. In Brazil, for example, both authoritarian and democratic governments opted for more 'heterodox' policies than in Uruguay. Yet in the light of the empirical evidence available, it is certainly not possible to maintain that democracy hinders development, or that authoritarian regimes implement more efficient economic policies. I believe that Przeworski and Limongi are right to argue that 'politics does matter, but regimes do not capture the relevant differences . . . it does not seem to be democracy or authoritarianism per se that makes the difference but something else'.[34] But in any event, democracies do not show a greater propensity for economic stagnation or populist policies which increase the public deficit. That is, while it is not possible to infer very illuminating conclusions concerning the connection between political regimes and economic performance from comparative quantitative analyses, no support can be drawn for the pro-authoritarian theses.

Further evidence for this conclusion comes from Table 1.3, which shows regressions referring to the degree of democracy in 82 countries during the 1980s and a series of economic indicators. The independent variable consists of an index based on the extent of

---

[34] Adam Przeworski and Fernando Limongi, 'Political Regimes and Economic Growth', *Journal of Economic Perspectives*, 7/3 (1993), 65.

political and civil rights and political participation measured on a scale of 1 to a 100.[35] The three economic indicators used are:

(*a*) economic growth rates between 1980 and 1987;
(*b*) annual inflation rates between 1980 and 1990; and
(*c*) the budget deficit as a percentage of the GDP in 1990.[36]

The results of the regressions show that the nature of the regime had a negligible impact on growth rates (although democracy had a slight positive effect). Thus, the degree of democracy in 1980 explains 11.1% of the variation in the economic growth rates between 1980 and 1987; an increase of one point in the democracy index produces an increase of .052 in the economic growth rate. At the same time, there is no statistically significant relationship between inflation or the public deficit and the degree of democracy in the different countries.

Empirical studies offer a further conclusion: independently of the fact that the institutional characteristics of democracy do not prejudice economic performance, this type of regime is more likely to implement policies promoting education and equality which, in turn, reinforce democracy. According to the World Bank,

by developing human resources and, more particularly, by investing in education, countries have been found to strengthen the basis for open political systems . . . , for a given level of income, improvements in social indicators are associated with freedom and liberty . . . political instability declines not only as incomes rises, but also as education improves.[37]

The results of a regression analysis between the index of democracy and three indicators of social expenditure are given in Table 1.4. The three indicators of social expenditure are:

(1) public expenditure on social welfare as a proportion of the GDP in 1980;
(2) public expenditure on health as a proportion of the GDP in 1986; and
(3) public expenditure on education in the same year as a proportion of GDP.[38]

---

[35] This index has been calculated from the data contained in the study by Charles Humana, *World Human Rights Guide*, 2nd edn. (London, Economist Publications, 1986).

[36] The three economic indicators have been taken from United Nations, *Human Development Report* (New York, Oxford University Press, 1990).

[37] World Bank, *World Development Report 1991* (Washington DC, World Bank, 1991), 134.

[38] As in Table 1.3, the index of democracy has been taken from Humana, *World Human Rights Guide*. The indicator of public social welfare expenditure comes

TABLE 1.4. *Effects of democracy on social welfare, health, and education expenditure (as percentage of GDP)*

	Public expenditure on welfare (1980)	Public expenditure on health (1986)	Public expenditure on education (1986)
Constant	−1.832	−1.017**	2.802*
	(2.576)	(.543)	(.576)
Index of	.194*	.059*	.025*
Democracy (1980)	(.038)	(.008)	(.009)
R^2	.236	.373	.085
Signif. F	.000	.000	.006
No. of observations	85	89	88

* Statistically significant at 5% or less.
** Statistically significant at 10% or less.

Note: Standard errors in parenthesis.

As the index of democracy rises, so too does public expenditure on social welfare and education. The index of democracy accounts for 23.6% of the variation in expenditure on social welfare, 37.3% of that on health, and 8.5% of that on education in 1986. A rise of one point in this index is linked to an increase of .19 in expenditure on social welfare, .059 on health, and .025 on education.

Democratic regimes, therefore, do not manage their economies to the detriment of social policies. The relationship between political regimes and equality has been widely debated,[39] but the

from Richard J. Estes, *The Social Progress of Nations* (New York, Praeger, 1984) and refers to 90 countries. The indicators of public health and education expenditure have been taken from the United Nations, *Human Development Report*, which was also used in Table 1.3 and are based on 93 and 94 countries respectively.

[39] The thesis that democracies promote equality has been advanced from both conservative and socialist standpoints since the end of the 18th century. For example, it was defended by John Stuart Mill during the debate on the Reform Bill of 1832, by Alexis de Tocqueville with respect to democracy in the United States, by Karl Kautsky and Friedrich Engels when they discussed the effects of universal suffrage. It was also sustained by Gerhard Lenski in *Power and Privilege* (New York, McGraw-Hill Book Co., 1966). This thesis is usually based on the arguments that the extension of the electorate brings egalitarian consequences, since by transferring political influence to less privileged social groups, regimes become more exposed to distributive conflicts, socialist parties win greater support and influence, elections act as the expression of democratic class struggle, and all parties need to win workers' votes.

comparative statistical evidence suggests that democratization does not necessarily take place at the expense of equality. On the contrary, economic efficiency and social policies appear to be more compatible under democratic than under authoritarian regimes. This has important consequences for the nature of the states. In democracies, these tend to be more complex, as well as to spend and raise more resources, largely in order to finance the more extensive social policies. As is well known, Alexis de Tocqueville argued that, under democracy, wider social demands and a greater public sensitivity to these should result in greater public expenditure and taxation.[40] Democracies have usually given rise to stronger civil societies, but also to states with more resources. The case of Southern Europe is paradigmatic of this tendency,[41] but as can be

Others, in contrast, have pointed out that lower-class voters do not necessarily perceive inequality as unjust, nor do they automatically demand income redistribution. It has also been argued that political rights (and political participation) are not exercised equally by all social groups, but to a greater extent by the more privileged. Political authoritarianism may therefore be more egalitarian, since it limits these political differences. Examples of these arguments can be found in Charles R. Beitz, 'Democracy in Developing Countries', in Raymond Gastil (ed.), *Freedom in the World: Political Rights and Civil Liberties* (New York, Freedom House, 1982), as well as in Samuel P. Huntington and Joan M. Nelson, *No Easy Choice: Political Participation in Developing Countries* (Cambridge, Mass., Harvard University Press, 1976). More recently, Stephen Haggard has argued from his study of South-East Asia that equality increases when labour organizations are excluded from the political arena, there is no strong corporatism, and labour markets are very flexible, since all these factors prevent social dualism (at the expense of unorganized groups which are also normally the most disadvantaged). These conditions are more likely to exist under authoritarian regimes. See Haggard, *Pathways from the Periphery*, 253.

Comparative statistical studies tend to provide greater support for the thesis that democracy has egalitarian effects, even though these studies normally suffer from technical problems relating to the sample of countries considered, the measurements of democracy, and the evaluation of inequality. Examples of comparative quantitative studies published over the years include Phillips Cutright, 'Inequality: A Cross-National Analysis', *American Sociological Review*, 32 (1967); Harold Wilensky, *The Welfare State and Equality* (Berkeley, University of California Press, 1975); Robert W. Jackman, *Politics and Social Equality* (New York, John Wiley and Sons, 1975); Kenneth Bollen and Robert W. Jackman, 'Political Democracy and the Size Distribution of Income', *American Sociological Review*, 50 (1985); Edward N. Muller, 'Democracy, Economic Development and Income Inequality', *American Sociological Review*, 53 (1988); Larry Sirowy and Alex Inkeles, 'The Effects of Democracy on Economic Growth and Inequality', in Alex Inkeles (ed.), *On Measuring Democracy* (New Brunswick, NJ, Transaction Publishers, 1991).

[40] Alexis de Tocqueville, *Democracy in America* (New York, Harper and Row, 1988), 211, *passim*.

[41] See the study of the Southern European experience in Luiz Carlos Bresser Pereira, José María Maravall, and Adam Przeworski, *Economic Reforms in New Democracies* (Cambridge, Cambridge University Press, 1993), 77–131.

TABLE 1.5. *Effects of democracy on public revenue and expenditure (as percentage of GDP in 1990)*

	Public expenditure			Fiscal revenue		
	(1)	(2)	(3)	(4)	(5)	(6)
Constant	20.547	4.158	12.295*	10.932	–4.954	3.602
	(5.577)	(5.840)	(5.249)	(4.456)	(4.071)	(3.744)
Index of Democracy						
(1980)	.139			.179*		
	(.080)			(.064)		
(1991)		.352*			.384*	
		(.077)			(.054)	
(1993)			7.650*			8.494*
			(2.191)			(1.574)
R^2	.046	.256	.164	.111	.453	.315
Signif. F	.089	.000	.001	.007	.000	.000
No. of observations	64	63	64	64	63	65

* Statistically significant at 5% or less.

Note: Standard errors in parenthesis.

seen in Table 1.5, greater public expenditure and revenue appear to be common characteristics of democracies.

This table shows the results of a regression analysis between, on the one hand, three indices of democracy (two referring to respect for human rights in 1980 and 1991 on a scale of one to a hundred, and the third to political participation in 1993 on a scale of one to three), and on the other, public expenditure and tax revenue as a percentage of the GDP in 1990.[42] It can be seen that whilst there was no relation between the degree of democracy in 1980 and public expenditure, in 1991 the former explains 25.6% of the variation; an increase of one unit on the scale of democracy is associated with a change of .35 in the level of public expenditure as a proportion of GDP. This independent variable, both in the 1980 index and in that of 1991, was linked to increased taxation; in 1991 it explains 45.3% of the variation, and an increase of one unit in the scale of democracy led to a rise of .38 in fiscal revenue as

[42] The first of these indices of democracy is based on the information contained in Humana, *World Human Rights Guide*. The second is based on the data in Freedom House, *Freedom in the World: Political Rights and Civil Liberties* (New York, Freedom House, 1993). The data on public expenditure and taxation has been taken from United Nations, *Human Development Report* (New York, Oxford University Press, 1993).

a proportion of GDP. If we consider the effect of the third index of democracy in 1993, this explains 16.4% of the variation in public expenditure, and an increase of one unit on the scale is linked to an increase of 7.65 in expenditure; on the other hand, this index accounts for 31.4% of the variation in fiscal revenue, and an increase of one unit produces a rise of 0.18 in revenue as a proportion of GDP. In short, different indicators of the degree of democracy suggest that the state tends to have more resources under democracy than under authoritarian regimes. Hence democracies appear to be characterized by no less efficient economies, by more extensive social policies, and by states which administer, through their revenue and expenditure, greater resources.

Finally, these comparative empirical studies also suggest that democracies are more resilient than dictatorships to economic crises. Not only did they prove less vulnerable and fragile than was expected during the 1980s, but this was also the case over longer periods. It is true that democracies with a very low level of economic development and negative growth rates are much more vulnerable than authoritarian regimes. However, their chances of survival increase considerably once a certain minimum threshold has been reached. For example, considering the experience of Latin America between 1945 and 1988, Limongi and Przeworski have shown that after three years of negative economic growth, 91% of the democracies survived the following year, compared to only 67% of the dictatorships; and after five years of negative growth, 75% of the democracies, but none of the dictatorships, survived the following year.[43] Similarly, Remmer's analysis of 114 stabilization programmes in nine Latin American countries over a period of 30 years[44] reveals that these more frequently led to the collapse of dictatorships than of democracies. The latter, therefore, appear to enjoy a certain autonomy with respect to economic conditions. Juan Linz has argued that this is a consequence of the fragmentation of power and responsibility in democratic regimes, which helps to ensure that inefficiency does not directly impinge on the regime's legitimacy.[45] Huntington has explained the same phenomena in terms of the separation between the 'legitimacy of the rulers', which

[43] Limongi and Przeworski, 'Democracy and Development in South America', 6–11, 20–4.

[44] Karen Remmer, 'The Politics of Economic Stabilization: IMF Standby Programs in Latin America, 1954–1984', *Comparative Politics*, 18 (1986), 1–24.

[45] Juan J. Linz, 'Legitimacy of Democracy and the Socioeconomic System', in Mattei Dogan (ed.), *Comparing Pluralist Democracies* (Boulder, Colo., Westview Press, 1988), 65–113.

is based on performance, and the 'legitimacy of the regime', based on rules: a crisis of the former would lead to a change of government, but not to a challenge to the regime itself.[46] Albert Hirschman, in turn, has linked it to the reserves of political support which a new regime counts on when it replaces a repressive and discredited dictatorship, as well as to the fact that democracy provides 'political goods' which may compensate for a fall in per capita incomes.[47] In any event, the result would be that democracies have more room for manœuvre than dictatorships.

Let us now consider the theoretical arguments in favour of democracy. The empirical evidence on economic results achieved by regimes of this kind may be explained by the operation of democratic markets and the character of democratic political institutions. On occasions, some economists have maintained that whilst economic markets function well, political markets do not. However, it can be argued that democratic political markets can be very competitive, that political actors may be rewarded for performing efficiently, and hence that democracy may produce comparatively better results.[48] Electoral competition may reduce the opportunist potential of politicians to lower levels than those found in dictatorial regimes: on the one hand, politicians win reputations and suffer from their failure to fulfil promises in democratic political markets; on the other, voters have relatively more information on the politicians' identity, the party ideologies, and candidates' reputations, as well as access to critical viewpoints from different organizations and groups. Democratic political institutions can also reduce transaction costs and facilitate the efficient exchange of rights. Majority rule itself may reduce the particularistic distortions which pressure groups can introduce into the political system. Political parties may act as aggregative agencies which universalize interests and hence counterbalance the influence that sectorial or local interests may have on politicians. Parties and trade unions may accept inter-temporal trade-offs and hence moderate their demands. And political leaders in democratic regimes usually have greater legitimacy in the event of having to appeal for austerity from society. Reform measures proposed by the communist government in Poland in 1987 were rejected in a referendum, but were supported in 1990 when they were proposed by Tadeusz Mazowiecki's democratic government.

[46] Huntington, *The Third Wave*, 46–58.

[47] Albert Hirschman, 'The Political Economy of Latin American Development: Some Exercises in Retrospection', *Latin American Research Review*, 22/3 (1987), 28.

[48] Donald Wittman, 'Why Democracies Produce Efficient Results', *Journal of Political Economy*, 97 (1989), 1, 395–424.

Thus, the relative efficiency of dictatorships is explained in terms of their capacity, autonomy, and insulation from society, whilst that of democracies is related to the existence of incentives, the responsibility of the institutions, and the predominance of universalistic interests. State autonomy from society is not necessarily a prerequisite for efficiency; not only does it fail to guarantee that the correct policies will be adopted, but beyond a certain point, it has harmful consequences for the economy. In this sense, Douglass North has argued that democratic institutions are those best able to restrict the state's 'predatory' instincts in the name of general interest.[49] According to North, since the political process conditions economic decisions, institutions have an important effect on economic exchanges. Despite the inadequacies of the voters' information and unequal access to the decision-making process, democracies constitute the institutional framework most closely resembling a political market, in which transaction costs permit efficient exchanges. Democratic institutions facilitate information about the costs and benefits of different policies; due to the incentives resulting from political competition, they also transmit the most efficient preferences and decisions better than authoritarian institutions do.

Jean Drèze and Amartya Sen have used similar arguments to explain why democracies may be more economically efficient. Their analysis focuses on extreme cases: the prevention of famines and the reduction of severe hardship in the Third World. In dictatorships, leaders do not suffer the consequences of their policies.

The contribution of political pluralism relates to the importance of adversarial politics and social criticism in influencing state action in the direction of greater sensitivity to the well-being of the population. . . . it is clear that the scope for effective public influence on the activities of the state tends to be greater in political systems that make room for opposition and criticism.[50]

In contrast, when there are no elections, when opposition parties are not tolerated, nor public and uncensored criticism permitted, governments do not have to pay politically for their mistakes. If democracy is defined as a regime endowed with a system of incentives capable of making governmental policy sensitive to results, then economic efficiency would not only benefit from the

---

[49] Douglass C. North, *Institutions, Institutional Change and Economic Performance* (Cambridge, Cambridge University Press, 1990), 107–12.

[50] Jean Drèze and Amartya Sen, *Hunger and Public Action* (Oxford, Clarendon Press, 1989), 17–19, 257–79 (the quote is from p. 278).

economic incentives introduced by the market, but also from the political incentives derived from democracy. If a free press is able to disclose information which might influence policies, it may also act as an early warning system and cause mistakes to be corrected. Thus, political incentives and information may help to explain the contrast between the experiences of famine in India before and after 1947, or in Botswana and Zimbabwe in comparison to Sudan, Ethiopia, Somalia, Chad, Mali, or Uganda, despite the existence of similar material conditions.

It is true that these arguments concerning the reasons for the greater economic efficiency of democracy assume the existence of perfect information among voters and perfect competition among parties. Yet it is equally true that these assumptions need only be relative; the arguments remain valid provided that dictatorships and democracies differ in terms of the degree of competition and information found within them. And in so far as these arguments are plausible, they undermine both the thesis that markets require authoritarian regimes and the sequence which gives priority to economic rather than political reforms. That is, they invalidate the ideas that defend an authoritarian path to an efficient market economy. In its 1991 report on the comparative perspectives for economic development, the World Bank noted that

there is suggestive evidence that links features of democratic systems positively with overall aspects of development and welfare. . . . Political checks and balances, a free press, and open debate on the costs and benefits of government policy could give a wider public a stake in reform. The need to produce good results in order to be reelected could help, rather than hinder, economic change.[51]

However, these arguments focus above all on the incentives which explain why democracies may generate better outcomes. In contrast, they have little to say about their capacity to do so. To what extent are democracies able to manage their economies in the face of the pressures of electoral interests and particularistic groups? Obviously, there is no simple answer to this question. Although Haggard argues that authoritarian regimes are relatively more capable, he recognizes that 'there are no theoretical reasons to think that authoritarian regimes are *uniquely* capable of solving the collective-action problems associated with development', and that 'there are no *unique* institutional solutions for reducing the political constraints on economic policy.'[52] What alternatives to the

[51] World Bank, *World Development Report 1991*, 134, 133.
[52] Haggard, *Pathways from the Periphery*, 256, 267.

authoritarian mechanisms, therefore, may provide democracies with the capacity to implement their policies?

These alternatives depend on four conditions: the gravity of the economic crisis, the breadth of the mandate, the extent of the political consensus, and the sequence of decisions. When economic crises were profound and prolonged, and were not caused by uncontrollable external circumstances, governments more readily accepted that economic measures had to be taken, that these represented the best available option, and that they had no room for manœuvre or delay in taking decisions.[53] This mechanism of urgency helps explain many democratic governments' responses to the economic crises of the 1980s: it operated in Spain in 1982, in Portugal in 1983, in Argentina in 1989, and in Poland in the same year. When crises were accompanied by a frustrating experience of partial reforms that had failed to modify the evolution of their economies, governments proved more willing to abandon this type of response and opt for a radical change of economic policy. The policies of macroeconomic adjustment and structural reform applied in Latin America and Eastern Europe were the response to many years of timid reforms and voluntarist experiments. In countries such as Hungary or Poland, partial reforms designed to give enterprises a degree of autonomy, introduce greater competition, and further open up economies to foreign trade, failed to resolve the basic structural problems. Economic decisions were still taken according to political criteria, autonomy remained limited, the power of the state monopolies was not reduced, competition hardly increased, unprofitable enterprises continued to survive on the basis of subsidies and considerable fiscal laxity, and labour costs carried on rising. In countries such as Argentina, Brazil, or Peru, the heterodox experiments of the 1980s ended in failure: after an initial period of euphoria provoked by the apparent fall in inflation, the economic crises worsened due to the absence of fiscal reforms, undisciplined monetary policies, acquiescence in the face of demands for consumption, and the growing burdens on the states. In both Latin America and Eastern Europe the situation became unsustainable. Paradoxically, as the crisis deepened, the governments' capacity to initiate policies of macroeconomic austerity and structural transformation increased, since both politicians and society as a whole came to the conclusion that there was no other

[53] Nelson, *Economic Crisis and Policy Choice*, 325–7; John Waterbury, 'The Heart of the Matter? Public Enterprise and the Adjustment Process', in Haggard and Kaufman, *The Politics of Economic Adjustment*, 196–8, 215–17.

alternative. Deep and prolonged crises can generate processes of collective learning from previous experiences. Learning processes of this type occurred in Southern Europe: in Portugal, derived from the failure of the economic policies of the 'revolution of the carnations'; in Spain, after various years of economic decline and in the light of the failed experiences of Portugal, of France between 1981 and 1982, and of Great Britain during the 1970s. The crisis forced decisions to be taken and experience helped when choosing between different policies.

However, the economic crisis was not usually a sufficient condition for the implementation of drastic economic reforms. In many cases, coalitions of groups that had benefited from existing policies organized to block any change of direction. This was clearly true in Russia, but many other examples also exist. In this context, a breakdown of the existing political formula, in the sense of a transformation of the *status quo*, or the end of a 'historical compromise', became necessary to enable a new government to choose a new economic policy paradigm. The mandate enjoyed by democratic governments was therefore another essential condition that reinforced their political capacity. As Peter Gourevitch has put it, 'the strong state is the one with the political support to be strong'.[54] The breadth of the government's mandate depended on the extent of its electoral victory and was manifested in two ways: through the government's parliamentary strength and the social support it enjoyed. John Keeler has shown that this strength and support, which he terms 'empowerment' and 'authorization', were the principal explanatory factors behind the very different reforms initiated by Roosevelt, Blum, Attlee, Johnson, Allende, Reagan, and Mitterrand.[55] Broad mandates, combined with acute economic crises, generally imply that the opposition is thrown into temporary disarray and previous policies are discredited. In addition, innovative teams, backed by strong leaders, are able to seize the reins of the economy. This is what happened in the cases of Pedro Aspe in Mexico, Miguel Boyer and Carlos Solchaga in Spain, Leszek Balcerowicz in Poland, three examples of what John Waterbury has labelled 'change teams'.[56] The protection they received from a leader with wide popular and political support granted them a considerable degree of autonomy.

[54] Peter Gourevitch, *Politics in Hard Times* (Ithaca, NY, Cornell University Press, 1986), 238.
[55] John T. S. Keeler, 'Opening the Window for Reform: Mandates, Crises, and Extraordinary Policy Making', *Comparative Political Studies*, 25/4 (1993), 427–86.
[56] Waterbury, 'Heart of the Matter?', 191.

Thus, the capacity of democratic governments increased when they had broad mandates, when parliamentary and social resistance receded, and when alternative policies had been discredited. These effects multiplied when the political institutions provided governments with additional leeway for decision-making. The choice of different electoral systems, presidentialism or parliamentarism, centralism or federalism, constitutionalism or the majority principle, neo-corporatism or pluralism, have significant implications for economic policy. At one extreme, the institutions may paralyse decisions and their implementation. But at the other, they may engender governments which are insensitive to the balance of forces in parliament, or uninterested in dialogue and negotiation. Whilst a government's capacity may increase under conditions which promote 'decisionism', these may also foment political insulation which reduces the information and incentives necessary for the selection of efficient policies. For this reason, Nelson argues that 'economic reform cannot long be isolated from politics and . . . politics is not always the enemy of such reforms.'[57] Governments have to listen, negotiate, and persuade, both to increase the information at their disposal and to win greater support for their policies. Once the time when a situation of acute crisis that may require urgent economic measures is past, governments need to consult and reach agreement if their policies are to be viable and they are to obtain information and co-operation from key social actors. In this way, whilst broad mandates help, they do not constitute a necessary or sufficient condition for the implementation of economic reforms. As illustrated by the case of the Aníbal Cavaco Silva government in Portugal after the 1985 elections, minority governments with an initially limited mandate may also be both capable and efficient. The empirical evidence available on the relative economic performance of majority and minority governments is, in fact, far from conclusive. Consensus, both among politicians and in society as a whole, may therefore be a functional alternative to a broad electoral mandate. Politicians may share the view that there are no options other than those proposed by the government; and society may also come to believe that there is no alternative to these policies, that they will probably lead to a better future, that it is rational to maximize the present value of future consumption, and that the costs and benefits of these policies are fairly distributed.

[57] Joan Nelson, 'The Politics of Economic Transformation: Is Third World Experience Relevant in Eastern Europe?', *World Politics*, 45/3 (1993), 459.

In this case, consensus and agreement may open a 'window of opportunity' for ambitious economic policies to be initiated.

However, neither mandates nor consensuses last forever. In time, 'windows of opportunity' close, honeymoon periods come to an end, and governments wear themselves out. For this reason, strategies are of crucial importance. A government's capacity and efficiency are not solely dependent on political and economic conditions, but also on the temporal sequences of policies. Policies do not take place in a single moment of time, but constitute a process which develops in changing circumstances. The strategic dilemmas concern, above all, two interrelated issues. On the one hand, the calendar of initiatives, on the other, negotiation or 'decisionism'. Generally speaking, initiatives taken early on in a mandate have more chance of success, since governments are new, they enjoy public confidence which has yet to be exhausted, and are supported by cohesive parties, whilst the opposition has only recently been defeated. Rapid reforms will meet with less resistance, their costs will be absorbed more quickly, and policies will appear more difficult to reverse. However, the passing of time will erode trust in governments and their initiatives, and cracks may appear in their party support. For all these reasons, lost opportunities usually prove expensive for policies. Hence Przeworski has argued that economic reforms must be both rapid and radical. In Eastern Europe, 'radical programs are more likely to advance reforms farther under democratic conditions'; since 'bridges have been burned', reforms will prove harder to reverse.[58] Initiatives will be more readily accepted by society if they scrupulously follow channels of democratic debate and are complemented by social polices that lessen the costs involved.[59]

The second dilemma refers to the choice between 'decisionist' or 'pactist' strategies. This dilemma is connected with the previous one. In the early days of a government, the 'decisionist' option will generally be easier. Later, in contrast, as the 'windows of opportunity' gradually close, governments tend to opt for a strategy based on agreement and pacts. The erosion caused by time and the shrinking of the mandate are not the only factors influencing this dilemma, however. Both the ideology of the governments and the

---

[58] Adam Przeworski, *Democracy and the Market* (Cambridge, Cambridge University Press, 1991), ch. 4.

[59] The importance of the democratic process and social policies for economic reform strategies has been heavily emphasized in Bresser Pereira, Maravall, and Przeworski, *Economic Reforms in New Democracies*, esp. 199–220.

nature of the reforms influence the choice of strategies. Thus, social democracy has tended towards negotiation and neo-corporatist strategies. In contrast, Margaret Thatcher's strategy was a very clear example of 'decisionism'; as she herself would say, 'social dialogue' means voting every five years. Certain reforms, in turn, require decisiveness and surprise, whilst others demand negotiation and persuasion. A devaluation is one thing, fiscal reform quite another.

The economic efficiency of democracy may, therefore, be a product of both the functioning of incentives and political information, and of mechanisms which reinforce its political capacity. Among these, I have emphasized the gravity of the crisis, the breadth of the mandate, the extent of the consensus, and the election of temporal strategies. These mechanisms may be both accumulative and compensatory: they offer possibilities but determine nothing; it is unlikely that they operate as a necessary cause and they certainly do not constitute a sufficient one. Ultimately, other, rather intangible factors, such as leadership and the cognitive maps of politicians, play a decisive role. It is up to leaders to take advantage of political conditions: many waste favourable opportunities, whilst others, in contrast, are able to develop their economies even under unfavourable conditions. In any case, Gourevitch is right to argue that 'policies need politics';[60] the thesis that strong or authoritarian governments generate more efficient economies is usually based on a very crude conception of politics.

To sum up, in this chapter I have explored the relationship between political regimes and economies from two perspectives. On the one hand, I have examined the economic conditions which usually precede democratizations and the extent to which they favour or hinder political change and the consolidation of a new regime. On the other, I have considered the relative capacity of both types of regime to manage their economies and reform these when they enter into crisis. I have argued that the fatalistic thesis regarding the economic efficiency of the new democracies and their possibilities of surviving amidst serious difficulties is quite unfounded. In many places in Latin America and Eastern Europe these observations are neither obvious nor irrelevant. I have also argued that economic outcomes have not been combined with greater inequality. Democracies have tended to be associated with broader social and fiscal policies. Important differences have, of course, existed between the new democracies in terms of the

---

[60] Gourevitch, *Politics in Hard Times*, 17.

political strategies and the socio-economic formula they have adopted in response to crisis. These differences have influenced, in turn, both the level of political support as well as the social distribution of the economic costs and benefits of policies. However, this variation within the new democracies is quite a different question to that discussed in this chapter, and one which will be examined later on.

The Economic Effects of Dictatorships

How did economic conditions affect the political regimes in Southern and Eastern Europe? And what effects did the regimes have on the economies? Evidently, economic conditions in these countries varied very considerably. Prior to the change of political regime, the economies were affected to very different degrees by the excessive burden of the states' falling competitiveness, public deficits, and unemployment. In Southern Europe, there was no system of public ownership and state economic planning. Currencies were convertible, exchange rates were not artificial, black markets did not exist, and generally speaking, prices reflected supply and demand. Inflation was high, but not out of control; at the beginning of the transition it stood at around 20% in Portugal, Greece, and Spain. The per capita foreign debt was also relatively low; at its highest, in Greece, it amounted to $331 per person in 1974. Similarly, although the Eastern European economies shared a number of basic characteristics, there also existed notable differences between them. Thus in 1989, whilst inflation was running at 251.1% in Poland, it stood at only 17% in Hungary, and 1.4% in Czechoslovakia. Whilst the per capita foreign debt in Hungary and Poland was immense ($1,656 and $1,113, respectively), it was much lower in Czechoslovakia ($444). Although the period of economic expansion had come to an end in all these countries, whilst Romania and Bulgaria had negative growth rates (–5.8% and –0.4%, respectively), Czechoslovakia maintained a positive rate of 1.5%.

It is obvious that economic polices are to a large extent determined by the conditions of the respective national economies. However, variations in these conditions do not prevent the comparative analysis of economic reforms. The nature of these reforms also depends on political factors such as a government's political support, and the priorities, ideologies, and competence of decision-makers. These factors affect both the design of reforms (regarding privatization, the state sector, public expenditure, taxation, the combination of state and market), and their implementation, rhythms, and outcomes. In Southern and Eastern Europe, policy options were not totally determined by economic conditions. Furthermore, if policies merely reflected the specificities of these conditions it would be impossible to understand why the programme of reforms implemented in each country shared a number of elements. In other words, if the conditions were so different, why were the programmes so similar? The Balcerowicz Plan in Poland applied policies which had already been experimented with in Bolivia. The Spanish experience was also carefully studied in Eastern Europe. In Hungary, at the beginning of the political and economic reform process in November 1989, the then prime minister, Miklos Nemeth, declared that 'the Spaniards' experience of eliminating a dictatorship and carrying out a transition to democracy is important for us. Moreover, it interests us because we have dismantled the obsolete structures of the Stalinist social and economic order and we wish to embark on democratic politics in a market economy'.[1] And after winning the general elections in May 1994, the new prime minister Gyula Horn declared that the Moncloa Pacts (the economic agreements signed by the Spanish government and opposition parties in 1977) were an instructive example of economic strategy. In other words, different economic conditions do not necessarily give rise to reform programmes in which there are no common elements.

In this chapter, I am going to examine the relationship between politics and the economy in regime changes by studying the experiences of Southern and Eastern Europe from a comparative perspective. I will discuss economic conditions before democratization in the light of these experiences. Were the changes of regime preceded by periods of growth, or by economic crisis? Did the political institutions of the dictatorships find it increasingly difficult to manage their economies, or, on the contrary, did their independence from electoral support and supposed autonomy from particularist interests result in greater economic efficiency? Did economic change under the dictatorships give rise to a more plural social order and a more complex civil society that smoothed the way towards democratization? These are the three main questions I will consider in relation to the period before the change of regime. I will argue that the dictatorships experienced problems of capacity and, above all, of incentives which hindered efficient economic

---

[1] *El País*, 9 Nov. 1989.

management, and that these problems became more acute at a certain stage of the regimes' history. Difficult economic circumstances constitute the *experimentum crucis* for the capacity of a regime. For this reason, I will focus on the different regimes' responses to the economic crisis of the 1970s. I will also defend the thesis that the *raison d'être* of political change in Southern Europe was that reforms should not merely be economic, but also political, whilst in Eastern Europe, one of the objectives of political change was to carry out radical economic reforms which appeared impossible under the existing regimes.

When examining these two experiences, I will pay only limited attention to the influence of the international environment on the regime changes. This is mainly because the dependent variable I am studying is economic policy rather than the democratic transition itself, while the independent variables that interest me are domestic in character. As will become clear below, the European Community exercised considerable influence on events in Southern Europe, and geo-political developments played a crucial role in shaping the processes of change in Eastern Europe, especially the influence of Gorbachev and his decision not to intervene in these processes. Yet in spring 1989 the leaders of Poland and Hungary were uncertain about the tolerance of the Soviet Union *vis-à-vis* their strategies for political change, and whether Gorbachev had indeed decided to abandon the 'Brezhnev doctrine'. Moreover, the removal of Soviet dissuasion does not explain why these countries took the path of democracy and the market. Rather than the cause of the changes, the disappearance of the USSR as a political deterrent under Gorbachev signified the elimination of a decisive veto on change.

2.1. Autarky, Development, and Crisis: Southern Europe

Let us begin by analysing the mutual influences between the economies and the dictatorships. In the previous chapter I discussed in general terms whether democratizations were caused by economic crisis or by the consequences of economic development. The Southern European experience has often been seen as a paradigmatic case of political change facilitated by social effects of development that were neither expected nor intended by the dictatorships, and which led to increasing social and cultural pluralism. Whilst I believe this explanation to be broadly correct, it should nevertheless be qualified in a number of important respects.

Although significant differences existed between the three Southern European countries, the economies of Greece, Portugal, and Spain shared a long history of relative backwardness with respect to other Western European countries. In comparative terms, their per capita incomes were low, their technologies under-developed, and their labour forces relatively unskilled, with a large part employed in an inefficient primary sector. In terms of the composition and balance of trade, the nature of foreign investment, and the importance of tourism and emigration, they belonged to the 'semi-periphery' of the developed core of Europe. The economies of all three countries largely stagnated for decades: between 1913 and 1950 the Greek economy grew at an average annual rate of 0.2%; the Portuguese at an average of 0.9%, whilst the Spanish economy shrunk at a rate of –0.3% annually.[2]

After the Second World War, the regimes adopted an autarkic economic model based on insulation from international markets and the protection of domestic production through tariffs, duties, and import quotas. Rather than a temporary strategy to weather passing difficulties, this model was conceived as the definitive form of economic organization. The goal was to achieve self-sufficiency through a policy of import substitution; according to the Spanish Protection and Promotion of New Industries Act of 1939, this would 'redeem Spain from the importation of exotic products which can be produced and manufactured within our Nation'.[3] The Institute of National Industry (INI), created in Spain in 1941 and modelled on the Italian Istituto per la Riconstruzione Industriale (IRI) set up by Mussolini in 1933, embodied this statist and protectionist conception of promoting industrialization at any price.[4] This was

[2] Allan Williams (ed.), *Southern Europe Transformed: Political and Economic Change in Greece, Italy and Spain* (London, Harper and Row, 1984), Table 1.1, p. 2. These aggregate data, however, conceal important variations over time. In the Spanish case, for example, growth in industrial production outstripped the European average between 1913 and 1922, and roughly matched it between 1922 and 1935. Yet, as a result of the Civil War and the first decade of Francoism, only in 1951 did output return to its pre-war level. See Francisco Comín, 'La economía española en el período de entreguerras (1919–1935)' and Albert Carreras 'La industria: atraso y modernización' in Jordi Nadal, Albert Carreras, and Carles Sudrià (eds.), *La economía española en el siglo XX: una perspectiva histórica* (Barcelona, Ariel, 1987), 109–14 and 303–9.

[3] Another Spanish law, the 1939 Regulation and Defence of Industry Act, restricted consumption to domestic products and services.

[4] The INI was originally to be called the National Institute of Autarky. See Pablo Martín Aceña and Francisco Comín, *INI: 50 años de industrialización en España* (Madrid, Espasa–Calpe, 1991), 52.

also the objective of the Portuguese Industrial Development and Reorganizaton Act of 1945. In both countries this economic model was linked to a political model, a key component of which was the regimentation of the working class through the corporative institutions of the dictatorship. In Portugal 'state corporatism'[5] was established in the 1933 constitution and the National Labour Statute enacted later that year. In Spain it was instituted in the 1938 Labour Charter and in the Syndical Unity Act of 1940. All workers were forced to join the state unions, independent unions were banned, and collective bargaining and the right to strike abolished. The state assumed responsibility for the regulation of labour relations, working conditions, and wages. The latter remained very low: in Spain for example, real wages in 1953 still stood at less than half their pre-war level.

There was very little political and social resistance to this model of economic organization. Repression (which in the case of Spain had been preceded by civil war) prevented any significant organizational activity. The labour movement had practically been destroyed: after the end of the war, seventeen executive committees of the anarcho-syndicalist Confederación Nacional del Trabajo (CNT) were arrested between 1940 and 1947, and seven of those of the socialist Unión General de Trabajadores (UGT) shared the same fate between 1939 and 1954.[6] The modification of the corporatist-autarkic model essentially depended on the relationship between the international environment and the politics of the dictatorships. Initially, this model reflected the preferences of the regimes' support coalitions (the Catholic Church in the 1930s and 1940s, and the Falange, the single party under the dictatorship), which were reinforced by international conditions (Franco's sympathy for Mussolini and the regimes' isolation after the Second World War). Whilst it was conceived as the definitive form of economic organization, the model was also instrumental in the dictatorships' political survival after 1945. Nevertheless, the changes

---

[5] See the study of corporatism in Portugal in Peter J. Williamson, *Varieties of Corporatism* (Cambridge, Cambridge University Press, 1985), ch. 7; see also, Philippe C. Schmitter, *Corporatism and Public Policy in Authoritarian Portugal* (London, Sage, 1975). For corporatism in Spain, see Juan J. Linz, 'A Century of Politics and Interests in Spain', in Suzanne Berger (ed.), *Organising Interests in Western Europe* (Cambridge, Cambridge University Press, 1981), and Charles W. Andersen, *The Political Economy of Modern Spain* (Madison, University of Wisconsin Press, 1970).

[6] José María Maravall, *Dictatorship and Political Dissent* (New York, St Martin's Press, 1978), 22, 24, 66–70.

in economic conditions and the international environment which took place in the 1950s had decisive repercussions for the political model of the economies.

These corporatist institutions and autarkic policies were an obstacle to long-term economic development. They gave rise to an uncompetitive private sector, incited short-term speculation at the expense of industrial investment, made production dependent on domestic markets with limited purchasing power, and obstructed the supply of the capital goods and raw materials necessary for industrialization. The slow pace of Spain's economic recovery after 1939 was a consequence of the political economy of the dictatorship. In this sense, Gabriel Tortella has argued that

the democratic alternative would have been superior to the dictatorial one in post-Second World War Spain for at least two reasons. Firstly, because a democratic Spain would have benefited from the Marshall Plan and from economic co-operation with the rest of Europe, including membership of the European Economic Community, advantages which it was deprived of because of Francoism. Secondly, because a democratic government would have spared the country the hugely expensive encumbrance of the autarkic, interventionist, and xenophobic economic policy that was consubstantial with Francoist ideology. This policy cost the country at least a decade of economic stagnation; Italy's and France's economic recovery after the Second World War was achieved in some three years. That of Spain after the Civil War took between eleven and fourteen years.[7]

Changes in the international environment were the principal factor behind the transformation of the autarkic model. These changes were related, first, to the new international alignments that developed in the context of the Cold War. Thus, Portugal joined NATO in 1949 and EFTA in 1959, whilst at the same time Spain began to break out of the diplomatic isolation of the immediate post-war years with the signing of a co-operation agreement with the United States in 1953, admission into the United Nations in 1955, and the IMF, the World Bank, and the OECE (later OECD) in 1958. A second change in the international situation was the

---

[7] Gabriel Tortella, *El desarrollo de la España contemporánea: historia económica de los siglos XIX y XX* (Madrid, Alianza Editorial, 1994), 205 and 20. With two homogeneous industrial production indices for Spain and Italy, Carreras demonstrates that Italy grew faster between 1947 and 1960 and that these different rates of growth had prolonged consequences for the economies of the two countries; thus, he concludes that 'if Spanish industry had followed the path of that of Italy between 1947 and 1975, its overall output would have been more than 26% higher than it actually was'. Carreras, 'La industria: atraso y modernización', 306.

period of strong economic growth which began in Western Europe in the 1950s. This expansion had important consequences for the economies of Southern Europe. It brought great influxes of tourists, created opportunities abroad for vast numbers of emigrant workers, and facilitated a significant increase in direct foreign investment, which would account for 52% of total manufacturing investment in Portugal in 1968, and finance one out of every five jobs in Spain in 1973.

As a result, the Iberian dictatorships found themselves in a more favourable environment. On the one hand, the regimes benefited from the new alignments of the Cold War; on the other, their economies had the opportunity to open up to an expanding international economy. The regimes' responses to these changes in international conditions were determined by pragmatic rather than ideological considerations: their first priority was survival. As long as the regimes were not challenged (but rather strengthened) by reform, they were willing to adapt to the new circumstances; that is, to reform their institutions, change economic strategy, and alter the internal balance of their support coalitions. Thus in Spain, Franco tempered the more totalitarian features of the regime's institutions, relegating the Falange to less prominent positions, and entrusting the regime's foreign policy to conservative monarchists and economic policy to Opus Dei.

In the mid-1950s, the autarkic model suffocated the further growth that this more favourable environment made possible. Statism and production at any price in autarkic conditions had led to inflation; the labour institutions prevented the operation of an efficient labour market; large wage rises were tolerated in order to avert social tensions; supply remained rigid and scarcely competitive; the INI had amassed debts amounting to over 8% of the national income;[8] and the trade imbalances eventually drove the economy into a cul-de-sac, with minimal currency reserves, unable to continue paying for imports. In these conditions, the autarkic model was abandoned in favour of gradual integration into the international economy and the progressive substitution of state regulation by market mechanisms. Economic liberalization began in Spain in 1959, with the implementation of a stabilization plan lasting three years; in Greece it started in 1953, with the reforms introduced by Spyros Markezinis in a regime of restricted democracy; Portugal also took this path, timidly towards the end of the 1950s, and more resolutely after 1966.

---

[8] Tortella, *El desarrollo de la España contemporánea*, 277.

It is this change of economic strategy which has given rise to the thesis that market reforms preceded political change in Southern Europe.[9] It has also been put forward in support of the argument that dictatorships have a particular capacity to introduce this type of reform. Proponents of this idea, however, tend to neglect a number of important issues. One is that the reforms were overwhelmingly determined by external factors: in the first place, the economic influence of Western democracies, and secondly, the balance-of-trade crisis. The Spanish stabilization plan of 1959 was indispensable if Spain was to have access to the international loans it required, and clearly responded to the recommendations issued by the OECD and the World Bank. Equally, the new economic policy was adopted in imitation of the European experience, and that of France and Italy in particular. This influence was further strengthened by the creation of the European Economic Community after the signing of the Treaty of Rome in 1957. Moreover, such interpretation tends to overlook the fact that economic reforms were intended to reinforce the dictatorships, by protecting them from the economic crisis and facilitating the typical authoritarian pact of consumption in return for acquiescence. As Raymond Carr has written of the Spanish case, 'the "dictatorship of victory" became the "dictatorship of development".'[10] And thirdly, in the same period democratic regimes were able to develop their economies from what were undoubtedly critical situations: Italy, Japan, and Germany are all obvious examples, whilst in the Greek case too, the democratic characteristics of the regime before 1967 proved no obstacle to economic development. The question is, therefore, whether hypothetical democratic governments in Portugal and Spain would have adopted a different economic policy. I think that José Luis García Delgado is right to argue that the economic development that took place in the 1960s only represented the 'recovery of previously wasted opportunities'.[11] In the context of Europe during the one and a half decades after the Second World War, if democracies had existed in both countries they would surely not have opted for an economic model of autarkic protectionism.

In any event, the new economic strategy adopted at the end of

[9] See Victor Pérez Díaz, *The Return of Civil Society: The Emergence of Democratic Spain* (Cambridge, Mass., Harvard University Press, 1993), ch. 1.

[10] Raymond Carr, *Modern Spain, 1875–1980* (Oxford, Oxford University Press, 1980), 165.

[11] José Luis García Delgado, 'Industrialización y desarrollo económico durante el franquismo', in Nadal, Carreras, and Sudrià (eds.), *La economía española en el siglo XX*, 177.

TABLE 2.1. *Economic performance in Southern Europe, 1960–1975*

	Spain	Greece	Portugal	European Community
GDP growth at constant prices (% per annum)				
1961–70	7.3	7.6	6.4	4.8
1971–5	5.2	5.2	4.5	2.9
Transition year	0.5	–3.6	1.1	1.9
Annual variation in job creation				
1961–70	0.6	–0.7	0.4	0.2
1971–5	0.4	0.4	–0.7	0.2
Transition year	–1.6	0.1	–0.5	0.4
Evolution of retail prices (% per annum)				
1961–70	5.9	2.5	2.8	3.8
1971–5	12.0	11.5	12.3	10.2
Transition year	15.5	23.5	23.4	13.8

Source: Commission des Communautés Européennes, *Économie Européenne*, 54 (1993), Tables 2, 10, and 24.

the 1950s led to very rapid development. As can be seen in Table 2.1, between 1961 and 1970 the GDP grew at an average rate of 7.6% per annum in Greece, 6.4% in Portugal, and 7.3% in Spain. However, this economic growth suffered from a number of major weaknesses. First, it was heavily reliant on European expansion, and the effects this had on tourism, remittances of emigrant workers, and foreign technology and investment. Only in a phase of international development could these countries compensate for their lack of domestic technology and savings. Initially, Southern European growth was also based on the availability of abundant and cheap labour. However, this comparative advantage diminished as labour emigration (that involved some 8% of the workforce in Spain) began to provoke shortages in the labour supply. The balance of trade and inflation always constituted a problem, as a result of the limited capacity of domestic production to satisfy overall rising demand and persistent state economic interventionism. This remained considerable in the capital and labour markets, whilst protectionist tariffs continued to shield goods markets. The industrial sector was made up of a myriad of small- and

medium-sized companies, highly protected from competition. Furthermore, industrialization was reliant on imported energy: in 1973
Spain's domestic supply of primary energy satisfied only 20.1% of
demand; in the same year, Greece had to devote two-thirds of her
export income to oil imports.

Political factors aggravated some of these economic weaknesses.
This was the case for the public sector, which always had little
room for manœuvre within the constraints imposed by a primitive,
rigid, and extremely inequitable tax system. It was also true of the
financial system, which constituted an obscure circuit of clienteles,
favouritism, and privileged channels for official credit. Political
factors also explain the limited development of the public services
and the paucity of the regimes' social policies. Nevertheless, economic growth did radically alter the social structure. There was a
drastic reduction in the agricultural workforce which dropped from
49% to 25% of the active population in Spain between 1950 and
1970, and from 42% to 28% in Portugal between 1960 and 1973.
At the same time, both the industrial working class and the urban
middle class grew very rapidly. The per capita income tripled in
real terms between 1960 and 1975. Student numbers in Spanish
universities rose from 76,000 in 1961 to 229,000 in 1971. However,
economic development not only had economic consequences, but
gradually political ones too, as it modified the characteristics of
civil society as well as the relationship between this and the state.
As Juan Linz has put it, 'economic and subsequent social change
made the organized representation of interests increasingly necessary'.[12] And with this, the economy and the new dynamic of social
relations would eventually undermine the corporatist model and,
in the long run, the Portuguese and Spanish authoritarian regimes themselves.

The political consequences of economic development became
increasingly apparent. The ever more complex economies could
hardly be governed by the political framework of the dictatorships.
This explains why the military regime established in Greece in
1967 never took root.[13] In the cases of Portugal and Spain, the
corporatist institutions became an ever greater obstacle to the
demands of competition. Rising productivity and the evolution of
wages could no longer be founded on bureaucratic imposition, but

[12] Linz, 'A Century of Politics and Interests in Spain', 390.

[13] Edward Malefakis, 'Southern Europe in the 19th and 20th Centuries: An
Historical Overview', *Working Paper 1992/35* (Madrid, Center for Advanced Study
in the Social Sciences, Instituto Juan March de Estudios e Investigaciones, 1992),
59–64.

required negotiation between employers and workers. Dahl is right when he notes that 'in an advanced economy, long-run performance under threat or coercion is less productive at all levels than a more willing performance based upon voluntary compliance.'[14] Albeit with considerable political precautions, a limited form of collective bargaining was regulated by law in Spain in 1959 and through a decree-law passed in Portugal in 1969. However, despite the precautions taken, collective bargaining introduced a fundamental contradiction into the corporative edifice of both countries, since if agreements were to be effective, some form of democratic workers' representation was inevitable.[15]

Thus, these economic and social changes created previously unknown opportunities for a democratic labour movement.[16] A new form of unionism began to emerge from below, that is, from the new industrial relations which developed in the workplace, and was heavily influenced by the possibilities generated by collective bargaining. In Spain, the reorganization of the labour movement was helped by the legalization of collective contracts and the modest autonomy conceded to shop stewards and works councils within the state union. This, therefore, was a paradigmatic case of the way in which institutional contradictions can have political consequences.[17] Labour conflict spread rapidly: the number of working hours lost through strike action rose from 1.4 million in 1966 to 14.5 million in 1975. Conflict also became increasingly political: solidarity, or politically motivated strikes accounted for just 4% of the total between 1963 and 1967, but some 45% between 1967 and 1974. Repression intensified after 1968: examples include the High Court's prohibition of the nascent Comisiones Obreras (CCOO), or Workers' Commissions, the prosecution of the movement's leaders

[14] Robert A. Dahl, *Polyarchy* (New Haven, Conn.: Yale University Press, 1971), 77.

[15] Maravall, *Dictatorship and Political Dissent*, ch. 2.

[16] For Spain see Robert M. Fishman, *Working Class Organisations and the Return to Democracy in Spain* (Ithaca, NY, Cornell University Press, 1990), chs. 4 and 5; for Portugal, see John R. Logan, 'Worker Mobilization and Party Politics: Revolutionary Portugal in Perspective', in Lawrence S. Graham and Douglas L. Wheeler (eds.), *In Search of Modern Portugal: The Revolution and its Consequences* (Madison, University of Wisconsin Press, 1983), 135–48.

[17] This is a classic theme in sociology. Marx considered it in the Preface to *A Contribution to the Critique of Political Economy*. In modern sociology it has been developed by Robert K. Merton in *Social Theory and Social Structure* (Glencoe, Ill., Free Press, 1957), as well as by David Lockwood in 'Social Integration and System Integration', in George K. Zollschan and William Hirsch (eds.), *Explorations in Social Change* (London, Routledge and Kegan Paul, 1964); and by Frank Parkin in 'System Contradiction and Political Transformation', *Archives Européennes de Sociologie*, 13/1 (1972).

in 'Trial 1,001', or the declaration of a State of Emergency in 1969. But in the decade before the political transition the conflict put down roots which the regime found impossible to eradicate.[18] In Portugal the labour movement first developed in the new industrial areas of Lisbon, Setúbal, and Oporto, whilst conflict also spread in the expanding tertiary sector. As was the case in Spain, workers' committees and commissions began to appear in the workplace, voicing demands that became increasingly political in character. Strike action intensified after 1968 and peaked between 1973 and 1974. However, in contrast to Spain, where strikes became less frequent after 1977, in Portugal the greatest social mobilizations came after the fall of the dictatorship. Finally, in Greece, economic liberalization had similar consequences, although under a different regime. Thus, whilst strike action was responsible for the loss of 48 working days per 1,000 workers in 1959, by 1966 this figure had risen to 519.[19] In Southern Europe, therefore, economic development generated a new social dynamic and, in the cases of Portugal and Spain, gave rise to important institutional contradictions within the corporative system itself, contradictions which would have political consequences.

The economic reforms ultimately failed to achieve their political objectives, namely, to widen support for the regimes by bringing improvements in material living conditions, to promote political apathy through consumption, and to de-activate demands for a political transformation. This strategy was very similar to that János Kádár would pursue in Hungary. By the 1960s the authoritarian regimes of Southern Europe no longer claimed legitimacy on ideological grounds, but on the basis of their economic performance. This eventually made them vulnerable to problems of efficiency. Dahl has noted that dictatorships which develop their economies usually find it harder to survive politically.[20] In the case of Southern Europe, economic development and its consequences ultimately favoured democratization, despite the very different

[18] The final years of the Francoist dictatorship were a period of increased political repression. Between 1968 and 1974 no fewer than 500 labour leaders were under arrest at any one time. In 'Trial 1,001', nine leaders of the Workers' Commissions (CCOO) were condemned to between 9 and 20 years imprisonment. Three states of emergency were declared after 1968 (one in the whole of Spain, two in the Basque Country) and, two months before his death in November 1975, Franco ordered five executions on political grounds.

[19] Nicos Mouzelis, *Politics in the Semi-periphery: Early Parliamentarianism and Late Industrialization in the Balkans and Latin America* (New York, St Martin's Press, 1986), 138.

[20] Dahl, *Polyarchy*, 78.

intentions of those who had promoted it. The subsequent economic crisis of 1973 was an enormous blow to the regimes' claims to legitimacy.

The crisis was particularly acute in Southern Europe. Despite the steps taken towards liberalization, state intervention in productive factors and goods markets and heavy reliance on imported energy meant that the economies were still less flexible than those of the advanced European countries. Hence, after a long period of economic growth, all three countries experienced a sharp economic decline. As can be seen in Table 2.1, at the end of the dictatorships the GDP growth rate per annum dropped to 1.1% in Portugal, 0.5% in Spain, and –3.6% in Greece. In terms of GDP growth, inflation, and job creation, the European Community as a whole performed better. In Portugal investment and exports fell by 37% and 21%, respectively, in 1974 alone.[21] In Spain the energy bill tripled in 1974, whilst (if we take 1973 as the base-point of 100), the real exchange rate plummeted twenty points in a single year. Fig. 2.1 shows the scale of the crisis in Spain in terms of the evolution of production, inflation, the foreign current account balance, and unemployment. At the end of the dictatorship the economy had deteriorated considerably in all four dimensions.

To what extent were the dictatorships able to respond to the economic crises? At this particular stage of their history, specific characteristics of the authoritarian regimes of Southern Europe had negative consequences for their economic policies. In other words, political factors aggravated the economic crises.

One factor was the governments' obsession with avoiding any economic initiative that might create political problems. In contrast to what the pro-authoritarian theses would suggest, the politicians' independence from electoral results did not reinforce their concern for general interests. Economic reforms were acceptable as long as they were located in what Richard Gunther has called 'the zone of political indifference', that is, as long as they did not threaten the regime's stability.[22] One example of this was fiscal policy, for tax rises were vetoed.[23] The taxation system was primitive

---

[21] Eric M. Baklanoff, *La transformación económica de España y Portugal: la economía del franquismo y del salazarismo* (Madrid, Espasa–Calpe, 1980), ch. 9.

[22] Richard Gunther, *Public Policy in a No-Party State* (Berkeley, University of California Press, 1980), ch. 3.

[23] To give an example from the Spanish case, in June 1973 the Finance Minister, Alberto Monreal, was removed from office because of his attempt to introduce tax reforms which, whilst economically necessary, might have provoked middle-class discontent and generated tension within the regime.

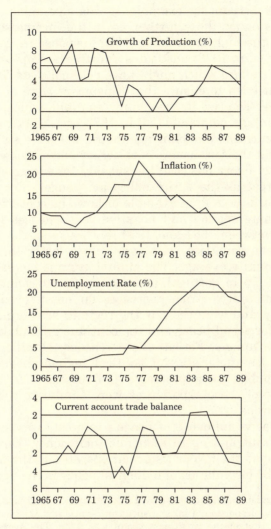

FIG. 2.1. *Spanish economic indicators, 1965–89*
Source: Banco de España.

and regressive, consisting essentially of indirect taxes and social security contributions. In fact, indirect taxation accounted for a higher proportion of total revenue at the end of Francoism than in the nineteenth century.[24] Tax pressure was relatively low, less than

[24] In 1971 indirect taxation produced 54.1% of total revenue, compared to 47.5% between 1850 and 1890; see Tortella, *El desarrollo de la España contemporánea*, 355–64.

half that of Britain, for example. It was also unjust, in so far as it was greater for those further down the income scale than for those with the highest incomes.[25] The response to the increase in the price of oil in 1973 constitutes a further example of this resistance to any reform which might have political costs. The Francoist government tried to ensure that consumers were not affected by the increase. The rise in the country's oil bill, which amounted to three percentage points of GDP in 1973, was paid from public resources. Hence the economic agents did not have sufficient information about the seriousness of the crisis and oil consumption was subsidized at enormous cost; the subsidy, for example, was almost twice as great as the entire education budget. The evolution of wages constitutes a final example of how the concern to preserve an illegitimate regime had negative consequences for economic efficiency. Between 1961 and 1973 real wages in the three Southern European countries rose significantly faster than the European Community average. The annual average increase was 5.8% in Greece, 6.7% in Portugal, and 7.1% in Spain, compared to 4.5% in the Community.[26] Wage increases far outstripped the rise in productivity, and were seen by the regimes as the price that had to be paid for social peace and the continued prohibition of democratic trade unions. For all these reasons, Gunther is right to argue that 'characteristics of political regimes have a profound impact on public policy processes and outputs'.[27] As we shall see below, some of these experiences were similar to those found in Eastern Europe.

The pervasive influence of private interests was another political factor contributing to economic inefficiency. Various studies have portrayed the favouritism that operated in the financial sector and in the formulation of industrial policy in the Spanish case.[28]

[25] If the Spanish population is divided into seven income groups, in 1964–5 the tax burden (the proportion of income spent on taxation) of the poorest group was 14.5%, whilst that of the wealthiest group was 9.6%. The average figure was 13.5%, compared to 30.1% in Great Britain: see Gunther, *Public Policy in a No-Party State*, 58–62.

[26] Commission des Communautés Européennes, *Économie Européenne: Rapport économique annuel pour 1993*, 54 (1993), Table 20, p. 224.

[27] Gunther, *Public Policy in a No-Party State*, 288.

[28] For financial interventionism, see José María Serrano Sanz and Antón Costas Comesaña, 'La reforma del marco institucional', in José Luis García Delgado (ed.), *Economía española de la transición y la democracia* (Madrid, Centro de Investigaciones Sociológicas, 1990), 505–25; see also Arvid Lukauskas, 'The Political Economy of Financial Restriction: The Case of Spain', *Comparative Politics*, 27/1 (1994), 67–89. For industrial interventionism, see Oscar Fanjul, 'Política industrial, competencia y crecimiento (1960–1980)', in Fernando Maravall (ed.), *Economía y política industrial en España* (Madrid, Pirámide, 1987), 171–83.

This worked against the transparent operation of markets and rational economic decision-making: 'the industrial lobbies did not now compete in prices, quality, or costs, but in winning official favours; and the politicians of development administered these like almost enlightened despots.'[29]

In opposition to the thesis that economic policy in authoritarian regimes is more autonomous from the pressures of interest groups, pluralist channels of interest representation were replaced by

the incessant articulation of disaggregated, particularistic demands. ... Personalistic or clientelistic factors acquire a disproportionate impact in the policy-making process and on public policy outputs. Given the absence of other sources of political power, those groups with numerous personal ties to state officials will hold an advantage in the competition over the distribution of the nation's wealth and over the other policy outputs.[30]

Political factors also reduced the availability of economic information. To give an example, in 1972 the government banned a World Bank report on the state of the Spanish economy because it criticized the management of the INI and the regime's industrial policy. Political factors also explain why the government did not have the legitimate authority to demand inter-temporal trade-offs from society and wage moderation from workers. In consequence, support spread for the ideas that the potential for economic development was severely limited, as it generated contradictions in the political system; that major economic reforms were urgently required, but that these could scarcely be initiated by the regime; that social conflict could become an important threat, since there was a profound desire in society for political freedom which would neither be satisfied by economic liberalization alone nor eradicated through repression; and that outside the European Community the future seemed very uncertain.

This last idea reflected another political factor with consequences for the economy. The entry of the United Kingdom, Ireland, and Denmark into the Community in 1973 represented a great leap forward for European integration. In 1974 this process gained further momentum after the meeting between Valéry Giscard

[29] Manuel Jesús González, *La economía política del franquismo (1940–1970): Dirigismo, mercado y planificación* (Madrid, Tecnos, 1979), 300.

[30] Gunther, *Public Policy in a No-Party State*, 265 and 270. Many other specialists agree with this assessment of the role of private interests in the Francoist economy. Enrique Fuentes Quintana, for example, has referred to 'the decisive presence of interest groups which became pressure groups when economic policy measures were being decided'. See his chapter 'Tres decenios de la economía española en perspectiva', in José Luis García Delgado (ed.), *España: Economía*, ii (Madrid, Espasa–Calpe, 1988), 30.

d'Estaing and Helmut Schmidt in Paris. The three Southern European countries were then in the midst of a profound economic crisis and excluded from the European integration process. Yet, following the opening up of their economies, some two-thirds of Spain's and Portugal's foreign trade was conducted with Western European countries. Outside the European Community the future certainly appeared rather bleak. At the same time, the criteria for admission were quite clear: as the 1962 Birkelbach Report confirmed, only those states which guaranteed truly democratic practices and respect for human rights and fundamental liberties would be admitted into the Community. Thus, the European Community represented a particular form of political 'conditionality'.

Increasingly, therefore, the political regimes came to be seen as an obstacle to further economic development. As has been said of the Portuguese dictatorship, they were systems which were 'too archaic, too disconnected and inflexible to be able to respond to changes in the environment.'[31] At the same time, the regimes were also held responsible for the very backward state of these countries' social policies in comparison to the welfare states of Western Europe. It is true that differences may exist among the authoritarian regimes as well as among democracies in terms of their distributive outcomes, due to variations in the character of their support coalitions and in the economic contexts in which they operate. Nevertheless, the Southern European experience provides no support for the thesis that authoritarian regimes generate egalitarian effects. This thesis has rested on two main arguments. On the one hand, that the generalized restriction of political rights and democratic participation means that these are not exercised to a greater degree by privileged groups; as a result the latter will not be able to accumulate a disproportionate share of material resources. On the other hand, that by banning labour organizatons, authoritarian regimes prevent the consolidation of corporative privileges and labour-market rigidities which generate social dualism and inequalities.[32] In all three countries the dictatorships had negative consequences for both social policies and equality. If we take the Spanish case, the social legislation introduced during the first third of the twentieth century had not lagged significantly behind

[31] Thomas C. Bruneau, *Politics and Nationhood: Post-Revolutionary Portugal* (New York, Praeger, 1984), 26.

[32] The first argument appears in Samuel P. Huntington and Joan M. Nelson, *No Easy Choice: Political Participation in Developing Countries* (Cambridge, Mass., Harvard University Press, 1976), and the second in Stephen Haggard, *Pathways from the Periphery: The Politics of Growth in the Newly Industrializing Countries* (Ithaca, NY, Cornell University Press, 1990), ch. 9.

TABLE 2.2. *Social policies and inequality in Southern Europe at the end of the dictatorships*

	Social expenditure (% of GDP) (1976)	Rate of enrolment in education (1965)		Ratio of highest to lowest income quintiles
		Secondary	Tertiary	(*c.*1970)
Spain	9.9	38	6	10.4
Greece	—	49	10	—
Portugal	—	42	5	—
Italy	22.6	47	11	7.1
France	22.9	56	18	7.7

Sources: World Bank, *World Development Report* (New York, Oxford University Press, 1992), Table 29; Malcolm Sawyer, *Income Distribution in OECD Countries* (Paris, OECD, 1976); Ministerio de Trabajo y Seguridad Social, *Análisis económico-financiero del sistema español de la Seguridad Social 1964–1985* (Madrid, Ministerio de Trabajo y Seguridad Social, 1985).

most other European countries: the Instituto de Reformas Sociales, a para-statal body responsible for studying and resolving social problems, was set up in 1903; the first compulsory social insurance scheme was approved in 1919 (at the same time as in Italy, eight years after Great Britain); sickness insurance was established in 1931 (three years after Italy, one year after France); and unemployment insurance was introduced in 1932 (five years after Germany). But with Franco's victory in 1939, this synchronicity was broken. Before the dictatorship, the state had financed 25% of the cost of workers' pensions; this figure fell to 3.8% in 1950 and 1% in 1960. Social security and workers' mutual insurance schemes were organized along corporative occupational lines rather than according to universalistic principles. The Social Security Act of 1963 represented an attempt to reorganize the multitude of mutual insurance schemes and the chaotic social insurance arrangements. Yet the state subsidy remained minimal, covering a mere 4.3% of the Social Security budget in 1975, compared to 25% in Italy and the Federal Republic of Germany, and 40% in Britain. In 1976 social expenditure accounted for only 9.9% of the Spanish GDP, compared to an average of 24% in the European Community. Table 2.2 provides further data on the scope of social policies and the degree of inequality in Southern Europe at the end of the dictatorships.

The limited scope of social policies in the Southern European dictatorships was not only due to these countries' relative economic backwardness, but to political factors too. These were derived from the nature of both the regimes themselves and of their support coalitions. Their structures of interests and institutional systems blocked any increase in fiscal resources and social expenditure, and prevented these from becoming more redistributive. The economic development of the 1960s had raised overall living standards, but, at the end of the dictatorships, the societies of Southern Europe had nothing to match the systems of social services and income transfer which accompanied economic prosperity in Western Europe. The limitation of liberties which were confined to the economic sphere, the restrictions on social policies, and the collapse of development, played a decisive role in the crisis of all three dictatorships.

The Southern European experience offers a number of elements of interest for comparative purposes. First, economic liberalization had important unintended consequences for pluralism, conflict, and social expectations. Secondly, the authoritarian regimes had negative effects for the economies, as exemplified by the implantation of the autarkic model, the limits of the economic reforms, or the inadequate response to the crisis of the 1970s. Thirdly, this crisis, which came in the wake of a prolonged period of growth, undermined the dictatorships' claims to legitimacy on the grounds of their alleged economic efficiency. Finally, the European Community exerted great influence on the different phases of both economic policy and politics itself. Hence, the supra-national factor, the long-term consequences of economic development, and the short-term effects of the economic crisis combined in a complex way over a period of some fifteen years, conditioning the process of political change in all three countries.

The analysis of Southern Europe provides no support for the theses that authoritarian regimes are economically more efficient, and that economic change should precede political change. Let us remind ourselves of the reasons why. These regimes possessed only very limited legitimacy to impose austerity policies. In the absence of a free press and a political opposition, the information and debate required for decision-making (concerning the autarkic model, taxation, or the public sector) were highly inadequate. The lack of incentives associated with democratic political markets promoted a pattern of procrastination in decision-making and frequently led to the subordination of the general interest to private interests. The systems of labour relations in Salazar's Portugal and Franco's Spain fostered considerable labour-market rigidities and hindered productivity. Many economic reforms were still pending when democracies were reestablished. Moreover, these were related to the generalized demand in these societies for liberties not confined to the economic sphere alone.

2.2. The Politics of Command Economies: Eastern Europe

The experience of Eastern Europe was, of course, very different. Here, rather than just shaping the corporatist institutions and giving rise to specific problems of efficiency, politics determined the design of the entire economic system. The basic features of this are well known. One was state ownership of industrial enterprises, energy resources, financial institutions, and transport. Another was the existence of imperative planning, carried out by a central authority which determined production and prices, took all important economic decisions, and fixed priorities relating to production and consumer goods. A third characteristic was the successive disaggregation of economic directives down through the vertical relationship between planning authorities and firms. These were issued with hundreds or thousands of mandatory objectives each year, stipulating products, inputs, production costs, profits, and prices. A final characteristic was the absence of markets, of a free relation between supply and demand.

This model was always very tentative in character. Marxist thinkers paid much more attention to the capitalist economy than to the transition to communism. The first studies of the statist economic model and central planning were those produced by Bebel, Kautsky, and Bauer, later to be followed by the works of Lenin, Bukharin, Preobrazhensky, and Strumilin. The model developed from a combination of dogma, on the one hand, and trial and error on the other. For a long time the dogma asserted that economic laws did not exist under communism, that in this system political economy lost all meaning as a science. It was not only Rosa Luxemburg and Bukharin who defended this position: many years later Oskar Lange wrote that 'economic laws can be made to operate in accordance to human will'.[33] Political will, therefore, was the key to the construction of communism, and it was hoped that this voluntarism would compensate for the notable theoretical

---

[33] Oskar Lange (ed.), *Problems of Political Economy of Socialism* (New Delhi, People's Publishing House, 1962), 5.

weakness of communist economics. However, this weakness accentuated the anti-democratic characteristics of communism. It would also be the root cause of the crisis of communism once totalitarian political control and the deterrent of force disappeared. The social and economic costs of the trials and errors could only be met in the conditions of impunity existing in a dictatorship;[34] terror was a characteristic particular to Stalinism, but dictatorship was a necessary component of communism. The economic model, in fact, would have been impossible in a pluralist environment of regular and competitive democratic elections; it could only be implemented within the protective mantle of a dictatorship. Both the tentative character and the radicalism of the experiment demanded that, whatever the relative role assigned to private property or the market, the party had necessarily to hold all power if an economic system was to be defined as communist. For many years the limits of experimentation were fundamentally political in character; eventually, as Deng Xiaoping demonstrated later on in China, the system was found to be more incompatible with democracy than with the market.

In Eastern Europe the political and economic models were established simultaneously between 1946 and 1950. To take the example of Hungary, whilst a plurality of parties competed in the elections held in November 1945,[35] by spring 1949 just one party controlled 96% of the votes. In the same period, parliament ceased to be a central institution in the political system,[36] and the judiciary, civil service, and mass media lost all political independence.

---

[34] Of the 145 members of the Central Committee of the CPSU between 1912 and 1969, 69 were eliminated; 1,108 of the 1,966 delegates to the XVII Congress in 1934 were shot; on the eve of the Second World War, some three and a half million workers were held in prison camps; see David Lane, *The Socialist Industrial State* (London, George Allen and Unwin, 1976), ch. 5. See also Barrington Moore, *Authority and Inequality under Capitalism and Socialism* (Oxford, Clarendon Press, 1987), 57–62.

[35] The Smallholders' Party (FkgP) won 57% of the vote in the 1945 elections. In March 1946 its leaders began to suffer intense persecution: in February 1947 the party general secretary, Béla Kovács, was arrested; the prime minister, Ferenc Nagy, was forced into exile in May that year; the president of the Republic, Zoltán Tildy, resigned in July 1948; and finally, in February 1949 the party was absorbed by the Communist Party's front organization, the Hungarian National Independence Front (MFN). The other three main political organizations, the Social Democratic Party, the Popular Democratic Party, and the Hungarian Independence Party, shared a similar fate.

[36] The number of parliamentary questions dropped from 220 in 1946 to zero in the entire period between 1950 and 1955. See Elemer Hankiss, *East European Alternatives* (Oxford, Clarendon Press, 1990), 19.

The economy was transformed by a wave of nationalizations that took place between March 1948 and January 1950, the number of private companies falling from 4,049 to just 37. The economic model was a faithful reproduction of the Soviet one. Thus, it responded to specific conditions and objectives: a backward and basically agricultural economy and a hostile international environment. The economic efficiency of the model was greatest when the main task was accumulation, the level of development low, and the priorities few and simple. In these circumstances it was possible to mobilize domestic resources, control popular consumption, generate high levels of savings and investment, and transfer resources towards high priority objectives. But when the problem was no longer one of accumulation and investment rates, but the productivity of these, the rationality of resource allocation, and innovative activity, the model was inefficient. In more complex economies, the communist system could not solve problems of information, co-ordination, and incentives. In part these problems were derived from the fact that the economies were communist, and in part from the fact that the regimes were dictatorships.

For these reasons, the imposition of the Soviet model had much more dramatic consequences in the more developed countries, in Czechoslovakia and the German Democratic Republic, for example, than in Romania or Bulgaria. Calls for change surfaced after Stalin's death in 1953. In Poland, Hungary, and Czechoslovakia, proposals were formulated that sought to rectify the structural deficiencies of the economic model within the limits set by the communist political system. They aimed to make enterprises more autonomous, assign a more important role to prices, introduce incentives for performance, and tolerate certain forms of private economic activity. More generally, they constituted an attempt to introduce market mechanisms within the framework of state ownership of the means of production and imperative planning. As Maurice Dobb wrote

What is required, therefore, is a combination of centralized direction and decentralized decision-making, which, in turn, implies a combination of planning and market, in the sense that, even if planning employs market mechanisms, allowing itself to be guided by the prices fixed by them and consumers' preferences between different goods, it considers these mechanisms subordinate to the general objectives of planning.[37]

---

[37] Maurice Dobb, *Argumentos sobre el socialismo* (Madrid, Ciencia Nueva, 1967), 100.

This was the essence of Oskar Lange's theses on the introduction of a price system which would serve to distribute resources, reflect demand, and evaluate economic results. Lange believed that this price system was compatible with a statalized economy and central planning. His arguments led to a famous debate with Friedrich Hayek and Ludwig von Mises, who maintained that market mechanisms can only function efficiently when the means of production are privately owned.[38] Proposals for 'market socialism', notably those defended by Włodzimierz Brus in Poland, Evsey Liberman in the USSR, and Ota Šik in Czechoslovakia, have been seen as an attempt to create 'capitalism without capitalists', or 'simulated capitalism'.[39] However, they still assume that communist economies have a greater potential for efficiency since their rates of savings and investment should be more stable, and state ownership should allow externalities to be taken into account more systematically. Moreover, they should also lead to more equal societies, since all private wealth would consist of earned income.

Economic reform under communism also responded to political factors. Nikita Khrushchev's denunciation of Stalinism at the XX Congress of the Communist Party of the Soviet Union (CPSU) in February 1956 opened a brief period of expectations of change, both economic and political. But the end of Stalinism also led to greater social mobilization, and to traumatic conflicts in Eastern Europe. The Communist leaders responded by using the economy to quell political demands. After the riots in Poznań in Poland in June 1956, Władysław Gomułka slowed down the collectivization process, tolerated a certain degree of private economic activity, and placed more emphasis on the production of consumer goods. In Hungary, after the repression of the 1956 uprising, Kádár also began to introduce economic reforms. After Gÿorgy Peters's proposals dating from 1956–7, the Hungarian economy began to evolve towards a model of socialism with a decentralized market. Hungary would become the best example of the scope for reform in a communist economy. The 'New Economic Mechanism' of 1968 put

[38] Oskar Lange, 'The Economist's Case for Socialism', in Irving Howe (ed.), *Essential Works of Socialism* (New Haven, Conn., Yale University Press, 1976), 699–717; Friedrich A. Hayek, 'Socialist Calculation: The Competitive "Solution"', *Economica*, ns 7 (1940), 125–49; Ludwig von Mises, 'Economic Calculation in Socialism', in Morris Bornstein (ed.), *Comparative Economic Systems* (Homewood, Ill., Irwin, 1974), 120–7.

[39] Leszek Balcerowicz, 'The "Socialist Calculation Debate" and Reform Discussions in Socialist Countries', in János Mátyás Kovács and Márton Tardos (eds.), *Reform and Transformation in Eastern Europe* (London, Routledge, 1992), 5–17.

an end to imperative central planning, permitted enterprises to draw up their own annual plans in accordance with demand and choose their own inputs, and allowed prices to partially reflect shortages. Thanks to the greater flexibility, decentralization, and autonomy of the economy, the number of people employed in the private sector increased five-fold between 1954 and 1984, the number of co-operatives grew rapidly until they accounted for 51% of the gross agricultural product, and opportunities for consumer choice rose significantly. By 1984, 87% of homes were privately owned, whilst car sales were fourteen times higher than in 1966.

The economic reforms had a political objective: to reinforce the regimes' legitimacy by creating escape valves through consumption and greater tolerance of private activities. Coercion and indoctrination had failed to avert traumatic episodes such as those in Hungary and Poland in 1956. The alternative strategy was the typical choice of bureaucratized authoritarian regimes, namely an implicit pact offering prosperity in return for acquiescence. The goal was political apathy, no longer ideological mobilization. This change of strategy was summed up in Kádár's famous phrase in a speech in December 1961, 'he who is not against us is for us', in contrast to his predecessor, Mátyás Rákosi, who had declared that 'he who is not for us is against us'. In this way, objectives were assigned to the economy which properly corresponded to politics; the market was seen as an alternative to democracy. This was not only the vision of the governments: as Brus has argued, until the mid-1980s pessimism about the possibilities for democratization encouraged many economists in their support for the market, as an instrument to weaken the political centre.[40] Thus, whilst governments saw the reforms as a means of promoting their own legitimacy, others believed they would help to erode the total control exercised by communist power.

The limits of the reforms were also both political and economic in character. Economic changes generated significant political resistance from within the party and state bureaucracies, from ideologues, managers of the large state-owned enterprises, and within the official unions. In Hungary, for example, this resistance led to the suspension of the 'New Economic Mechanism' in 1972. Thus reforms were either inconsistently applied (in Hungary and Poland), or abandoned after a traumatic experience (such as that

---

[40] Włodzimierz Brus, 'From Revisionism to Pragmatism: Sketches to a Self-Portrait of a "Reform Economist"', in Kovács and Tardos, *Reform and Transformation in Eastern Europe*, 136–42.

in Czechoslovakia in 1968). Their economic outcomes were always unsatisfactory. They failed to resolve the disconnection between production and individual needs, the problems created by the generalized excess demand, the chronic shortages, the forced substitution in consumption, the queues of consumers, or the production bottlenecks. Prices still did not reflect supply and demand. Central planning had been discarded on the grounds of inefficiency, but it had not been substituted by a real market.

The bureaucracies retained overall control of investment, prices, incomes, the appointment of company managers, and foreign trade. After the Hungarian reforms, the companies themselves still only decided one-fifth of all investment in the public sector. The bureaucracies were dominated by inertia, conformist behaviour, and rent-seeking strategies. Their aversion to risk-taking hindered innovation in processes and products. Rather than strengthening the autonomy of the states, the dictatorships made them more vulnerable to interest group pressure. The economies were still characterized by a high degree of monopolization: for example, the average number of workers per factory in Hungary was twice as high as in France, Italy, or Japan.[41] As a result, company managers could limit production in order to raise prices, or cut costs by lowering the quality of their products. They tended to conceal the productive capacity of their companies from the government in order to make it easier to meet production targets. Loans from the state banks were often made on political grounds rather than according to profitability, and were systematically used to keep inefficient companies afloat. Even though the reforms had given enterprises greater autonomy, they still received vast subsidies from the government; the persistence of what János Kornai has termed 'soft budget constraints' reflected the lack of economic discipline.[42] Efficiency could hardly be raised through greater competition: since the state owned all capital, new enterprises could not be created, while a liberalization of imports would have dramatic consequences for the balance of payments. Partial reforms, therefore, did not resolve the endemic problems of the communist economies: the inefficient allocation of resources; the restrictions on the 'entry' and 'exit' of agents; insufficient innovation; the absence of incentives; or the lack of adequate information. It has been argued

[41] János Kornai, 'The Hungarian Reform Process: Visions, Hopes and Reality', *Journal of Economic Literature*, 24 (1986), 1, 687–737.

[42] Kornai, 'Hungarian Reform Process'; Ellen Comisso, 'Market Failures and Market Socialism: Economic Problems of the Transition', *Eastern European Politics and Society*, 2/3 (1988), 433–65.

that 'decentralized decision-making under a soft budget constraint may lead to worse results than central planning'.[43]

Nevertheless, the reforms did have social consequences. From the beginning of the 1970s, in Kádár's Hungary and Edward Gierek's Poland societies became somewhat more plural. This social pluralism developed around what was known as the 'second economy', which comprised a growing number of informal activities beyond the state sector, under 'hard budget constraints', corresponding to a myriad of family firms and small co-operatives. Despite their limitations, therefore, the economic reforms facilitated the emergence of areas of greater autonomy from the states, of more complex civil societies. In the case of Poland, these social changes were related to the upsurge in social unrest and 'pressure from below' from the beginning of the decade onwards. If the conflicts of 1970 had provoked the replacement of Gomułka by Gierek, ten years later the mobilizations by Solidarnośc were responsible for the latter's substitution by Stanisław Kania. In Hungary, in contrast, changes were more narrowly restricted to the economic sphere and to tensions among the political élites.

The political causes of economic inefficiency became particularly evident with the onset of the international economic crisis in the 1970s. As in the case of Southern Europe, the dictatorships failed to respond adequately to the crisis, and, in consequence, the chronic problems of the communist economies worsened dramatically during the last fifteen years of the regimes' existence. Rather than attempting to adjust their economies to the new circumstances, many of the governments sought to maintain rapid growth in the belief that they could avoid the effects of the international crisis. This they did by resorting to foreign loans, then relatively easy to obtain: as a result, their foreign debts spiralled. Their foreign trade suffered seriously from the effects of the general crisis, and rather than expand, their share of international markets shrank. Under the crisis, budgets were laxer than ever and public deficits escalated. The states protected increasingly inefficient enterprises at great expense to the public coffers: in Poland, for example, subsidies accounted for one-third of the state budget. Governments also adopted very permissive wage policies: whilst from 1971 to 1980 nominal wages rose by an average annual rate of 6.5% in Hungary and 9.5% in Poland, per capita output grew a mere 2.3%

---

[43] Christopher Clague, 'The Journey to a Market Economy', in Christopher Clague and Gordon C. Rausser (eds.), *The Emergence of Market Economies in Eastern Europe* (Cambridge, Mass., Blackwell, 1992), 4.

and 2.6%, respectively.[44] Their response to the crisis shared a number of common characteristics with that of the dictatorships of Southern Europe. On the one hand, they failed to diagnose the crisis correctly, or design adequate economic policies with which to combat its effects. On the other, in a context of economic difficulties and of a major erosion of their support, governments were unwilling to impose budget and wage austerity, but rather attempted to buy their survival at enormous cost to their economies.

Thus, the regimes were incapable of responding to the crisis. They could not stabilize their economies, nor impose fiscal austerity, price increases, or wage discipline. In Hungary, as early as 1977 the Central Committee of the Hungarian Socialist Workers' Party (HWSP) had recognized the need to change its economic policy. However, the measures of economic stabilization and liberalization introduced in 1979 were only limited. As can be seen in Table 2.3, there was little economic growth after that date. Moreover, the rise in interest rates decreed by the creditor countries doubled Hungary's foreign debt. After twenty years of partial reforms, there was widespread pessimism and weariness with economic policies, and the system lost even more credibility. Many of those responsible for the reforms were abandoning Kádár, including figures such as Imre Pozsgay, Rezsö Nyers, and Miklós Németh who would later initiate the 'changes from above' that characterized the Hungarian transition. If we turn to Poland, attempts to stabilize the economy from the mid-1970s onwards were repeatedly rejected by the population. When Gierek replaced Gomułka he attempted to expand his support by ordering a 40% rise in real wages. The austerity measures which inevitably came in the wake of this move had to be abandoned in the face of popular protest. Several attempts to introduce economic discipline were similarly dropped due to social resistance, as in the case of the failed initiative to increase food prices by 70% in June 1976. After another wave of strikes, the 'Gdańsk Accords' signed by the government and Solidarność in August 1980 represented a further economic capitulation in exchange for social peace. Salaries were raised and index-linked to inflation, the working week was shortened, and food subsidies increased. As a result, the economic situation continued to deteriorate and hence social conflict did not come to an end. A new attempt was made to stabilize the economy following the military intervention led by General Wojciech Jaruzelski in

---

[44] János Kornai, *The Socialist System* (Princeton, Princeton University Press, 1992), 533.

Table 2.3. *Economic performance in Eastern Europe up to 1989*

	Czechoslovakia	Hungary	Poland
Growth of net material product			
(% per annum)			
1951–60	7.5	5.8	7.6
1961–5	1.9	4.1	6.2
1966–75	6.1	6.6	7.8
1976–80	3.6	3.2	—
1981–5	1.8	1.8	—
1986	2.6	0.9	4.9
1987	2.2	4.1	1.9
1988	2.5	0.5	4.9
1989	1.5	−1.8	−1.5
Gross investment			
1986	1.4	6.5	5.1
1987	4.4	9.8	4.2
1988	4.5	−7.7	6.0
1989	1.0	−5.7	0.0
Net debt ($M.)			
1986	3,037	12,898	31,866
1987	3,724	16,230	35,806
1988	4,029	15,926	35,572
1989	5,370	19,446	37,520

Sources: Tamas Bauer, 'The Second Economic Reform and Ownership Relations', *Eastern European Economics*, 22/3–4 (1984), 33–87; OECD, *Financial Market Trends*, 45 (1990); Miroslav Hrnčíř, 'The Transition to a Market Economy: Lessons from the Experience of the CSFR', in Michael Keren and Gur Ofer (eds.), *Trials of Transition: Economic Reform in the Former Communist Bloc* (Boulder, Colo., Westview Press, 1992), 151–72.

1981. However, fear of renewed outbreaks of social conflict meant that the new government was unable to reduce the foreign debt burden or prevent inflationary wage agreements. Its attempt to win popular support for new reforms failed in the referendum of November 1987. The gravity of the economic situation led the Minister of the Economy, Władysław Sadowski, to try to implement the reforms even in the face of popular opposition. However, he was unable to halt the decline in the net material product, the escalating public deficit, the growing foreign debt which reached $1,113 per capita, the soaring inflation which eventually turned into hyperinflation (53% in October 1989), or the spiralling wage increases. If we consider the period between 1981 and 1989, nominal wages rose an average of 8.1% annually in Hungary and 60.8% in Poland, whilst per capita output only increased by 0.9% per annum in Hungary and fell by −0.4% in Poland.[45]

Political factors contributed decisively to this economic failure. There was extensive opposition to the partial reforms among the party and state bureaucracies. The expansion of the private sector, the introduction of market mechanisms, the restriction of *nomenklatura* positions, and tighter budgetary controls would limit their possibilities of extracting rents from the public sector.[46] Yet even though the interests of these bureaucracies were tied to the old system, they were in charge of implementing the reforms. Moreover, as against the thesis that dictatorships enjoy greater autonomy, the Hungarian and Polish regimes turned out to be very vulnerable to pressure from interest groups. They proved incapable of altering a course which was leading to unsustainable public deficits, overwhelming foreign debts, and very high inflation. Nor were they able to impose disciplined fiscal and monetary policies. Rather than guaranteeing efficiency, the high degree of discretion which these regimes apparently enjoyed constituted a source of insecurity. This discretion certainly did not assure individual rights; people only enjoyed those rights which the political power was willing to tolerate in any given circumstances. Olson has argued that the discretionary nature of power and the insecurity surrounding rights constitute the major sources of dictatorships' economic fragility.[47] And as Brus has noted, 'macroeconomic choices are by their very nature political, and without a pluralist polity they will remain arbitrary'.[48] The restrictions on information also limited these governments' economic efficiency, making it harder to detect and rectify incorrect diagnoses and policies.[49] Finally, the dictatorships'

[45] Stanisław Gomułka, 'Polish Economic Reform: Principles, Policies and Surprises', in Michael Keren and Gur Ofer (eds.), *Trials of Transition: Economic Reform in the Former Communist Bloc* (Boulder, Colo., Westview Press, 1992), 111; Kornai, *Socialist System*, 533, n. 44.

[46] Barry W. Ickes, 'Obstacles to Economic Reform of Socialism: An Institutional-Choice Approach', *The Annals of the American Academy of Political and Social Science*, 507 (1990), 62.

[47] Mancur Olson, 'Dictatorship, Democracy and Development', *American Political Science Review*, 87/3 (1993), 567–76; and by the same author, 'The Hidden Path to a Successful Economy', in Clague and Rausser (eds.), *Emergence of Market Economies in Eastern Europe*, 66 and 67.

[48] Brus, 'From Revisionism to Pragmatism', 138.

[49] See the discussion, in relation to the communist countries, of the problems of information and incentives under dictatorships, in Gordon G. Rausser, 'Lessons for Emerging Market Economies in Eastern Europe', in Clague and Rausser (eds.), *Emergence of Market Economies in Eastern Europe*, 315–17.

illegitimacy had consequences for the economies too, since in the midst of a crisis, the governments could not appeal for austerity, and this could only be imposed with difficulty. As Sachs has written

the timidity of the reforms; the power of the *nomenklatura* to avoid a real opening of the economy to international competition, and even the introduction of domestic competition; the political illegitimacy of the regime; and the corruption and arrogance of the Communist party all contributed to the failure of the pre-1989 reforms. . . . The government could not appeal to the public for restraint, patience, and trust.[50]

In this way, during the years of deepening crisis and failed reforms, Eastern Europe's economic problems were increasingly interpreted in political terms, as the consequence of obstacles stemming from the communist system. This explains why, in Longworth's words, 'every grievance, every mistake tended to be blamed on the regime.'[51] On the one hand, the concentration of power resulted in a concentration of responsibility. On the other, the political monopoly blocked any possibility of effective change in the economies and was rejected not only for political motives but on economic grounds too. Towards the end, reformist elements within the communist regimes in Hungary and Poland made contact with the democratic opposition in order to establish a consensus which could only be achieved through democratization. There was widespread agreement in these societies that economic reforms were no substitute for political ones, that democracy was essential in order to overcome the resistance of the political bureaucracy, to limit the discretionary use of power, and guarantee civil rights. In other words, whilst in Southern Europe society demanded political changes from economic change, in Eastern Europe societies demanded political change for economic change.

Moreover, a major erosion of egalitarianism had taken place in all these societies, a process which was linked to their economic decline. A characteristic feature of the communist systems had been the coverage of 'social rights without citizenship': that is, the satisfaction of such rights depended on the authoritarian paternalism of the state-party. There was no welfare system based on universal criteria: entitlement to, and provision of, social benefits were mainly based on the individual's job, were closely tied to one's working life, and largely managed by enterprises. Thus, social costs accounted for around 50% of enterprises' wage costs.

[50] Jeffrey Sachs, *Poland's Jump to the Market Economy* (Cambridge, Mass., MIT Press, 1993), 33 and 35.
[51] Philip Longworth, *The Making of Eastern Europe* (New York, St Martin's Press, 1992), 58.

Since inflation was not officially recognized, benefits were not regularly revised, and increases were arbitrary and sporadic. Nor was unemployment recognized, and for many years the existence of poverty was denied. In Hungary, for example, discussion of this problem was only tolerated after the congress held by the Hungarian Sociological Association in 1981. During the following decade, it was estimated that some 10% of the population lived below subsistence level.[52] Anthony Atkinson and John Micklewright have shown that, in comparative terms, there was a very similar degree of relative poverty in Western and Eastern Europe,[53] although the policies adopted to fight poverty did vary (in Western Europe these were more directed towards old people, whilst in the East they were focused more on large families and couples of working age). However, since the average incomes used in these calculations were much lower in Eastern Europe, in absolute terms the poor had fewer resources and experienced greater real necessity. When the economies collapsed, there was a major increase in poverty: in the Soviet Union, for example, the number of people at or below the poverty line rose from 68 million to 80 million. And not only were there more poor, but they also had even fewer resources. The end of communism, therefore, took place in the context of enormous social hardship.

If we consider incomes, Table 2.4 shows that they were more evenly distributed in the communist economies than in Western Europe. In contrast, taxation and public expenditure had a much more limited egalitarian impact. Income tax did not exist, confiscatory levies from firms constituted the principal source of public revenue, and hence taxation had no redistributive function. Similarly, social expenditure had only a slight effect on inequality; in Hungary, for example, only 22.7% of social expenditure was redistributive.[54] Thus, 'social income' accounted for a lower proportion of labour incomes than in most Western European countries,

[52] Xavier Gaullier, 'Modernisation et État-Providence en Europe Centrale: Réflexions à partir de la situation en Hongrie', *Revue Française des Affaires Sociales*, 46/1 (1992), 3–19.

[53] In other words, the proportion of the total population with an income below a certain percentage of the average income: see Anthony B. Atkinson and John Micklewright, *Economic Transformation in Eastern Europe and the Distribution of Income* (Cambridge, Cambridge University Press, 1992), ch. 7.

[54] The redistributive impact has been estimated on the basis that the lowest decile receives more than 10% of the budget of the programme and the two lowest deciles obtain more than 20%; see David M. Newbery, 'The Safety Net during Transformation: Hungary', in Clague and Rausser (eds.), *The Emergence of Market Economies in Eastern Europe*, 197–221.

TABLE 2.4. *A comparison of social indicators in Eastern and Western Europe*

	Infant mortality rate[a]	Life expectancy at birth[b]	Rate of enrolment in tertiary education[c]	Ratio highest to lowest income quintiles[d]	Proportion of total income of the wealthiest 10%[e]
Czechoslovakia	12	71.8	18	—	—
Hungary	15	70.9	15	3.2[e]	20.7[e]
Poland	16	71.8	20	3.6[f]	21.0[f]
Spain	11	77.0	32	5.8[g]	24.5[g]
France	7	76.4	37	6.5[h]	25.5[h]
Great Britain	8	75.7	24	6.8[h]	23.3[h]
Federal Republic of Germany	7	75.2	32	5.7[i]	23.4[i]
Sweden	6	77.4	31	4.6[j]	20.8[j]

Source: United Nations Development Programme, *Human Development Report* (New York, Oxford University Press, 1993), Tables 28, 29, and 31.
   [a] Per 1,000 births in 1990.
   [b] In years; data for 1990.
   [c] Percentage of age-group.
   [d] Referring to family income units.
   Data years as follows: [e] 1987–9, [f] 1987, [g] 1980–1, [h] 1979, [i] 1984, [j] 1981.

representing, for example, 20% in Hungary compared to 35% in France.[55] As a result, the final pattern of inequality does not appear to have been qualitatively very different from that of many market economies. Income distribution after taxes and public expenditure in a country like Hungary was a little more equitable than in the Federal Republic of Germany or Sweden, but basically similar to that found in the Netherlands or Belgium.[56] On the other hand, the degree of income equality varied in the different communist countries. It was, for example, higher in Hungary and Czechoslovakia than in Poland or the USSR. It appears, therefore, that Barrington Moore was right to conclude, on the basis of his study of the Soviet Union during the Brezhnev era, that 'the

[55] Pierre Kende and Zdenek Strimska, *Égalité et inégalités en Europe de l'Est* (Paris, Presses de la Fondation Nationale des Sciences Politiques, 1984).
   [56] Rudolf Andorka, 'Hungarian Sociology in the Face of the Political, Economic and Social Transition', *International Sociology*, 6/4 (1991).

system of equality under prevailing forms of socialism has turned out to be not very different from that under liberal capitalism... The number of rungs in the ladder and the differences in life styles between the high and low rungs are very similar'.[57]

However, despite comparatively low standards of living and shrinking resources, there was a basic level of protection. As Jacek Kuroń notes, 'The old system had established a certain order which assured everyone social protection.... It is a prison in which one finds more security and better social protection, where one is guaranteed a roof over one's head and three meals a day.'[58] At the end of communism, the collapse of central planning and the crisis of the state-owned enterprises seriously affected social policies. Table 2.4 shows that in comparison to various Western European countries, life expectancy was lower in Hungary and Poland, as was the proportion of the age-groups enrolled in secondary and tertiary education. During the 1980s not only did the regimes fail to generate material prosperity, but inequality and poverty were increasing and social rights were being restricted. In this way, the desire for liberty fused with these material factors in the regimes' legitimacy crisis. Political and economic change could come through 'reform from above' (as in the Hungarian case), or from 'pressure from below' (as in Poland), but it was always motivated by these factors, and it began as soon as Gorbachev removed the deterrent of force.

In Czechoslovakia, of course, the experience was very different. External factors played a much more important role in the change of regime, whilst Stalinism always had a much stronger grip. The Communist Party had interpreted any conflict, whether the popular revolt in Pilsen in 1953 or the 'Prague Spring' of 1968, as the result of excessive tolerance: reforms were not seen as the response to political crises but rather as their cause. After Alexander Dubček's experiment had ended in Soviet intervention, Gustav Husák carried out a major purge of reformists and reinforced central economic planning. Over the following two decades, Czechoslovak politics remained under the protection and tutelage of the USSR. This was a period of great discipline within the ranks of the communist *nomenklatura*, political intimidation exercised through a strict security system, extensive social demobilization, and ideological rigidity (to the extent that the Czech Academy of Sciences

[57] Moore, *Authority and Inequality*, 118–19.
[58] Jacek Kuroń, 'Aider ceux qui en ont vraiment besoin', *La Nouvelle Alternative*, 23 (1991).

banned the term 'economic reform' in 1972). The economy did not decline as dramatically as in Hungary or Poland. Moreover, a system of planning still existed and the Communist Party continued to act as an instrument of economic co-ordination. Although the foreign debt doubled after 1985, it remained relatively low ($444 per capita) due to a strict austerity programme implemented in the early 1980s. Nevertheless, this resulted in a major deterioration of social benefits, infrastructures, and the environment. In the absence of reforms, Czechoslovakia continued to display the classic features of communist economies: in 1987 only 0.6% of workers were employed in the private sector; the mono-bank system survived until 1989; and the economy remained highly monopolized.[59] With the exception of Bulgaria, Czechoslovakia was the country which relied most heavily on the Mutual Economic Assistance Council. This dependence led to the 'regressive specialization' and fossilization of the Czechoslovak economy, and hindered its adaptation to the changing shape of international demand.[60]

Unlike Hungary and Poland, Czechoslovakia remained stable at the macroeconomic level until the last years of the communist regime. However, neither the institutions, production, nor foreign trade were modified in any way. Hence the economy revealed the typical problems of communist systems: namely, excess demand, hidden inflation, obsolete productive capital, and international isolation. And as can be seen from Table 2.3, growth rates fell steadily from 1970 onwards.

Thus, the crisis of the Czechoslovak economy was not due to experiments in partial reforms. Equally, the crisis had less serious political consequences than in Poland or Hungary. The democratization process proved much more abrupt and also more dependent on the 'USSR factor'. When this factor began to work in favour of change, the Czechoslovak leaders tried to distance themselves from *perestroika* and *glasnot*. When Husak was removed from his post as first secretary of the Communist Party in December 1987, he was replaced by a 'hardliner', Miloš Jakeš. A few monthš later, in September 1988, the prime minister Lumobir Strougal was dismissed as a result of his excessive sympathy towards Gorbachev. The cautious demonstrations of political dissent which took place in August 1988 and January 1989 were brutally repressed.[61] But

[59] The average Czech enterprise employed close to 2,000 workers, compared to 1,200 in Poland.

[60] Miroslav Hrnčíř, 'The Transition to a Market Economy: Lessons from the Experience of the CSFR', in Keren and Ofer (eds.), *Trials of Transition*, 156.

[61] Over 800 people were arrested following the demonstrations in January 1989.

the regime could not survive the transformations then taking place in the USSR, the changes in Poland and Hungary, and the collapse of communism in the German Democratic Republic. The citizens perceived the nature of these changes and took to the streets; there came a point when the regime lost its capacity to repress. Without repression, it had no alternative but to capitulate. The process was extremely rapid. On 17 November a massive demonstration was once again fiercely repressed, but on this occasion the crowd responded by occupying the streets. Caught in a cul-de-sac, on 10 December the government was replaced by another of 'national concord' under a reformed communist, Marian Calfa. Nineteen days later the Federal Assembly elected Václav Havel president of the Republic.

The last phase of communism saw a blossoming of political traditions which had survived under the dictatorships. I shall discuss this phenomenon in Chapter 5, but the impact of the economy or other exogenous factors on the regime change can only be understood in this cultural context. Archie Brown and Jack Gray were right to conclude in their 1970s study of the political culture of the communist systems (and of Czechoslovakia in particular) that

the attempt to create a new socialist man, the end product of the official political culture, has been on the whole a depressing failure. . . . Almost everywhere apathy, privatism and 'economism' are prevalent and tolerated. . . . Perhaps the most striking implication of our study is the relative failure of Communist processes of socialization and education, in spite of the enjoyment of all the institutional powers which a Communist political system bestows.

And, they continue

in countries where there has in the past been experience of the fruitful play of competing ideas and competing interests, experience of Communist government has not weakened but actually strengthened the conviction among the population that political freedom brings both greater justice and greater efficiency.[62]

The crisis of economies whose efficiency had become their major source of political legitimacy, the uselessness of a history of partial reforms, the all-encompassing fatalism with regard to the nonviability of the system, the erosion of social policies, the obsolescence of the original values of communism, and the survival of political traditions constituted, therefore, a complex series of factors

---

[62] Archie Brown and Jack Gray (eds.), *Political Culture and Political Change in Communist States* (New York, Holmes and Maier, 1977), 270–2.

which contributed to these regime changes. However, the Eastern European case has enabled us to explore a little more deeply the questions as to whether these changes of regime were preceded by economic crises or economic growth, and whether dictatorships have a greater capacity to improve economic conditions. In Eastern Europe political factors aggravated the regimes' economic problems: the crises not only affected systems which were communist, but regimes which were dictatorships. As was the case in Southern Europe, in time these regimes modified their claims to legitimacy, basing them on technical grounds more than on ideology. And, in turn, as in Southern Europe, they became more vulnerable to social pressures, proved incapable of altering a path that led to spiralling public deficits and inflation, and adopted very lax fiscal, wage, and monetary policies. Their capacity to implement reforms was rigidly restricted by political considerations, as was their response to the new economic circumstances of the 1970s. One might argue that all this was because in Poland and Hungary, and later in the Soviet Union, the dictatorships became too permissive. However, this argument immediately raises the question as to how repressive they should have been to generate efficient economic results. We all know that dictatorships often have the power to sacrifice entire generations in the name of a future paradise, whether under communism or the market. However, dictatorships have no mechanisms to guarantee that these sacrifices will not simply lead to even more sacrifices.

3

The Political Economy of Democratization

What was the economic scenario facing the new democracies of Southern and Eastern Europe on the collapse of the dictatorships? What consequences did the newly established regimes have for the economies? How far did the type of democratic transition, the strength of electoral support, and the nature of the political consensus influence the economic policies governments adopted and the problems they encountered? To what extent did economic policies converge or diverge in terms of the content and pace of reform? These are the main questions to be examined in this chapter. It will be argued that the type of transition, although initially important in some cases, became increasingly less significant for economic performance, and that this was much more dependent on electoral results and the quality of governments. I will also maintain that electoral support was an important, but not a decisive factor in the formulation of economic policies, and that forms of consensus and certain experiences of political learning sometimes had more influence on these. It will be further suggested that, whilst there was a significant degree of convergence of macroeconomic policies, they diverged notably in terms of the role assigned to social policies and the state. Finally, I will defend the thesis that, in time, democracies were generally able to improve the economic situation.

3.1. Southern Europe: Politics, Economics, and Policy Paradigms

Basic differences existed between the experiences of Southern and Eastern Europe on the return to democracy. One had to do with the intellectual maps of economic policies: when the Southern European democracies were established, consensus on policy paradigms was much more limited than it would be during the 1980s. These different intellectual environments were reflected in the greater experimentation with heterodox policies in Portugal than in Poland, Hungary, or Czechoslovakia. Another difference concerned the scale of the tasks facing the new regimes. In Greece, Portugal, and Spain, inflation and the foreign debt were lower, and the reforms did not imply the total transformation of the economic system. Yet the agenda of economic reforms was still heavily loaded in the three Southern European countries. As I noted in the previous chapter, the crisis of the 1970s had hit their economies very hard, the very lax policies of the dictatorships only aggravating the problems. Growth had ground to a halt, whilst both inflation and unemployment rose rapidly. The economies were still heavily protected, above all in Spain and Greece, and scarcely competitive.[1] In none of these three countries had the dictatorships tackled industrial reconversion or the reorganization of the public sector. Public provision of education, active manpower policies, and health care was very limited. In contrast, the states intervened extensively in economic life, regulating labour markets and prices, subsidizing firms, and directly participating in production, generally in unprofitable sectors, through the public business sector.[2] Wages had risen sharply, whilst the tax systems remained primitive and regressive. Capital markets, competition between banks and financial institutions, and savings instruments were all relatively underdeveloped. Furthermore, all three countries were excluded from the European Community on political grounds.

These were the reforms pending when democracy was re-established in Portugal, Greece, and Spain. Let us examine the way the new political conditions affected economic policies by considering first the consequences of the different types of transition. Table 3.1 summarizes the principal characteristics of the three Southern European democratizations.[3] The most important

[1] Bénédicte Larre and Raymond Torres, 'Is Convergence a Spontaneous Process? The Experience of Spain, Portugal and Greece', *OECD Economic Studies*, 16 (1991), 177–8. In Spain and Greece the combined total value of imports and exports amounted to some 17% of the GDP in 1980, compared to 28% in Portugal.

[2] In Spain in 1976 the INI accounted for 10% of the GDP and 6% of employment; in 1980 state-owned companies represented 22% of investment and 5% of employment in Spain, 18.3% and 5.2% in Portugal, and 12.7% and 3.5% in Greece.

[3] For a study of the three transitions, see e.g. Guillermo O'Donnell, Philippe C. Schmitter, and Laurence Whitehead (eds.), *Transitions from Authoritarian Rule: Southern Europe* (Baltimore, Johns Hopkins University Press, 1986), chs. by Nikiforos Diamandouros, José María Maravall and Julián Santamaría, and Kenneth Maxwell. See also the interesting typologies of Alfred Stepan, 'Paths towards

TABLE 3.1. *Characteristics of the transitions in Southern Europe*

Spain	Greece	Portugal
Protracted dictatorship.	Shorter dictatorship.	Protracted dictatorship.
Failed liberalization (Arias).	Failed liberalization (Papadopoulos).	Failed liberalization (Caetano).
Mobilization 'from below'.	Some mobilizations 'from below'.	Few mobilizations 'from below'.
Divisions within the regime.	Internal divisions within the regime.	Military crisis in Angola and Mozambique.
Reforms 'from above'.	Military crisis in Cyprus (July 1974).	Abrupt rupture led by the armed forces as a movement (April 1974).
Interaction reformists/moderates.	Initiative to terminate the regime from the armed forces as an institution.	Initial importance of extra-parliamentary politics.
Decisive leaderships.	Decisive leadership of Karamanlis.	Intense struggle over the rules of the game.
Transactions and consensus 1977–9 (Constitution, State of the Autonomies, Moncloa Pacts).	Gradualist but rapid transition.	Provisional governments.
No provisional governments.	No cross-party consensus.	Long period of unstable governments.
Initial electoral predominance of the right (1977 and 1979).	No provisional governments.	Initial electoral predominance of the left (1975–6).
Threats of involution.	Initial electoral predominance of the right (1974 and 1977).	Changes in the rules of the game (constitutional reforms in 1982 and 1986).
Existence of regional nationalisms.	Changes in the rules of the game (constitutional reform in 1985).	
Stable rules of the game.		

differences lay in the duration and character of the previous regime, the abruptness or gradualism of political change, the predominance of strategies of consensus or imposition, and the importance of mobilizations 'from below' or political reforms 'from above'. Thus, the dictatorship of the Colonels in Greece was comparatively short and never became fully institutionalized; the final years of the Francoist regime constituted a peculiar combination of repression, institutionalization, and developmentalism; and, finally, the Salazar regime more closely resembled a nineteenth-century conservative dictatorship. Whilst in Portugal the rising led by the Movimento das Forças Armadas (MFA) in April 1974 marked a radical break with the past, in the other two cases political change was more gradualist and transactional; in Spain, for example, free elections were only held twenty months after Franco's death, and a further eighteen months went by before the new constitution was approved. Whilst Spain represents the paradigmatic case of a transition carried out by transaction, and of the use of strategies of consensus to establish the rules of the game and the institutions of the new regime, Portugal, in contrast, was an example of imposition. In Greece, in turn, Constantin Karamanlis hardly negotiated with the opposition. In Spain, mobilizations 'from below' were much more significant than in the other two countries,[4] even though reforms 'from above' were crucial for the transition; in Portugal, although the change was more revolutionary in character, most of the mobilizations took place after the change of regime.

In Southern Europe, during the phase of the transition itself, politics took precedence over the economy; that is, political considerations decisively influenced the choice of economic policies. The reasons for this, however, were very different in the three countries. In Portugal, the sharp break with the past, the subsequent wave of popular mobilizations, the MFA's revolutionary rhetoric, and the ideology of the provisional governments all had profound consequences for the orientation of economic policy. Above all during

Redemocratization: Theoretical and Comparative Considerations', in Guillermo O'Donnell, Philippe C. Schmitter, and Laurence Whitehead (eds.), *Transitions from Authoritarian Rule: Comparative Perspectives* (Baltimore, Johns Hopkins University Press, 1986), 64–84, and of Terry L. Karl and Philippe C. Schmitter, 'Modes of Transition in Latin America, Southern and Eastern Europe', *International Journal of Social Science*, 128 (1991), 269–84.

[4] See José Maria Maravall, *Dictatorship and Political Dissent* (New York: St Martin's Press, 1978), 18–43, and by the same author, *The Transition to Democracy in Spain* (New York, St Martin's Press, 1982), 4–18.

the first two years of the new regime, there was considerable political experimentation with the economy, since the goal was not merely to establish a new regime, but also the rapid and radical transformation of capitalism.[5] The type of transition thus had important consequences for economic policy. The new governments embarked on a massive nationalization programme, which affected 22 Portuguese banks and more than one-quarter of all firms, as well as a major redistribution of income through increased public spending and wage rises (these went up by some 25% in real terms during the first two years). This first stage of the transition was characterized by a high degree of political voluntarism; many of the radical elements behind the 'revolution of the carnations' were convinced that political will was all that was required to modify economic laws.

However, the economic results of these policies turned out to be disappointing. Rather than promoting economic development via increased state activity and expanded domestic demand, they fuelled public and trade deficits, massive capital outflows, and an investment crisis. Exports, for example, fell by 21%, and investment by 37% in 1974 alone.[6] During 1974 and 1975, growth fell by 3.2%, prices rose by 43.3%, and unemployment went up two points.[7] Moreover, emigration no longer provided an economic escape-valve: 192,200 emigrants returned to Portugal between 1973 and 1974, whilst the scale of the problem grew over the next few years with the decolonization of Angola and Mozambique.[8]

These economic problems overlapped with considerable political instability. For a time this was the fruit of the tension between conflicting models of direct and representative democracy, of economic collectivism and a mixed market economy. The clashes between the radical and moderate elements in the new regime, which were mirrored within the ranks of the MFA itself, reflected these tensions. The failure of the radical *putsch* in November 1975 marked the beginning of a shift towards representative democracy and the market. The results of the successive elections reinforced this

[5] Thus, article 91 of the 1976 constitution established the 'creation of a socialist society' as an objective. The provisional government's economic programme was defined in the Decree-Law of 15 May 1974.

[6] Eric M. Baklanov, *La transformación económica de España y Portugal: La economia del Franquismo y del Salazarismo* (Madrid: Espasa–Calpe, 1980), ch. 9.

[7] Commission des Communautés Européennes, *Économie Européenne*, 54 (1993), Tables 3, 10, and 34; pp. 198, 205, and 219.

[8] Hans D. Schmitt, 'Economic Stabilization and Growth in Portugal', *IMF Occasional Paper*, 2 (Washington DC, International Monetary Fund, 1981), Table 1.

tendency: from the start most votes went to a centre-left party (the Partido Socialista (PS)) or to the centre-right (the Partido Popular Democrático (PPD), later renamed the Partido Socialdemócrata (PSD)). Successive elections and experiences of governments gradually weakened the impact the type of transition had initially had on Portuguese economic policy. Thus, although for a time the sharp break with the past encouraged economic experimentalism, from 1976 onwards the governments began to modify the orientation of their policies.

In Greece and Spain the more gradualist transitions, the non-existence of provisional governments, the absence of radical military movements, and the political parties' greater control of the process of political change all contributed to the adoption of more cautious economic policies. In both cases, the transitions took place through transaction, that is, they were based on implicit or explicit pacts of coexistence between sectors situated within and outside the dictatorial regime. In Greece, although the military crisis provoked by the Cyprus fiasco gave the new regime greater room for manœuvre than in Spain, Karamanlis faced an attempted *coup d'état* in February 1975. In the case of Spain, the transition was seriously threatened by the presence of strong anti-democratic groups, the persistent appearance of involutionist conspiracies ('Operation Galaxy' in November 1978, an attempted coup in February 1981, and a military plot in October 1982), and intensified terrorist activity under democracy. In both countries, conservative parties won the first two elections. Political change did not extend to the economic terrain. Neither Karamanlis[9] nor Adolfo Suárez attempted any kind of economic experimentation. Indeed, both gave priority to the task of building a viable democracy rather than economic reform. In both cases the result was a brilliant political transition. This, however, was achieved at the cost of postponing essential economic decisions.

Certain features of this pattern of procrastination in economic policies differed in the two countries. For one, the degree of support enjoyed by the governments varied. In the case of Greece, Karamanlis obtained an absolute parliamentary majority in the November 1974 general elections, in which he won 54.4% of the vote. Although his share of the vote dropped to 42.9% in the next elections, Nea Demokratia retained its absolute majority until 1981.

[9] Nevertheless, Karamanlis, who was heavily influenced by Gaullist policies, implemented an extensive programme of nationalizations. For his political strategy, see Nikiforos Diamandouros, 'Transition to, and Consolidation of, Democratic Politics in Greece, 1974–1983', *West European Politics*, 7/2 (1984), 50–71.

In Spain, in contrast, Suárez won both the 1977 and 1979 elections with a little more than one-third of the votes, although with 47% of the seats in Congress. Thus, the type of transition helps to explain why the economic policies initially adopted in Greece and Spain differed from those in Portugal. However, it does not account for other variations and similarities found in the economic policies of these three countries. We must therefore consider other political conditions in the new democracies, starting with the evolution of electoral results. Table 3.2 shows the results of the various general elections held in the three Southern European countries.

If we examine the pattern of electoral results and the way these influenced governments and economic policies, the two extreme cases were Portugal and Greece. In the Portuguese case, results were very volatile during the first decade of the democracy; the governments were likewise very unstable. Although economic experimentation was gradually abandoned after the first general elections, the successive governments found it difficult to sustain coherent policies for any length of time. Mario Soares's socialist government, which won the first two elections in 1975 and 1976, failed to obtain the support of the IMF in 1977 due to the fragility of its parliamentary support. The attempt to reinforce the government by forming a coalition with the CDS only lasted a few months, namely, from January to July 1978, when Soares was ousted by Ramalho Eanes, a president of the Republic with extensive executive powers. However, the successive governments of 'presidential inspiration' proved equally short-lived. In 1979 the third general election ended in a triumph for the conservative coalition, Alianza Democrática, made up of the Centro Democrático e Social (CDS) and the PSD. Yet despite its large majority, the new government did little to tackle the profound economic crisis. As a result, for ten years neither the minority socialist governments, nor the coalition of the socialists and the right, nor the presidential governments, nor the conservative coalition, were able or willing to implement rigorous economic policies.

Only after 1983 did the Bloco Central, the PS–PSD coalition government led by Soares, initiate a stabilization programme and introduce structural reforms. The transitory costs of this programme were considerable: over the next two years the GDP dropped by 3.2%, unemployment rose by 4.5 points, real wages fell by 2.7%, and public expenditure was cut by 3.1 points of the GDP.[10] After

---

[10] Commission des Communautés Européennes, *Économie Européenne*, 54 (1993), Tables 2, 10, 29, and 55; pp. 197, 205, 224, and 248.

TABLE 3.2. *Electoral results in Southern Europe*

Spain	1977	1979	1982	1986	1989	1993	1996
AP-PP	8.8	5.9	26.2	26.0	25.6	34.8	38.8
UCD	34.6	34.9	7.1	—	—	—	—
CDS	—	—	2.9	9.2	7.7	1.8	—
PSOE	29.3	30.5	48.4	44.1	40.2	38.8	37.5
PCE-IU	9.4	10.6	4.1	4.6	8.9	9.5	10.5
CiU	3.7	2.7	3.7	5.0	5.2	4.9	4.6
PNV	1.7	1.5	1.9	1.5	1.3	1.2	1.3
Others	12.5	13.9	5.7	9.6	11.1	9.0	7.3

Greece	1974	1977	1981	1985	1989	1989	1993
Nea Demokratia	54.4	42.9	35.9	40.8	44.3	46.2	39.3
Centre (EDIK, EK, KODISO)	20.6	12.0	1.5	—	—	—	—
PASOK	13.6	25.3	48.1	45.8	39.1	40.7	46.9
KKE	9.5	9.4	10.9	9.9	13.1	10.9	4.5
KKE-ESO		2.7	1.4	1.8			
Others	1.9	7.7	2.2	1.7	3.5	2.2	9.3

Portugal	1975	1976	1979	1980	1983	1985	1987	1991	1995
CDS-PP	7.6	16.0	—	—	12.4	9.7	4.3	4.4	9.0
PPD-PSD	26.4	24.4	—	—	27.0	29.7	50.1	56.4	33.9
AD (CDS*PSD)	—	—	45.3	46.7	—	—	—	—	—
PS	37.9	35.0	27.3	27.8	36.3	20.8	22.3	29.3	43.9
PCP-CDU	12.5	14.6	18.8	16.8	18.2	15.5	12.2	8.8	8.6
PRD	—	—	—	—	—	18.4	4.9	1.7	—
Others	5.6	10.0	8.6	8.7	6.1	5.9	6.2	5.4	4.6

its victory in the 1985 general election, the PSD maintained this economic policy, despite the transitory costs involved and the minority support for the government. But there existed then in Portuguese society a widely held belief that the economic crisis was extremely serious and that decisive action was at last being taken. This boosted support for the prime minister, Aníbal Cavaco Silva, who won absolute majorities in the next two general elections. Moreover, the economic policy began to bear fruit in the second half of the 1980s, when Portugal was also able to benefit from the international economic expansion, falling oil prices, and her entry into the European Community. Economic development was very strong during the second half of the decade, with annual average growth of 4.6% between 1986 and 1990. The economy became more competitive and foreign investment multiplied. During the 1980s, therefore, both coalition and single-party governments, whether minority or majority, achieved much better economic results than those of the previous decade. Moreover, whilst fragile electoral support could hinder the implementation of economic policies, economic performance did, in turn, affect voting patterns. Thus, the thesis that broad electoral mandates are crucial for economic efficiency must be heavily qualified in the case of Portugal: For on the one hand, they were not a necessary condition for success, and on the other, they were an effect of efficiency.

During the 1990s the new international crisis shattered the late and fragile 'virtuous circle' linking the economy and politics in Portugal. The growth of the previous years dropped to 1.1% in 1991 and −1.2% in 1993. Unemployment rose from 3.9 to 6.5% between 1992 and 1994, and during the same period the public deficit more than doubled, increasing from 3.3 to 7.1% of GDP. This new crisis had political consequences: the PSD dropped far behind in the polls, eventually losing the next general election held in 1995 to the socialists. However, this pattern of crisis was by no means limited to Portugal, but was common to many other European countries. In this way, Portugal had lost its distinctiveness as a new democracy.

In the Greek case too, broad electoral mandates were not to prove a sufficient condition for economic efficiency. Karamanlis's absolute majorities did not lead his governments down the road of reform; growth remained limited and inflation doubled in the space of three years, averaging 15.7% during the years of conservative rule (1974–81). As public expenditure soared, increasing by 12 points of GDP, so too did the fiscal deficit. Labour costs rose and investment fell. The failure to carry out essential reforms led to a worsening of the economic situation during this period. Greece's economic difficulties were soon matched by political problems, as Nea Demokratia suffered the effects of internal divisions and Karamanlis's resignation from the party leadership on his election as president of the Republic. The result was the PASOK's triumph in the 1981 general elections, a victory which marked the culmination of the party's spectacular electoral progress since 1974.

Andreas Papandreou held an absolute parliamentary majority between 1981 and 1989. However, as had been the case with his predecessor, the strength of his support did not improve economic performance. The problem was no longer to do with political procrastination, but with the selection of policies. In fact, the PASOK's economic policy was very similar to that followed by Pierre Mauroy's first government in France between 1981 and 1983. Although Papandreou did not initiate a nationalization programme, he did adopt a similar policy of expansion-cum-redistribution. Both public expenditure and wages were increased significantly in a bid to stimulate demand and redistribute income. The outcome was also comparable to that seen in France: imports, rather than domestic production, increased, and the economy became less competitive. This economic policy had negative effects on growth, inflation, unemployment, and the trade and public deficits. However, only after his second electoral victory was Papandreou willing to rectify his policy, by introducing a two-year stabilization plan. In contrast to the French case, this rectification was both limited and temporary, as once again electoralism and populism became the guiding principles behind the PASOK's economic policy. The result was the return of high inflation, growing public deficit and trade imbalances, and limited growth. Thus Greece failed to benefit from the European economic expansion of the mid-1980s and her entry into the European Community. The difference between Greece and the Community in terms of per capita income widened during this period. The Greek governments' large majorities, which were magnified by an electoral system that drastically corrected the proportional allocation of seats to the benefit of the winner, did not therefore improve economic results. Governments either postponed introducing necessary reforms or failed to choose efficient policies. This pattern was not altered by a further change of government. Nea Demokratia hardly improved the country's economic performance after its return to power in 1989. Although inflation fell by around half over the next four years, economic growth averaged a mere 0.9% per year, unemployment rose by three points (from 7 to 10.1%), and the public deficit was not reduced (remaining at around 18% of the GDP). The prime minister, Constantin Mitsotakis, faced strong popular opposition, his party was racked by internal divisions, and he himself was too worn out to exercise political leadership. In 1993 the poor economic results, accentuated by the impact of the European crisis, returned the PASOK to power. After three majority governments had alternated in power, the Greek economy still faced serious problems.

The cases of Greece and Portugal suggest, therefore, that electoral support was neither a necessary nor a sufficient condition for determined economic policies to be chosen. However, a further difference existed between these countries, namely, that the passing of time had a much greater impact on policies in Portugal than in Greece. During the 1980s, Portuguese governments adopted a different strategy to the one followed during the 1970s. This was probably due to the very different international environment, which required much stricter economic discipline, but also to an intense process of political learning from the errors and difficulties of the first decade of democracy. In the Greek case, however, governments remained largely immune to the influence of both the international environment and their own negative economic experiences. In the following chapter I will return to this point when the distinctive characteristics of Greek economic policy under the PASOK will be compared with the experiences of other social democratic governments in Southern Europe.

If we turn to the Spanish case, it would seem to illustrate the possibilities and limitations of minority and majority governments. Not only did Suárez count on only minority support, but throughout the transition to democracy there was great concern about the political consequences of attempting to establish greater economic discipline.[11] Yet the economic situation continued to deteriorate: inflation rose from 11 to 25% between 1973 and 1977, investment fell from 1975 onwards, Spain's current account balance deficit reached 4% of the GDP in 1976, whilst the loss of foreign currency reserves and the growing external debt threatened to provoke a balance of payments crisis. In the light of these mounting economic difficulties, with a limited mandate, and facing serious political threats to the new regime, Suárez's strategy consisted of seeking pacts. In other words, he sought to safeguard an economic policy of austerity by securing a broad agreement with all the major political parties.[12] After the first general elections held in June 1977, Suárez had considerable room for manœuvre in which to negotiate this agreement. The Moncloa Pacts, signed that autumn, constituted a typical stabilization plan, whereby the peseta was devalued 20%, a stricter monetary policy was introduced, and wage bargaining was linked to predicted inflation rates.[13] Nominal wages,

[11] See e.g. Luis Angel Rojo's comments on the subject in 'La crisis de la economía española, 1973–1984', in Jordi Nadal, Albert Carreras, and Carles Sudrià (eds.), *La economía española en el siglo XX: una perspectiva historica* (Barcelona, Ariel, 1987), 199.

[12] As is well known, although the UGT and CCOO supported the Moncloa Pacts, these were signed by the political parties and not the unions.

[13] For a study of the Moncloa Pacts, see Joan Trullén, *Fundamentos económicos de la transición política española: La política económica de los Acuerdos de la Moncloa* (Madrid, Ministerio de Trabajo y Seguridad Social, 1993), chs. 4 and 5.

which had increased by 27% in 1977, rose by only 9% in 1979. The government managed to reduce inflation by almost ten points and convert the current account deficit into a surplus. In return, public expenditure was increased, mainly in order to finance an extension of social policies. The political significance of these agreements was twofold: on the one hand, they expressed all the political parties' acceptance of the mixed market economy prior to the drafting of the 1978 constitution; on the other, they demonstrated that the democratic government had the legitimacy required to demand economic austerity, something which the governments of the dictatorship had lacked.

The economic results of the Moncloa Pacts were nevertheless limited, largely due to a further increase in international oil prices in 1979. Labour costs continued to escalate,[14] the labour market remained very rigid, and unemployment rose from 4.5% in 1975 to 8.6% in 1979. The problem of industrial reconversion had yet to be tackled, and a large number of loss-making companies were being absorbed into the public sector.[15] The combination of rapidly rising public expenditure and the slow pace of fiscal reform caused an escalation of the public deficit which was financed through inflationary mechanisms.[16] The industrial crisis eventually provoked a banking crisis of vast proportions. The UCD government was more courageous in its policies than Franco's governments at the beginning of the decade; it reflected the increased cost of oil in domestic costs and prices, at the same time as it attempted to control the inflationary tensions through strict monetary management and an incomes policy. However, inflation stood at 15%, the public deficit tripled, and the current account deficit went up. The economy entered into recession, with a shrinking GDP between 1980 and 1982, and unemployment continuing to rise, from 8.6% to 16.2% between 1979 and 1982.[17]

For an account which reflects the government's view at the time, see Enrique Fuentes Quintana, 'De los Pactos de la Moncloa a la Constitución', in José Luis García Delgado (ed.), *Economía española de la transición y la democracia* (Madrid: Centro de Investigaciones Sociológicas, 1990), 23–34.

[14] The growing cost of labour was above all a result of increases in social security contributions, which counteracted the effects of wage moderation.

[15] This was especially true in the period between 1978 and 1982, and mainly affected companies in the metal and textile industries.

[16] Between 1977 and 1979 the public deficit rose from 0.6% to 2.6% of the GDP: see Commission des Communautés Européennes, *Économie Européenne*, 54 (1993), Table 62, p. 179.

[17] The public deficit reached 5.6%, and the current account deficit 2.5%, of the GDP, whilst production fell by 1% of the GDP.

These economic problems have often been attributed to the weakness of a government which lacked a parliamentary majority and was backed by a divided party.[18] Sometimes they have been blamed on the strategy of concertation which, it is suggested, sacrificed economic efficiency in order to bolster the legitimacy of the economic system itself.[19] In both cases the effect would have been the same, namely, to postpone decisions and limit the reforms. In any event, the economic crisis overlapped with a political crisis within the ranks of the UCD, and both contributed to the rapid deterioration of the government's political strength. A further pact, the 1981 National Agreement on Employment, was signed during Leopoldo Calvo Sotelo's term of office and was largely possible thanks to the support which the PSOE gave to a fragile government.[20] At that time, the thesis that a broad mandate was a necessary condition to tackle the economic crisis was widely shared in Spain. This thesis, and the absence of a strong electoral rival, goes a long way towards explaining the scale of the PSOE's electoral victory in October 1982, when it won an absolute parliamentary majority.

The experience of the Socialist government after 1982 appears to be a clear example of the importance that electoral support and mandates have for economic policy.[21] However, although the breadth

[18] See e.g. Miguel Angel Fernández Ordóñez and Luis Serven, 'Economic Reform in Southern Europe: The Spanish Experience', in Andrés Solimano, Oswaldo Sunkel, and Mario I. Blejer (eds.), *Rebuilding Capitalism: Alternative Roads after Socialism and Dirigisme* (Ann Arbor, University of Michigan Press, 1994), 279–308; see also Guillermo de la Dehesa, 'Spain', in John Williamson (ed.), *The Political Economy of Policy Reform* (Washington DC, Institute for International Economics, 1994), 123–40.

[19] As is argued by Victor Pérez-Díaz, *The Return of Civil Society: The Emergence of Democratic Spain* (Cambridge, Mass.: Harvard University Press, 1993), 215–35.

[20] The PSOE's support, which was decisive in convincing the UGT to sign the agreement, was essentially due to Felipe González, who convinced the very reticent Executive Committees of both the party and union to back it. Their reticence was due to the consideration that, given the likelihood of the PSOE winning the forthcoming election, the party should keep the concertation card up its sleeve, in order to play it when in power. González's argument reflected his assessment of the instability of the democratic system and the depth of the economic crisis in 1981.

[21] See e.g. the interesting study by Nancy Bermeo and José García Durán, 'The Political Economy of Structural Adjustment in New Democracies: The Case of Spain', in Stephen Haggard and Steven Webb (eds.), *Voting for Reform: Democracies, Political Liberalization, and Economic Adjustment* (New York, Oxford University Press, 1994), 89–127. These authors emphasize that the execution of economic policies was influenced by the phase of democratization, the cohesion

of the mandate may explain why the government was able to carry out a policy, it does not answer the question of why it chose a particular policy from the various possible alternatives. The Spanish Socialist government's choice was highly orthodox, as, in contrast to the PASOK, it spurned traditional anti-cyclical policies. In the next chapter I will analyse these different responses from two governments that shared the same ideological label. The Spanish government believed that demand-centred policies would not address the country's structural economic problems, and that the growing internationalization of the economy imposed constraints on national strategies. The objective was to make the economy more competitive in order to achieve stable, long-term growth; this required reducing inflation, maintaining a sound macroeconomic framework, cutting the public deficit, and carrying out a number of structural reforms.[22]

Thus the PSOE's macroeconomic policy differed little from that of the UCD, although it was more decisive, coherent, and comprehensive. In order to reduce inflation, the Socialist government adopted a stricter monetary policy and made repeated attempts to secure wage agreements with the unions, although these only met with success in the signing of the Economic and Social Agreement, in force during 1985 and 1986. The structural reforms, in contrast, were much more ambitious than under the earlier conservative governments. They included the reconversion of one-third of Spain's industrial activity, an energy plan which reduced dependence on oil imports by 20 points,[23] the reorganization and liberalization of the financial system,[24] and the creation of a more flexible labour

and duration of governments, the concentration of decision-making, and the executives' autonomy from unions and employers' organizations. They also argue that the constraints resulting from the international environment meant that there were virtually no differences between the economic strategies followed by the UCD and PSOE governments, a point I will examine in more detail in Ch. 4.

[22] The first decision taken by the new government was to devalue the peseta by 8% in order to curb currency outflows and capital exports, which were then running at $500 million a day.

[23] Dependence on imported oil fell from 74% in 1974 to 54% in 1991.

[24] In 1981 foreign banks were allowed to enter a very closed and uncompetitive financial system. Restrictions on long-term capital flows were lifted in 1983, and all limits on direct foreign investment were removed in 1985. For a good analysis of financial deregulation in Spain under democracy see Arvid Lukauskas, 'The Political Economy of Financial Deregulation: The Case of Spain', Ph.D. thesis (University of Pennsylvania, 1992). From the starting-point of the supposed self-interest of politicians (that is, to gain and maintain power and increase public resources), Lukauskas explains how the institutions (and in particular the Spanish electoral system) generated incentives for deregulation under democracy.

market.[25] In general terms, these reforms were intended to reduce bureaucratic regulation, reinforcing the role the market played in the economy.[26] The principal cost of these reforms was unemployment, which rose to 21.9% of the active population in 1985.

However, in addition to a stricter monetary policy and market reforms, the government also practised a new type of social democratic strategy based on supply-side policies.[27] This strategy, which reflected a particular conception of the role of the state in the economy, was increasingly shared by other social democratic parties over the course of the decade. The state should compensate for the limitations of the market in order to ensure both sustained economic growth and a fair redistribution of resources and life chances. An essential difference between social democratic and conservative policies were the ideas that there was no antagonism between development and equity, that market reforms were compatible with a major responsibility of the state in investing in physical and human capital. The largest increases in public expenditure during this decade were assigned to physical and human capital. Public sector investment rose from 2.9 to 5.2% of the GDP between 1982 and 1991, and it became highly redistributive in character.[28] Expenditure on education rose from 2.8 to

[25] More flexible forms of employment relations (apprenticeships, training, part-time, substitute and temporary job contracts) were legalized in 1984.

[26] For a general description of the reforms, see Michel Galy, Gonzalo Pastor, and Thierry Pujol, 'Spain: Converging with the European Community', *IMF Occasional Paper*, 101 (Washington DC, International Monetary Fund, 1993).

[27] See the excellent analysis of this combination of macroeconomic discipline and active supply-side policies in Carles Boix, 'Partisan Strategies and Supply-side Policies in Advanced Nations, 1960–1990', Ph.D. thesis (Harvard University, 1994), Part II, 'The Spanish Experience'. Using a stylized model of partisan preferences, Boix examines the distinct economic policies of the Thatcher and González governments, as well as their electoral consequences. He concludes that the partisan differences were more important than is suggested by mainstream institutional analysis. Social democratic economic policies during the 1980s were characterized by orthodox macroeconomic management combined with a particular emphasis on investment in fixed and human capital.

[28] Whilst the more prosperous Autonomous Communities, such as the Balearic Islands and the Basque Country, received less than 30,000 pesetas of public investment per inhabitant per year, Andalusia and Extremadura obtained more than 110,000 pesetas. Between 1975 and 1987 the disposable family income in Andalusia and Extremadura, the two poorest Communities throughout this period, increased from 77% and 67% of the national average to 83% and 76%, respectively. This redistribution had little to do with the impact of European Community funds, which only began to reach Spain in 1987. The principal redistributive mechanism was the Inter-territorial Compensation Fund, which was invested in negative correlation to the territorial per capita income ($r = .90$).

4.7% of the GDP, whilst the enrolment rate increased by 20 points among 14- to 18-year-olds, and by 11 points among those aged between 18 and 23.[29] The PSOE government implemented a highly aggressive fiscal policy: it did not try to reduce the public deficit by simultaneously cutting expenditure and taxation; it increased both. As a result, public expenditure, which had stood at only 24.4% of the GDP in 1975, and had then expanded rapidly under the UCD governments, reached 42.2% in 1985, at the same time as fiscal pressure rose from 24.4 to 35.2%, an increase largely due to the reduction of fraud and to fiscal drag. Both public expenditure and taxation became much more redistributive: this question will be examined in detail in the next chapter.

After three years of adjustment, and with the aid of a more favourable international environment,[30] the economy entered into a phase of rapid growth. As was the case in Portugal, but in contrast to Greece, the difference between the Spanish per capita income and the European Community average in purchasing power parities was narrowed considerably between mid-1985 and 1992. Inflation fell; the current account deficit turned into a surplus from 1984 onwards; and between 1985 and 1989 the public deficit dropped from 6.9 to 2.7% of the GDP. Investment also went up: the increase was most spectacular in the case of foreign investment,

The two prosperous provinces of Madrid and Barcelona recouped only half of what they contributed to public revenue through public expenditure, whilst Andalusia and Extremadura received between three and four times more than they contributed. See Xavier Calsamiglia, 'Descentralización del gasto público y financiación autonómica: Una valoración del sistema español', *Working Paper* (Barcelona, Instituto de Análisis Económico, CSIC/Universidad Autónoma de Barcelona, 1989). See also the special issue of *Papeles de Economía Española*, 48 (1991) on 'La España desigual de las Autonomías'.

[29] Ministerio de Economía y Hacienda, *1983–1992: El trabajo de una década* (unpublished report, Madrid, 1993). In 1991 the state spent 4.5% of the GDP on education according to the Consejo Escolar del Estado, *Informe sobre el estado y situación del sistema educativo, 1993–1994* (Madrid, Ministerio de Educación y Ciencia, 1995), 452–3, and to the United Nations, *Human Development Report* (Oxford, Oxford University Press, 1995), Tables 25 and 28, pp. 222 and 225. To this percentage should be added the 0.8% of the GDP spent by local councils. The United Nations' report gives the figure of 1.1% of the GDP for total public expenditure on education in 1960.

[30] The drop in oil prices and the expansion of the European economy were the main aspects of the more favourable international environment. In the European Community as a whole, economic growth reached an annual average rate of 1.4% of the GDP during the first half of the 1980s, and 3.2% in the second half of the decade. See Commission des Communautés Européennes, *Économie Européenne*, 54 (1993), calculations based on Table 10, p. 205.

which was five times greater during the second half of the decade than during the early 1980s.[31] Very large numbers of new jobs were also created, unemployment falling to 16.2% in 1990. As in the case of Portugal, therefore, Spain benefited from a combination of different circumstances: membership of the European Community, renewed European economic expansion, and a comprehensive programme of economic adjustment.

However, there is no such thing as a threshold beyond which economies are immune to crisis. And, what is more, a number of important reforms had still to be carried out: many of the state-owned companies were still unprofitable and represented a heavy burden on the public coffers;[32] there was little competition in the service sector and its prices were inflationary; the labour market remained very rigid in terms of both contractual relations and the mobility of workers; and despite the substantial increase in fiscal revenue, there had been only a limited restructuring of public expenditure. These structural problems contributed to inflation and the public deficit. They were also aggravated by the vast popular pressure for the further development of welfare policies, which were already expanding fast, as well as by strong wage demands, advanced by unions opposed to the policy of income restraint. As a result, public expenditure rose to 46.4% in 1992, and the public deficit again grew, reaching 4.5% of GDP. Equally, despite the high unemployment, real wages rose during the 1980s without trade-offs with the 'social wage' from 1987 onwards. Given the difficulties in establishing fiscal discipline and controlling wage rises, the government adopted a very strict monetary policy in response to the resurgence of the economic crisis.

The crisis became extremely serious after 1992. The economic decline which affected the whole of Europe from the beginning of the decade was felt particularly severely in Spain. Economic growth fell to 0.8% in 1992 and to –1.0% the following year. The consequences for jobs were immediate and dramatic, with unemployment returning to 21.5% in 1993. Despite these problems, the government was reluctant to trim social programmes and public investment in physical and human capital. As a result, public expenditure reached 48.9% of the GDP in 1993, and the fiscal deficit went up to 7.3%, largely as a consequence of the growing

[31] Foreign investment accounted for 9% of all private investment.

[32] In 1984, 80% of investment in state-owned enterprises still went to unprofitable sectors: see José Viñals *et al.*, 'Spain and the EC Cum 1992 Shock', in Christopher Bliss and Jorge Braga (eds.), *Unity with Diversity in the European Community* (Cambridge, Cambridge University Press, 1990), 145–234.

cost of unemployment benefits. Real wages, in turn, rose by 2.5% in 1990, 2.7% in 1991, and 3.4% in 1992. The trade unions launched two general strikes, the first in 1992 and another in 1994, in protest against the government's new austerity measures. In this situation, monetary policy became an even more important element of macroeconomic strategy. Interest rates rose significantly and the peseta became over-valued. This particular policy mix accentuated certain aspects of the crisis, particularly unemployment and the fall in domestic investment.

In 1993 general elections were called in a context of dramatically rising unemployment, serious conflicts with the unions, and political scandals (relating to the personal enrichment of some figures of the PSOE and illegal party funding). The PSOE lost its parliamentary majority but, unexpectedly, won the elections, mainly as a result of widespread mistrust of the conservative Partido Popular's (PP) social policies and political tolerance. However, the new minority government did not corroborate the thesis that broad political mandates lead to more efficient policies. The government, with the support of the Basque and Catalan nationalist parties, now embarked on reforms which had been postponed for years, involving the budget and the labour market. The result was that, in the context of the general European recovery, economic growth and net job creation resumed as from 1994. The difficulties experienced by this minority socialist government did not lie in its economic policy but in political problems of a very different nature— the major divisions within the party, the fatigue resulting from many years in office, the accumulation of a large number of corruption scandals, and revelations about a 'dirty war' against Basque terrorism involving high-ranking officials in the Interior Ministry. As a result of these problems, the PSOE lost the general election of 1996, although it still managed to retain 37.5% of the vote, while 38.8% voted for the Popular Party (PP), the conservative alternative.

Table 3.3 shows the evolution of the economic performance in the three Southern European countries since the transition to democracy. Data for the European Community as a whole are also included for comparative purposes. It can be seen that significant differences existed in the three countries in terms of growth rates, inflation, and fiscal balances. In the case of Greece, after an initial period of economic improvement under the new regime, the rate of growth dropped and the public deficit grew, whilst inflation remained persistently high. In the cases of Spain and Portugal, in contrast, their economic performance improved during the first fifteen years of democracy.

TABLE 3.3. *Economic performance in Southern Europe under democracy*

	Spain	Greece	Portugal	European Community
Economic growth				
First year	0.5	-3.6	1.1	1.9
Average until 1985	1.5	2.6	2.2	2.0
Average 1985–92	3.7	1.6	3.8	2.6
Overall average	2.4	2.2	2.8	2.2
Inflation				
First year	15.5	23.5	17.1	13.8
Average until 1985	15.3	17.5	22.3	10.5
Average 1985–92	6.5	17.3	11.4	4.3
Overall average	11.8	15.5	18.2	8.1
Public deficit				
First year	0.0	10.7[a]	1.4	5.1
Average until 1985	3.0	10.0[a]	7.2	4.1
Average 1985–92	4.1	14.6	5.8	3.9
Overall average	3.4	12.7[a]	6.6	4.0

Source: Commission Européenne, *Économie Européenne*, 54 (1993). Tables 10, 24, and 56; pp. 205, 129, and 249.

[a] Since 1981.

The differences between the three countries, after the first few years of the new regimes, can obviously not be explained in terms of the distinct character of their transitions; these did not leave an indelible stamp on their institutions and policies. Thus, during the course of the 1980s, the Portuguese economy would gradually overcome the consequences of its particular type of transition to democracy. In time, the policy paradigms in these three countries tended to converge. In Portugal, Greece, and Spain the evolution of electoral support and political mandates influenced the formulation of economic policy. This can been seen from the experience of the minority governments of Soares in 1977 and Suárez between 1977 and 1981, as well as that of the majority governments of González from 1982 to 1993, and Cavaco Silva between 1987 and 1994. But these conditions were neither necessary nor sufficient to explain these variations. For the economic policy of Cavaco Silva's government between 1985 and 1987 did not suffer as a consequence of having only minority support, nor did those of Karamanlis or Papandreou benefit from the fact they were majority governments. Nor was the economic policy followed by the González government after 1993 any less rigorous because of its lack of a parliamentary majority.

The policy options of these governments were also influenced by an international environment which narrowed their room for manœuvre during the 1980s. Greater economic interdependence accentuated the negative consequences of postponing necessary reforms, opting for an inadequate policy mix, or allowing fiscal or wage permissiveness. On joining the European Community, the menu of options available to the three countries became more limited. The greater need for competitiveness imposed stricter macroeconomic orthodoxy, at the same time as it made experimentation more difficult. The governments of the three new democracies did not make their decisions in isolation; their information and incentives were radically altered by a network of European economists, administrators, journalists, and politicians, which undoubtedly had much more influence than would have been the case if the authoritarian regimes had persisted. However, neither was this new economic framework the decisive factor for the orientation of economic policies.

Whilst the external environment may account for part of the convergence in the paradigms of economic policies, it does not explain the enduring discrepancies between them. To give just one example, major differences continued to exist between the economic strategies of González and Papandreou, despite the fact that both faced comparable economic problems, had similar political mandates, shared the same ideological label, and governed during overlapping periods. The differences between the two cases were largely due to their very distinct intellectual maps, that is, to the very different political learning from past experiences. In the Spanish case, the dictatorship had lasted longer, the notion that political democracy was the overriding priority was more widely accepted, and stronger relations existed with other European governments. Equally, a variety of experiences in the 1970s and 1980s were interpreted much more critically: for example, the economic policy of the 'revolution of the carnations', the British Labour government's crisis in the 1970s, and the economic failure of the French government during the early 1980s. Moreover, a group of post-Keynesian economists gained much more influence in the Ministry of Finance and the Economy.[33] In the Greek case, in

---

[33] The case of Miguel Boyer and Carlos Solchaga as ministers of the Economy and Finance accords with what Waterbury called 'change teams': see Waterbury, 'Heart of the Matter', in Stephen Haggard and Robert R. Kaufman (eds.), *The Politics of Economic Adjustment* (Princeton, NJ: Princeton University Press, 1992), 191.

contrast, the dictatorship was much more short-lived, the European influence more limited, and orthodox economic paradigms more widely questioned. The fact that the Greek government enjoyed majority support, therefore, is not in itself sufficient to explain the orientation or the results of its economic policies.

Despite such differences, the Southern European experience shows that new democratic regimes could learn from negative political lessons. Although it is true that the autarkic economic model had been abandoned long before, by the mid-1970s major structural reforms were still pending and economic problems had worsened during the final years of the authoritarian regimes. A decade later, under democracy, Greece, Spain, and Portugal had joined the European Community, and although they may have taken greater or lesser advantage of the new opportunities created by EC membership, all three countries had raised their per capita incomes. As can be seen in Table 3.3, although Greece possessed the lowest comparative growth rate, it was no lower than that of the European Community as a whole in the same period. The shape of economic policies, therefore, was the result of a complex combination of influences stemming from the economic conditions, the European environment, the governments' electoral support, and the intellectual maps of politicians.

Although in all three countries the democracies were consolidated and therefore increasingly autonomous of economic conditions, they still faced a number of major economic problems. In the Spanish case, the main problem was unemployment. Even after the period of strong growth during the second half of the 1980s, unemployment did not fall below 16% of the active population, whilst at times of crisis this figure rose above 20%. In other words, economic adjustment was not carried out at the expense of wages or social expenditure, but of employment. It is true that these percentages were to some extent deceptive, since 'irregular employment' accounted for around 22% of all job contracts and there was also widespread unemployment benefit fraud.[34] It is also true

---

[34] See Julio Segura, Federico Durán, Luis Toharia, and Samuel Bentolila, *Análisis de la contratación temporal en España* (Madrid, Ministerio de Trabajo y Seguridad Social, 1991); Juan Muro, José Luis Raymond, Luis Toharia, and Ezequiel Uriel, 'Estimación del empleo irregular en la economía española', in Samuel Bentolila and Luis Toharia (eds.), *Estudios de Economía del Trabajo en España*, iii., *El problema del paro* (Madrid, Ministerio de Trabajo y Seguridad Social, 1991), 253–306; see also Victor Pérez-Díaz and Juan Carlos Rodríguez, 'Inertial Choices: Spanish Human Resources Policies and Practices (1959–1993)', *ASP Research Papers*, 2(b)/1994 (Madrid, Analistas Socio-Políticos, 1994).

that demographic factors explained much of the increase in unemployment.[35] However, wage increases and labour-market rigidities also restricted the job supply. Moreover, the segmentation of the labour market, the centralized and rigid character of collective wage agreements, and the fact that, regardless of the evolution of the 'social wage' and unemployment, strong wage demands remained at the heart of the unions' strategies, all meant that widespread unemployment did not moderate rises in real wages. Esping-Andersen has argued that a system of job-related welfare provision based on traditional gender roles also contributed to high unemployment: rigid labour markets and wage structures protected the male earner's job, income, and entitlements, and thus family welfare, but at the cost of a suboptimal labour-force participation, more restricted job opportunities for other members of the family, sharp insider-outsider divisions within the labour market, and an unfavourable population dependency ratio.[36]

High unemployment, however, had only limited political consequences. Not only did it not weaken support for democracy, but neither did it prove politically catastrophic for the government. In the 1986 elections, for example, there existed no difference in the level of electoral support for the PSOE among employed and unemployed workers, with 48% voting for the party in both cases.[37] In the 1993 elections, held in the midst of a new economic crisis, 40% of employed workers and 35% of the unemployed voted for the PSOE. I have examined the political impact of the economic situation and unemployment on both the PSOE vote and the evaluation of democracy through a regression analysis based on evidence from a post-electoral survey taken in 1993.[38] The results are given

[35] As a result of the baby boom of the 1960s and 1970s, the cohort of young people aged 16 to 25 was 27% larger than the 26–35 age-group. Women entered the labour market in huge numbers during the 1980s, when their participation rate in the active population increased by 7 percentage points.

[36] Gösta Esping-Andersen, 'Welfare States without Work: The Impasse of Labour Shedding and Familialism in Continental European Social Policy', *Working Paper no. 1995/71* (Madrid: Center for Advanced Studies in the Social Sciences, Instituto Juan March de Estudios e Investigaciones, 1995); 'After the Golden Age: The Future of the Welfare State in the New Global Order', *Occasional Paper no. 7* (Geneva: United Nations Research Institute for Social Development, 1994), 16–18.

[37] Arnold J. Feldman, Jorge R. Menes, and Natalia García Pardo, 'La estructura social y el apoyo partidista en España', *Revista Española de Investigaciones Sociológicas*, 47 (1989), 7–72.

[38] The poll was conducted by DATA S.A. from a representative nationwide sample of 1,448 adults. The poll was taken on the occasion of the June 1993 general elections as part of the Spanish study for the *Comparative National Election Project*, carried out by a team including Richard Gunther and José Ramón Montero.

in Table 3.4. In this table, the first set of independent variables corresponds to respondents' assessments of the general economic situation, their personal economic situation, and their employment situation.[39] A second set of independent variables refers to their opinion of the government's economic policy and its education policy.[40] The three dependent variables considered are the vote for the PSOE or for other parties (the government's electoral support), the satisfaction with democracy, and the legitimacy of democracy.[41]

The first set of independent variables relating to economic conditions accounts for 11.6% of the variation in the vote. However, of the three variables, only the assessment of the general economic situation is statistically significant, a one-point increase in the positive opinion of the economy leading to a .96% increase in support for the PSOE. The second set of variables, relating to government policies, explains 20.2% of the variation in the vote. Both the variables included here are statistically relevant: a one-point increase in the positive assessment of economic policy leading to a 1.0% rise in the vote for the government; and in the case of education policy, each one point producing a 1.8% rise in the latter.

These variables had less influence on respondents' opinion of democracy than on their voting behaviour. The set of variables referring to economic conditions explains 9.4% of the satisfaction with democracy. Both the assessment of the general economic situation and that of the personal economic situation were statistically significant: a one-point variation in the former produced a change of .25 in satisfaction with democracy, whilst in the case of the latter, the change was .10. At the same time, the set of variables relating to government policies accounted for 13.8% of the satisfaction with democracy. The respondents' opinions of both economic and education policy were also statistically relevant: each one point increase in the former led to a rise of .41 in satisfaction with democracy, and in the case of the latter, a rise of .36%.

[39] The questions referring to this set of variables were as follows: (1) 'How would you describe the current economic situation in Spain?'; (2) 'How would you describe your own economic situation at the moment?'; (3) 'Are you employed or self-employed?'

[40] The following questions were used for this set of variables: (1) 'Do you think the government has performed well or badly with regard to economic development?'; (2) 'Do you think the government has performed well or badly with regard to education?'

[41] For these three dependent variables the questions were as follows: (1) 'Which party did you vote for?'; (2) 'Overall, are you very satisfied, quite satisfied, not very satisfied, or dissatisfied with the way democracy works in Spain?'; and (3) 'Tell me if you agree or disagree with the statement "democracy is the best political system for a country like ours"'.

TABLE 3.4. *The effect of economic conditions and policies on voting behaviour and attitudes to democracy in Spain*

	Vote for government	Satisfaction with democracy	Legitimacy of democracy
Set of variables 'economic conditions'			
Constant	−3.033*	1.537*	.934*
	(.763)	(.198)	(.139)
General economic situation	.958*	.246*	.010
	(.164)	(.041)	(.029)
Personal economic situation	−.128	.098*	.087*
	(.176)	(.046)	(.033)
Employment	.094	−.086	−.013
	(.389)	(.103)	(.073)
R^2	.116	.094	.016
Signif. F	.000	.000	.032
No. of observations	323	539	539
Set of variables 'government policies'			
Constant	−7.067*	.658*	.923*
	(.534)	(.133)	(.110)
Economic policy	1.041*	.409*	.047
	(.159)	(.043)	(.036)
Education policy	1.804*	.358*	.102*
	(.169)	(.044)	(.036)
R^2	.202	.138	.009
Signif. F	.000	.000	.001
No. of observations	929	1,400	1,400

* Statistically significant at 5% or less.

Note: Standard errors in parenthesis.

The legitimacy of democracy proved highly immune to the effects of these variables. Citizens believed that, regardless of the state of the economy or the government's policies, democracy still represented the best political system. Thus the set of variables referring to economic conditions accounted for only 1.6% of the legitimacy of democracy, and those relating to government policies, .9% of this. The only statistically relevant variables are, in the first group, the respondents' assessment of their own personal economic situation, and in the second, their opinion of the government's education policy. A one-point variation in the former produced a .09% change in the legitimacy of democracy, and in the second, a change of .10. Thus, the legitimacy of democracy was highly autonomous of efficiency, as citizens considered democracy to be a value in itself, and not just a means to an end.

Thus, the employment situation had only limited direct consequences for voting behaviour, the level of satisfaction with democracy, and the legitimacy of the regime. This is probably explained by the protection against material hardship provided by families and by the growing panoply of social policies. Both provided a network of support that alleviated the social costs of the economic crisis. Only one of every four unemployed people was a head of household; in other words, unemployment primarily affected second incomes and other family members. Thus, the average per capita household income of the unemployed stood at 72% of that of the population as a whole. Besides income from other family members, state provision of income maintenance and free services served to mitigate hardship. The coverage of unemployment benefits rose from 46.7% in 1982 to 79.3% in 1992; from 1987 onwards, the proportion of unemployed workers unprotected by social policies never reached 10%.[42] It is true that the provision of protection in a context of mass unemployment led to serious strains within families, and that the rapidly expanding system of social protection faced financial difficulties; nevertheless, both institutions decisively softened the political effects of unemployment on democracy. The expansion of social policies since the start of the transition could be seen in that, if we compare the number of their beneficiaries in 1975 and 1992, 1,539,784 more people were covered by some form of unemployment benefit, 9,644,000 by the national health system, and an additional 1,885,507 students now received secondary or higher education.

This trend formed part of a more general process: under democracy, the economic differences between both regions and individuals were reduced. In Spain, Portugal, and Greece, the dictatorships did have distributive effects: that is, they were not only associated with economic backwardness with respect to Europe, but also with greater social inequality. Hence it was widely expected that the

[42] See the analysis of unemployment protection in Luis Toharia, 'Unemployment in Spain: How can it be so high?' (unpublished manuscript, Universidad de Alcalá de Henares, 1995). Also, Luis Ayala, Rosa Martínez, Jesús Ruiz-Huertas, 'La distribución de la renta en España desde una perspectiva internacional: Tendencias y factores de cambio' (unpublished manuscript, Instituto de Estudios Fiscales, Madrid, 1995).

new regimes would make up the lost ground in welfare policies: this was an essential element of what was understood by 'modernization', one of the key concepts in the political culture of Southern Europe. A long and heterogeneous tradition of political thinkers, from J. S. Mill to Kautsky, and from de Tocqueville to Engels, argued that democracy promotes equality, since universal suffrage forces parties and governments to attend to the interests of the most disadvantaged social groups, increases the political power of the poor, and intensifies distributive conflicts. I have already argued that quantitative cross-national analysis confirms this thesis, and that inequalities were comparatively high in the Southern European dictatorships. After the transitions from authoritarian rule in Portugal, Greece, and Spain were over, no trade-off took place between democracy and equality.

As can be seen in Table 3.5, democracy led to a considerable increase in both the number of people benefiting from social policies and in the economic resources dedicated to these. In Greece public expenditure on education rose from 2 to 3.1% of the GDP between 1960 and 1990, whilst public expenditure on health increased from 3.2 to 4.8%. In Portugal during the same period, the education budget grew from 1.8 to 4.9% of the GDP, and the health budget from 0.8 to 6.1%. Economic inequality appears to have diminished under the new regimes, as can be seen from the figures for income distribution in Spain. Thus, there was no incompatibility in the new regimes between social equality and economic performance, although the two factors were not unrelated. Governments were forced to maintain a delicate balance between economic competitiveness, wages, employment, public expenditure, and fiscal revenue. But this balance was not necessarily achieved at the cost of social equity, nor, as will be argued in the next chapter, did this mean that political differences between the governments had become irrelevant. Democracy did not prove to be a necessarily conservative political formula.

This combination of economic and social policies was not particularly unusual in democracies. I have already argued that these regimes are usually associated with increased public expenditure and taxation, and more developed social policies. In the case of the Federal Republic of Germany after the Second World War, Ralf Dahrendorf has noted that the economic reforms were possible thanks to the social policies put into practice by Konrad Adenauer, Ludwig Erhard, and Hans Bökler.[43] The new democracies in

---

[43] Ralf Dahrendorf, *Reflections on the Revolution in Europe* (London, Chatto and Windus, 1990), 90–2.

TABLE 3.5. *The evolution of social policies and inequality in Southern Europe*

		Spain	Greece	Portugal
(1) Social welfare expenditure (as % of GDP)	1970	10.0	7.6	9.1
	1991	21.4	20.7	19.4
(2) Expenditure on old age pensions (as % of GDP)	1980	5.4	6.3	4.3
	1991	6.4	10.6	5.5
Extent of pension coverage (social security and public pensioners in 000's)	1975	3,404	—	—
	1992	6,859	—	—
(3) Expenditure on unemployment benefits (as % of GDP)	1980	2.7	0.3	0.4
	1991	3.7	0.3	0.4
Extent of unemployment benefits coverage (in 000's)	1975	167	—	—
	1992	1,708	—	—
(4) Public expenditure on health care (as % of GDP)	1960	2.3	3.2	0.8
	1992	6.4	4.8	6.1
Coverage of health care (in 000's)	1975	28,800	—	—
	1992	38,444	—	—
(5) Public expenditure on education (as % of GDP)	1960	1.1	2.0	1.8
	1988	4.7	3.1	4.9
Education coverage: Secondary education	1975	1,124	—	—
	1992	2,374	—	—
Higher education	1975	557	—	—
	1992	1,193	—	—
(6) Ratio of poorest to richest 20 per cent of families	1974	10.4	—	—
	1990	4.8	—	—
Gini Coefficient (of monetary income)	1974	0.52	—	—
	1990	0.30	—	—
Concentration of income among richest 10 per cent	1974	28.5	—	—
	1990	24.7	—	—
Concentration of income among poorest 10 per cent	1974	1.5	—	—
	1990	3.2	—	—

Sources: Comisión de las Comunidades Europeas, *La Protección Social en Europa 1993* (Brussels, European Commission, 1994); Alain Euzéby, 'La Protection Sociale en Europe', *Futuribles*, 171 (1992); Luis Ayala, Rosa Martínez, Jesús Ruiz-Huerta, 'La distribución de la renta en España en los años ochenta: una perspectiva comparada', in Fundación Argentaria, *Sector público y redistribución de la renta: I Symposium sobre igualdad y distribución de la renta y la riqueza*, ii (Madrid, Fundación Argentaria, 1993); Ministerio de Economía y Hacienda, *El gasto público en España* (Madrid, Ministerio de Economía y Hacienda, 1989); 'El gasto público en la democracia', *Papeles de Economía Española*, 37 (1988).

Southern Europe expanded the net of unemployment benefits, health and education services, pension systems, and active labour-market policies; they also reduced inequality in the distribution of incomes. This helped these societies to assume the costs of the economic crisis and the problems posed by democratization. Democracies are generally attributed an inherent value and not simply seen in instrumental terms; but that value also depends on the human face of these regimes, which constitutes an essential part of their legitimacy.

3.2. Eastern Europe: Crises, Reforms, and Consequences

In Eastern Europe demands for political change had a strong instrumental component; that is, as well as being seen by many as an end in itself, democracy was conceived as a means of promoting economic development. The successive partial reforms carried out by the authoritarian regimes had failed to resolve the chronic problems of these economies. As a result, shortages, soft budget constraints, the monopolistic concentration of production, and the absence of incentives remained characteristic features of communist economies until the very end of the regimes. The weight of the public sector was overwhelming, although its share of the net material product varied considerably, ranging from 97% in Czechoslovakia, to 81.7% in Poland, and 65.2% in Hungary.[44] Moreover, the economic situation became much more critical during the 1980s, as the external debt spiralled, the public deficit grew, and growth collapsed. In Poland, inflation reached 251.1% in 1989 and, in October that year it crossed the threshold of hyperinflation (53% that month, or the equivalent of more than 17,000% a year). Although inflation was much lower in Hungary (17% a year), the Hungarian per capita foreign debt was the highest in the world ($1,656). Whilst Czechoslovakia maintained a more balanced macroeconomic framework, here too the economic situation had

---

[44] In Western Europe in 1985 the public sector accounted for 16.5% of production in France, 14% in Italy, 11.1% in the United Kingdom, and 10.7% in the Federal Republic of Germany. Although, after twenty years of reforms, the market was more important in Hungary than in other Eastern European countries, the state still generated two-thirds of the added value: see Christopher Clague, 'Journey to a Market Economy', in Christopher Clague and Gordon C. Rausser (eds.), *The Emergence of Market Economies in Eastern Europe* (Cambridge, Mass.: Blackwell, 1992).

worsened considerably and the government led by Gustav Husák had resisted making any reforms.

The political transitions were the result of distinct combinations of economic crisis, the weakening of Communist party control, and the transformations provoked by Gorbachev. Table 3.6 outlines the principal characteristics of the transitions in Poland, Hungary, and Czechoslovakia. Whilst the economic crisis played a much more important role in the first two cases, the transformations taking place in the USSR had a greater impact in the case of Czechoslovakia. At the same time as the 'pressure from below' which Solidarność had led throughout the 1980s was important in the Polish case, in Hungary the initiatives taken by the reformist leaders of the HSWP were a decisive factor for political change. However, in all three countries the transitions were based on transactions and pacts. In Poland, the pact led to partially free elections in June 1989 and a period of shared government. In Hungary and Czechoslovakia, the pacts paved the way for the free elections held in March and June 1990, respectively. In all three cases, the opposition won these first elections. Yet, regardless of the differences in the economic situation in the three countries and the distinct nature of their political transitions, one common characteristic was the existence of a broad 'consensus of termination'. In other words, once the regime collapsed there was widespread agreement that communist economic organization also had to be abandoned.

The post-communist political agenda, therefore, encompassed both the construction of democracy and the establishment of a market economy. The general consensus which existed with regard to this twofold task was summed up in the concept of 'normalization'. 'Normalization' implied 'Europeanization', that is, turning back to Europe, making up the lost ground, eliminating the differences. Hence a general characteristic of these new democracies was their rejection of 'third roads', of anything that did not consist of tried and tested policies and programmes. In his first address as prime minister to the Polish parliament, or *Sejm*, Tadeusz Mazowiecki declared that his goal was to carry out 'the transition to a modern market economy, validated by the experience of the developed countries'. The new Minister of the Economy, Leszek Balcerowicz, added that 'Poland is too poor to attempt experiments. We are following the models already used elsewhere. The rich countries are free to experiment if they wish'.[45] This meant

---

[45] Quoted in Jeffrey Sachs, 'Vers une économie de marché en Pologne', *Pour la Science*, 175 (1991).

TABLE 3.6. *Characteristics of the transitions in Eastern Europe*

Poland	Hungary	Czechoslovakia
Economic crisis.	Economic crisis.	Exogenous influences (USSR, GDR).
Mobilization 'from below'.	Reforms 'from above' (promoted by Pozsgay, Nyers, Németh).	Mobilizations 'from below' at end of dictatorship (November 1989).
Military intervention (Jaruzelski, 1981).	Negotiations between government and opposition (June to September 1989).	Capitulation of the hardliners (Jakeš) and replacement by liberalizers (Urbanek, Adamec).
Negotiations between government and opposition and 'Magdalenka agreement' (February and March 1989).	Referendum in November 1989 on the holding of presidential and legislative elections.	Collapse of liberalization due to social resistance.
Free elections limited to 35% of the seats in the *Sejm* (September 1989).	Unlimited free elections (March 1990).	Consensus provisional government in December 1989 (agreed by Calfa and the opposition).
Opposition electoral victory, but shared government.	Electoral victory of the opposition, without power-sharing.	Indirect election of President in December 1989 (won by Havel).
Presidential elections in December 1990 (won by Wałęsa).	Parliamentary democracy.	Opposition electoral victory without power-sharing.
Semi-presidentialist democracy.		Parliamentary democracy.
		Nationalist pressure. Separation of Slovakia in January 1993.

separating the economy from politics, that is, creating an economic system governed by the rules of the market and not the preferences of the bureaucracy. In Hungary and Poland even the former communist parties, that is, Gyula Horn's Hungarian Socialist Party (MSZP), and the Social Democracy of the Polish Republic (SdRP), led by Aleksander Kwaśniewski, were included in this consensus. The strongest reservations with regard to this programme were found in those countries where the communists adopted a new nationalist identity, as was the case in Slovakia. However, the variations in the type of transition did not have lasting effects on these political conceptions. Both in those countries where the change began with reform 'from above' and negotiations among the élites (as in Hungary), and in those in which it was brought about by the rapid collapse of the dictatorship (as in Czechoslovakia), there was generalized acceptance of democracy and the market.

The consensus also extended to more concrete objectives, including macroeconomic stabilization, the liberalization of prices and foreign trade, budgetary discipline, and the creation of a new private sector. This explains why, for example, the former communists in Poland greeted the 'Balcerowicz Plan', the emblematic programme of market reforms, with the comment 'your government, our reforms'. It was also evident that the internal logic of the reforms made them interdependent. It would be impossible to stabilize the economy without strict budgetary discipline, which was all the more urgent because the partial reforms under communism had fuelled uncontrolled expenditure. Yet budgetary discipline was unfeasible if enterprises could not go bankrupt, since fiscal laxity was largely a consequence of the subsidies paid to firms and their frequent recourse to public funds. At the same time, budgets would continue to be permissive if prices were not liberalized. And the fastest way to establish a rational price structure was to liberalize foreign trade, since this would not only import the prices of the market economies, but would also encourage competition and break the monopolies' stranglehold on the economy. Under monopoly conditions, the simple liberalization of prices could lead to abuses, and in the absence of markets, economic mafias. On the other hand, only if prices reflected shortages would a new private sector be able to develop. This, then, was a prerequisite for an efficient, rather than simulated, market which, in turn, dictated that private initiatives should have access to the factors of production, and that new rules in the economy be established (that is, private property should be legalized, the fulfilment of contracts guaranteed, and economic rights in general regulated). At the same time, these rules required institutional changes: in particular the creation of an independent judiciary, the effective enforcement of civil rights, and a free press.

It was beyond these general notions that the consensus broke down and disagreements began. The principal issues at stake were the pace of reform, the political strategies to be adopted, and the role of social policies. The question of the pace of reforms pitted advocates of 'shock therapy' against those who defended more gradualist programmes. The former argued that only comprehensive, simultaneous, and rapid reforms could provide the economic actors with the necessary incentives, and create price systems which would allow firms to act independently under hard budget constraints.[46] As Jeffrey Sachs put it, 'a brutal method immediately clarifies the orientation of the new economic system'.[47] They called for sweeping privatization of state-owned enterprises, in the belief that the development of the new private sector might be limited to the interstices of the economy if only the conditions for the 'entry' of new companies were eased. Thus, on the grounds that all the reforms were both interrelated and urgent, advocates of 'shock therapy' proposed a comprehensive and simultaneous programme comprising price liberalization, the opening up to international trade, the creation of a convertible currency, the reduction of subsidies, and the privatization of the economy.

Proponents of this programme defended it on both economic and political grounds. On the one hand, if reforms were fragmented or implemented gradually over time, they would limit competition, distort the price system, lead to continued budgetary indiscipline, prevent the reduction of inflation, restrict the development of the private sector, and promote corrupt practices in a barely transparent economy. On the other hand, only rapid and comprehensive reforms would make it possible to overcome bureaucratic inertia and resistance, forestall the decline in social confidence, and avert involution. 'Shock therapy' was supported by the IMF, the World Bank, and by politicians such as Balcerowicz in Poland or Vaclav Klaus in the Czech Republic.

Proponents of more gradual programmes, in turn, argued that not all economic reforms could be carried out according to the

---

[46] The arguments in favour of 'shock therapy' can be found in Jeffrey Sachs, *Poland's Jump to the Market Economy* (Cambridge, Mass.: MIT Press, 1993), esp. ch. 2, and in David Lipton and Jeffrey Sachs, 'Creating a Market Economy in Eastern Europe: The Case of Poland', *Brookings Papers on Economic Activity*, 1 (1990), 75–149.

[47] Sachs, 'Vers une économie de marché en Pologne'.

same time-scale; whilst a macroeconomic stabilization plan could be introduced rapidly, the development of a new private sector and the reconversion of a country's productive structure would take much longer. If trade liberalization was rushed it could lead to the collapse of domestic industry, enormous foreign deficits, mass unemployment, and a dramatic fall in public revenue. At the same time, unless there existed competitive markets, and agents that maximized their profits and had perfect information, trade liberalization was unlikely to promote economic development. Equally, the introduction of excessively strict bankruptcy legislation could ruin perfectly viable companies temporarily suffering the consequences of domestic clients' failure to pay their debts due to the economic crisis. Whilst they defended the elimination of all restrictions on the creation of new private companies, they were sceptical about the benefits of privatizing state-owned enterprises. They believed that 'the key to success is not to change enterprise ownership but instead, to provide incentives for entry and exit that are credible'.[48]

The difficulties facing these privatization policies were undoubtedly very different to those existing in Western Europe. In the West, the most ambitious experiment in privatization, namely that carried out by the Thatcher government in Great Britain, involved a public sector which accounted for only 11.1% of production in 1985, and never affected more than five companies a year. In contrast, in Hungary, the post-communist economy in which the public sector was proportionately least important, the latter still accounted for 65.2% of production, and in 1990 the target had been to privatize 2,197 enterprises.[49]. Post-communist privatization was made particularly difficult by the weakness of the banking system and the financial markets, the lack of the economic information necessary to evaluate the companies on sale, and the paucity of domestic savings worth only between 10 and 20% of the value of the assets to be privatized. János Kornai was the main advocate of a gradual privatization process,[50] the policy option which was also chosen by the new Polish government after the

---

[48] Rausser, 'Lessons for Emerging Market Economies in Eastern Europe', 328.

[49] Domenico M. Nuti, 'Privatisation in Hungary', in Michael Keren and Gur Ofer (eds.), *Trials of Transition: Economic Reform in the former Soviet Bloc* (Boulder, Colo.: Westview Press, 1992), 193–202.

[50] János Kornai, *The Road to a Free Economy* (New York, Norton, 1990), 34–101; and the same author's *The Socialist System* (Princeton, Princeton University Press, 1992), 459–60, 511–12, 577–80.

Democratic Left Alliance's (SLD) electoral victory in September 1993. According to the Minister of the Economy, Grzegorz Kolodko,

the state that is transforming its economy should ... not behave with its productive assets like a bankruptcy syndicate charged with selling them as fast as possible through auctions or distributing them free, but should see them as a source of income and as the workplace of the majority of the working population (a function which will gradually become less important as privatization progresses). Therefore it is essential to rationalize the administration of the state's productive patrimony, regardless of the speed with which it is privatized.[51]

The disagreements over strategies had a more political content. Supporters of 'decretist' strategies believed that the governments should implement reforms after only minimal negotiation and by taking irreversible decisions. This strategy was generally linked to a preference for 'shock therapy'. It was also usually accompanied by arguments in favour of strong governments, presidentialist institutions, social demobilization, and surprise decision-making. 'Decretism', therefore, reflected a fundamental lack of confidence in society. Its supporters argued that it was the only strategy capable of preventing the paralysation of policies, negotiations from becoming bogged down, and crucial time from being wasted when it came to pushing through urgent reforms. In contrast, advocates of 'pactist' strategies maintained that governments should negotiate their policies, and secure parliamentary agreements and pacts with social organizations. In other words, instead of regarding society with suspicion, governments should seek its consent and complicity. They should do so for both political and economic reasons, for if citizens feel excluded from decisions which imply major social costs, not only might governments be weakened, but the regimes themselves might be too. Furthermore, if governments shy away from submitting their policies to political debate, the result might be that their design and execution will be less efficient.[52] As the United Nation's Economic Commission for Europe declared, 'no-one has ever demonstrated that a lack of openness improves the quality of economic policy-making'.[53]

Disagreements over social policies were more closely tied to

---

[51] Grzegorz Kolodko, 'Stabilisation, récession et croissance economique dans les economies post-socialistes', *Économie Prospective Internationale*, 51 (1992).

[52] Luiz Carlos Bresser Pereira, José Maria Maravall, and Adam Przeworski, *Economic Reforms in New Democracies* (Cambridge: Cambridge University Press, 1993), Conclusions.

[53] Economic Commission for Europe, *Economic Survey of Europe in 1992–93* (New York, United Nations Publications, 1993), 14.

ideological differences. On the one hand, there were those who called for the creation of a 'social security net' conceived in minimalist terms;[54] that is, a system based not on the rights of citizenship, but on the provision for specific groups in need.[55] Beyond these limits, social policies would be counter-productive for market reforms, not only due to their cost to the public purse, but also because equality would be economically inefficient.[56] On the other hand, there were those who defended broader social policies on both political and economic grounds. Advocates of this alternative believed that greater income equality and higher expenditure on health and education would favour economic growth, and that the equitable distribution of the social costs of economic reforms was essential if citizens were to continue to support the reforms. Social policies, it was argued, could both further the goal of economic reforms and contribute to the consolidation of democracy.

These were the basic options existing on the collapse of the communist regimes. Table 3.7 shows the results of the democratic elections in Czechoslovakia, Hungary, and Poland. The opposition won the elections in all three countries, although political parties were still barely organized as such. Above all in Poland and the former Czechoslovakia, the volatility of the vote and changes in the ranks of the competing parties resulted in highly unstable party systems. Partly reflecting the initial system of extreme pro-portional representation, partisan fragmentation was particularly acute in the Polish elections of 1991: in total, 29 parties obtained parliamentary representation, but none won more than 12% of the vote. In Hungary and Czechoslovakia, and despite relatively unfragmented parliaments, the largest party required the backing of at least two others in order to form a government. In all three countries, therefore, the first post-communist governments were coalitions, a formula which is generally considered to imply a limited capacity to undertake drastic reforms.

In Poland the reforms began in January 1990 with the 'Balcero-wicz Plan'. The initiative was taken by Mazowiecki's government, formed in September 1989 after the partial elections to the *Sejm*

---

[54] See e.g. Olivier Blanchard, Rudiger Dornbusch, Paul Krugman, Richard Layard, and Lawrence Summers, *Reform in Eastern Europe* (Cambridge, Mass., MIT Press, 1991), 90–1.

[55] David M. Newbery, 'The Safety Net during Transformation: Hungary', in Clague and Rausser (eds.), *Emergence of Market Economies*, 197–217.

[56] As Leszek Balcerowicz put it in a lecture delivered at Columbia University on 20 January 1994, 'if envy is not on the increase then economic progress is not being made.'

TABLE 3.7. *Electoral results in Eastern Europe*

Czechoslovakia	June 1990		June 1992 (Czech Rep. only)
Civic Forum/Public against Violence	46.6	Civic Party/Christian Democratic Party (ODS-KDS)	29.7
Communist Party	13.6	Christian Democrat Union/Popular Party (KDU-CSL)	6.3
Christian Democrat Union/Christian Democratic Movement	12.0	Movement for Democracy and Self-government (HSD-SMS)	5.9
Society for Moravia and Silesia/Movement for Democracy and Self-government	5.4	Czech Social Democracy (CSSD)	6.5
		Left Bloc (LB)	14.1
Slovak National Party	3.5	Social Liberal Union (LSU)	6.5
Others	16.1	Assembly for the Republic (SPR-RSC)	6.0
		Democratic Civil Alliance (ODA)	5.9
		Others	19.1

Hungary	March 1990		May 1994
Hungarian Democratic Forum (MDF)	24.7		9.8
Alliance of Free Democrats (SzDSz)	21.4		17.9
Independent Smallholders' Party (FKgP)	11.8		6.7
Hungarian Socialist Party (MSZP)	10.9		54.1
League of Young Democrats (FIDESZ)	8.9		5.2
Christian Democratic Peoples' Party (KDNP)	6.5		5.7
Others	15.8		0.6

TABLE 3.7. (*cont.*)

Poland	October 1991	September 1993
Democratic Union—from Solidarity (UD)	12.3	10.6
Democratic Left Alliance (SLD)	12.0	20.4
Polish Peasant Party/Programmatic Alliance (PSL)	8.7	15.4
Confederation for an Independent Poland (KPN)	7.5	5.8
Solidarity	5.1	4.9
Liberal Democratic Congress (KLD)	7.5	4.0
Centre Alliance—from Solidarity (PC)	8.7	4.4
Peasant Accord—from Solidarity (PL)	5.5	2.4
Catholic Electoral Action (WAK)/Ojczyzna	8.7	6.4
Labour Union (UP)	—	7.3
Bloc in Support of Reforms (BBWR)	—	5.4
Others	24.0	13.0

that had resulted in a major defeat for the Communist Party, and backed by a four-party coalition. The economic situation was critical, with hyperinflation, a plummeting net material product, and a rising public deficit. The 'Balcerowicz Plan' was not only the first programme of post-communist economic reforms to be introduced in Eastern Europe, but also the paradigm of 'shock therapy'. It was a radical and comprehensive plan combining stabilization policies with structural market reforms. The plan initially enjoyed considerable popular support; when approved in Parliament, it was supported by 50% of the Polish population and opposed by only 14%.[57] However, as people began to experience the costs, but not the benefits, of the Plan, this support rapidly dwindled and in the spring of 1990 various social groups began to protest against the reforms.

In Hungary, where there was extensive experience of price and trade liberalization, the reform process started later with the introduction of the 'Economic Programme for National Renovation' in September 1990. After the elections held in March 1990, József Antall had formed a government made up of three parties: the Democratic Forum, the Independent Smallholders' Party, and the Christian Democratic People's Party. The coalition was highly heterogeneous, as a result of the divisions among the three allies as well as within the ranks of the Democratic Forum itself. However, the reforms also had the backing of other parties outside the coalition, notably the Alliance of Free Democrats, which was rewarded for its support by Arpad Göncz's appointment as president of the Republic. For some time, stabilization and liberalization measures were postponed due to the doubts and divisions within the government's ranks over the direction of reform. Eventually, the removal of Ferenc Rabar from the Finance Ministry and his replacement by Mihaly Kupa marked the triumph of the 'gradualist' thesis. Kupa himself declared that 'we cannot risk social tensions that would put everything in question', whilst another member of the government, Bela Kádár, emphasized that 'it is better to wait one year more than to charge ahead and risk losing all by inciting violent political resistance'.[58] Opposition was not slow in appearing:

---

[57] See Judy Batt, *East Central Europe from Reform to Transformation* (London, Pinter, 1991), 83–8. In Jan. 1990 42% of the population supported the Plan, 8% opposed it, and 50% stated that they were not sufficiently well-informed to give an opinion.

[58] Interviews in *Le Figaro*, 4 June 1991 and *La Tribune de l'Expansion*, 7 July 1991, quoted in Bresser Pereira, Maravall, and Przeworski, *Economic Reforms in New Democracies*, 151 and 183.

in October 1990 a transport workers' strike forced the government to cancel a petrol price increase, and the government's popularity soon began to decline.

In the former Czechoslovakia, the initial delay in implementing reforms reflected the provisional character of the government of National Unity in power between December 1989 and June 1990, as well as the disagreements between 'shock therapists' and 'gradualists'. A package of global reforms, christened the 'Scenario for Economic Reform', was eventually announced in September 1990 by the government dominated by the Civic Forum and the Public against Violence. However, the latter, under the leadership of Vladimir Meciar, soon took up Slovak nationalist demands which put a brake on reform and culminated in the division of the country on 1 January 1993. After his election as prime minister of the newly created Czech Republic, Vaclav Klaus initiated a drastic programme of reforms that counted on a level of popular support that was much stronger than in Hungary and more stable than in Poland.

Which political factors encouraged these governments to initiate or defer reforms, to choose one option or another from the menu of possible programmes? The economic situation, the characteristics of the transition, the political condition of the governments, and foreign influences appear to have been the main factors conditioning political decisions. When the economic crisis became particularly serious, and reforms even more urgent, governments were forced to act, and the likelihood of them opting for 'shock therapy' and 'decretism' increased. This can be seen in the Polish case; as Grzegorz Kolodko has written, 'the situation must first deteriorate, i.e., destabilize to the point where the only way out is fundamental institutional transformation, because it is only then that both the population and the governing élite are ready for indispensable reforms'.[59] At the same time, the Polish government enjoyed extensive popular support, and the results of the partial elections to the *Sejm* were still fresh. In Hungary, in contrast, the crisis was less severe, since, although the foreign debt was immense, there was no hyperinflation and a large number of liberalizing reforms had already been carried out during the final years

---

[59] Grzegorz Kolodko, 'Transition from Socialism and Stabilization Policies: The Polish Experience', in Keren and Ofer, *Trials of Transition*, 146. Stanisław Gomułka defended a similar thesis: 'in a crisis situation the population is also more inclined to accept a large dose of sacrifice in exchange for some prospects, however distant and unclear, of an improvement': see his 'Polish Economic Reform: Principles, Policies and Surprises', in Keren and Ofer (eds.), *Trials of Transition*, 110.

of the communist regime. For these reasons the Antall government considered that 'shock therapy' could be avoided by introducing a strict monetary policy, extending the role of markets, and gradually transforming property relations. Moreover, the traditional conservatism of the Democratic Forum and the Independent Smallholders' Party had an ambivalent attitude towards the market. The negotiated character of the transition meant that many organizations from the previous regime (particularly the unions) remained strong. Hence the government feared that 'shock therapy' would meet with serious social and political resistance. Although the macroeconomic conditions were more stable in the Czech Republic, the nature of the transition made radical reforms a more viable option: civil society was very disorganized, and the capitulation of the communist regime had provoked the political collapse of the organizations and institutions of the former regime. These circumstances gave the Czech government a particularly high degree of political autonomy for decision-making.

The context of discredited past policies, abrupt political change, and generalized support for the market economy, helped to make democratic politicians particularly receptive to economic advice coming from abroad. At a time of profound political disorientation, the Polish, Hungarian, and Czech governments embraced the safest recommendations. These were the measures which the International Monetary Fund and the Western governments and banks argued were imperative if these countries were to become solvent members of the international economy and, eventually, be accepted into the European Community. These were also the recommendations that a group of foreign experts with domestic connections presented as infallible, and which appeared to be vouched for by the experience of the Western economies. In this way, this foreign factor operated through what Stallings has labelled 'leverage' and 'linkage'.[60] In other words, through pressures and influences which tended to encourage the choice of 'shock therapy' and 'decretism'.

Despite the fact that they depended on the support of coalitions, and the acute fragmentation of partisan competition, various circumstances strengthened these governments' political capacity. On the one hand, the collapse of the communist regimes and economies, the disorganization of the opposition, and the weakness of

---

[60] Barbara Stallings, 'International Influence on Economic Policy: Debt, Stabilization, and Structural Reform', in Haggard and Kaufman (eds.), *Politics of Economic Adjustment*, 41–88.

the structures of interest articulation gave them considerable room for manœuvre. On the other, the cross-party consensus on the need for a market economy and the desirability of European Community membership served as the functional alternative to a broad mandate. For these reasons, the course of the economic reforms was partially independent of the support for governments. At the same time, parliamentary fragmentation and coalitions did not generally result in chaotic policies. In Poland, for example, when the government headed by Jan Olszewski attempted to slow down the pace of reform by introducing a new economic programme in February 1992, the parliament forced a political crisis the following month, since it considered that this change of strategy would result in economic decline, higher inflation, and less foreign investment. When the budget was debated in parliament in early 1993, Hanna Suchocka not only had the support of her seven-party coalition, but also that of the Alliance of the Democratic Left, and was thus able to prevent President Wałęsa from replacing her with a prime minister more to his own liking. In Hungary, in turn, despite the growing divisions within the government itself, neither the Alliance of Free Democrats, nor the Socialist Party, nor the League of Young Democrats questioned the need for market reforms.

What were the costs and benefits of the post-communist economic reforms? It is true that the experience of Eastern Europe is still only a brief one, and also that an economy never crosses a threshold into a world without crises. However, predictions of the time needed for reforms to take effect were normally very optimistic. According to the IMF, for example, the Eastern European countries could expect to grow by 2.8% as early as in 1992, whilst the 'Balcerowicz Plan' calculated that Poland would experience renewed growth six months after the initiation of the reforms.[61] In practice, however, the impact of the reforms was much more severe and prolonged. Although the outcomes varied, they generally consisted of a major fall in output, lower living standards and salaries, higher unemployment, and a larger public deficit. Social inequality and poverty increased whilst the quality and extent of public services and social policies fell sharply. Thus, when the United Nations' Economic Commission for Europe reviewed the overall effects of

[61] The IMF's forecasts, referring to the six countries of Eastern Europe, also assumed that the GDP would fall by 1.5% in 1991 (the actual figure was 15.3%). The 'Balcerowicz Plan' estimated that unemployment would only rise to 2% (when in fact it reached 16% in 1994), and that there would be a 20% drop in real wages (when in 1990 alone they fell by 24.4%).

TABLE 3.8. *Economic performance in Eastern Europe under democracy* (%)

	Czechoslovakia	Hungary	Poland
Inflation (annual average)			
1990	10.0	28.4	553.4
1991	58.0	35.0	70.3
1992	80.0	23.0	43.0
GDP			
1990	−1.4	−3.3	−11.6
1991	−15.9	−11.9	−7.6
1992	−8.0	−6.0	−0.5
Change in real wages			
1990	−5.4	−3.7	−24.4
1991	−25.2	−8.0	−0.3
1992	10.1	—	−3.6
Unemployment			
1990	1.0	1.6	6.1
1991	6.8	7.5	11.5
1992	5.0	12.3	14.0

Sources: OECD, *Perspectives Économiques*, 52 (1992); Institut National de la Statistique et des Études Économiques, *La transition économique des pays de l'Est*, 260 (1992); Economic Commission for Europe, *Economic Survey of Europe in 1992–93* (New York, United Nations Publications, 1993).

the reforms it concluded that 'if the metaphor of "shock therapy" is taken literally, namely that it provides quick and lasting relief from a severe disorder, then the record is not a successful one'.[62] In contrast, the results were much more positive in terms of inflation, foreign trade, exchange rate stability, and the foreign debt.

Let us now consider these effects in a little more detail. Table 3.8 provides data on the evolution of inflation, the GDP, real wages, and unemployment during the first three years of the post-communist period. To begin with inflation, Poland, Hungary, and Czechoslovakia liberalized their prices between 1990 and 1992. They did so at a single stroke, at the same time as they cut subsidies, opened their economies to foreign trade, implemented a major currency devaluation, and introduced high interest rates. The immediate result was a sharp rise in prices. In the Polish

[62] Economic Commission for Europe, *Economic Survey for Europe in 1992–93*, 7.

case, for example, these increased by 78% during the first two weeks of the 'Balcerowicz Plan' alone. However, prices soon stabilized as demand began to adapt to supply, international prices were imported, the monetary policy was brought under control, and wage increases were limited through strict incomes policies.

If we consider the evolution of the GDP (or of the net material product), this fell in Eastern Europe as a whole by some 30% between 1989 and 1992.[63] However, it is possible that this figure underestimates the volume of 'informal production', which certainly expanded. Much of that decrease may have represented a qualitative readjustment of supply, in so far as it concerned uneconomic production or unwanted goods (which, according to different estimates, accounted for between 10 and 20% of total production). In any event, production stopped falling in 1993: the Polish economy then entered a period of rapid growth, expanding by some 4% per annum during the following two years; the Czech economy began to grow in 1994 at a rate of 3.5%; whilst the Hungarian economy only expanded by 1% that year. In other words, economic recovery came first in those countries in which the reforms had been introduced earlier and were more comprehensive.

The reforms had extremely severe consequences for wages and employment. In Poland, for example, wages fell by 27% during the three years after the introduction of the reforms, and unemployment rose to 16% of the active population in 1994.[64] Previously, of course, unemployment had been hidden inside companies. Equally, many unemployed workers in fact worked in the underground economy, and a large number received a supplementary income in the form of unemployment benefits. For these reasons, it has been argued that the effects of the reforms were less severe than the data on GDP, wages, and employment might suggest.[65] Nevertheless, the social costs of reforms should in no way be underestimated: in Hungary, for example, the number of people who declared that they did not have enough to get by till pay-day rose from 26 to 68% between 1989 and 1991, whilst a six point increase in poverty was recorded as a proportion of the total population.[66]

[63] *The Economist*, 20 Feb. 1993, 30. This signified for example, that two-and-a-half million Poles lost their jobs.

[64] *The Economist*, 3 Sept. 1994, 30.

[65] Reference is made, for example, to an increase in the consumption of consumer durables in Poland between 1988 and 1991, or a rise of 16% in retail sales in Czechoslovakia: see Sachs, *Poland's Jump to the Market Economy*, 71; *The Economist*, Survey of Eastern Europe, 13 Mar. 1993.

[66] Xavier Gaullier, 'Modernisation et État-Providence en Europe Centrale: Réflexions à partir de la Situation en Hongrie', *Revue Française des Affaires Sociales*, 46/1 (1992), 8–10.

The economic reforms redirected these countries' foreign trade towards the OECD and the European Community.[67] However, with the exception of Hungary first, and later that of the Czech Republic, there was less foreign investment than the new Eastern European governments had expected.[68] Although foreign support helped to keep exchange rates and reserves relatively stable,[69] investment arrived in limited quantities, largely due to the difficulties the economies found in absorbing capital productively and the still prevailing institutional framework.[70] However, the whole model of reforms, both economic and political, was constructed in reference to the West, and the European Community in particular. Although Poland, Hungary, the Czech Republic, and Slovakia became associate members of the Community in December 1991, the road to full membership would be a difficult one; in order for Poland, for example, to reach half of the European per capita income by the year 2000, it would have to grow some 4% above the European average.[71] Although nobody predicted the spectacular economic development of the Federal Republic of Germany after the Second

[67] In 1991 alone, exports to the OECD countries and European Community increased by 19% and 24% respectively; Norbert Holcblat, 'Europe Centrale et Orientale: Des situations de plus en plus diversifieés', in Institut de la Statistique et des Études Économiques, *La Transition économique des pays de l'Est*, 260 (1992), 19–28.

[68] Although foreign investment rose from $2,300 million to $11,000 million between 1990 and 1992, the latter figure was still relatively low. Hungary attracted over half of all foreign investment in these countries, thanks to its longer history of market reforms, its more experienced business sector, and its more developed commercial banking system. See International Monetary Fund, *IMF Survey*, 22 Mar. 1993, pp. 81, 85, and 86.

[69] In the case of Poland, for example, a stabilization fund of $1,000 million played an important role in supporting the *zloty*.

[70] The rate of growth generated by capital investment was very limited. It has been estimated that, if four times as much capital were invested and this produced returns of 10%, the growth rate would only rise by 1%. In order to achieve growth of 7% of the GDP, the six Eastern European countries would need $107,000 million of investment per annum during a period of ten years, that is, ten times more than the foreign investment they attracted in 1993, or the equivalent of 43% of the total investment in the European Community in 1990. The equivalent requirements of the former USSR would amount to some $230,000 million per annum. It is worth remembering that the Marshall Plan consisted of some $20,000 million over a period of four years, the equivalent of 10% of the total investment. See Lawrence Summers, 'The Next Decade in Central and Eastern Europe', in Clague and Rausser (eds.), *The Emergence of Market Economies in Eastern Europe*, 25–34.

[71] For these calculations, see Sachs, *Poland's Jump to the Market Economy*, ch. 1, and Institut de la Statistique et des Études Économiques, *La Transition économique des pays de l'Est*, 260 (1992), 19–28. Such calculations assume that these countries' populations grow at the same rate, and are based on purchasing power parities.

World War, it is also true that output in that country only returned to its 1939 level a decade after the end of the war.

How did the economic reforms affect the states? The central objective of slimming down the state initially led to a reduction in public expenditure, which was mainly achieved by cutting production subsidies.[72] Yet, public expenditure soon began to rise again in relative terms, in part as a consequence of the fall in the GDP, and partly because of the growing cost of social transfers. Thus, the Polish state budget rose from 29 to 33% of the GDP between 1991 and 1992, whilst in Hungary it increased from 31 to 37%.[73] However, at the same time, fiscal revenue also fell. Under communism this had come above all from the contributions extracted from the state-owned enterprises, whilst prices and salaries had been subject to direct control. Yet as state intervention was reduced, prices liberalized, and the situation of the enterprises worsened, this system began to break down.[74] One of the most pressing economic problems facing the post-communist countries, therefore, was the need to create an efficient fiscal system. Yet, governments postponed fiscal reform for a long time: Value Added Tax, for example, was only introduced in Poland in January 1993. The result of this combination of rising public expenditure and falling revenue was the rapid increase in the fiscal deficit: in 1992 this reached 6% in Poland and 7.4% in Hungary.

The privatization of state-owned enterprises was intended both to reduce the weight of the state and obtain revenue in order to improve public finances. This second objective, however, has been strongly criticized. It has been argued that

it is always a bad policy to finance current deficits by the sale of assets rather than by the review of revenue and expenditure policies, and the government is likely to delay indefinitely the task of creating a modern system of tax collection as long as it can sell off state properties instead.[75]

[72] In a single year, price subsidies in Poland dropped from 15% to 6% of the GDP. See Gomułka, 'Polish Economic Reform', 119.

[73] Economic Commission for Europe, *Economic Survey of Europe in 1992–93*, 143–4.

[74] George Kopits, 'Fiscal Reform in European Economies in Transition', *IMF Working Paper 91/43* (Washington DC, International Monetary Fund, 1991); see also, Sebastian Edwards, 'Stabilization and Liberalization Policies for Economies in Transition: Latin American Lessons for Eastern Europe', in Clague and Rausser (eds.), *The Emergence of Market Economies in Eastern Europe*, 139.

[75] Joseph S. Berliner, 'Strategies for Privatisation in the USSR', in Keren and Ofer (eds.), *Trials of Transition*, 236; for the economic and ideological reasons for privatization, see Vincent Wright, 'Redrawing the Public-Private Boundary: Privatization in the United Kingdom, 1979–92', *Working Paper 1992/37* (Madrid, Center for Advanced Study in the Social Sciences, Instituto Juan March de Estudios e Investigaciones, 1992).

Moreover, whilst the creation of new private enterprises advanced at a good pace, so that by 1994 the private sector accounted for 40% of the GDP in Hungary and 50% in Poland,[76] the sale of state-owned enterprises was either very slow or not very profitable for the states. Hungary opted to sell these at a price fixed through an elaborate process of evaluation and auctions, without a massive distribution of shares or opening the doors to foreign capital. As a result, in 1993 only 4% of these enterprises were privately owned. In Poland and the Czech Republic, in contrast, privatization was carried out by distributing vouchers which entitled citizens to purchase shares in state-owned companies,[77] a formula, however, which did not generate revenue for the state. Furthermore, whilst the privatization programmes were intended to reduce the weight of the state, to create markets which would make enterprises more competitive and accountable, subsequent trading in vouchers and shares very soon gave rise to a concentration of control of companies: in the Czech Republic, for example, three-quarters of the vouchers issued to citizens were managed by bank investment funds, which eventually secured control of the companies.

The problems posed by the fiscal systems and privatization demonstrated that economic reform in Eastern Europe could not merely be limited to the promotion of markets in areas where only the state existed. It was not enough just to reduce the presence of the state, since this was not simply the opposite of the market. On the one hand, it was inevitable that a substantial public sector would continue to exist alongside the new private sector in the

---

[76] See the data in *The Economist*, 23 Jan. 1993, pp. 21–2; 13 Mar. 1993, in the supplement entitled 'Survey of Eastern Europe'; 21 Aug. 1993, pp. 16–18; and 3 Sept. 1994, p. 30. In the mid-1980s, the private sector had contributed a mere 10% of the GDP in Hungary, and 20% in Poland.

[77] In Hungary the state-owned enterprises were first decentralized and then split into different corporations; the shares in these were then transferred into private hands through a process in which investment banks and international consultants played an important role. The final result was a complex mix of shares owned by banks, by public and private firms, and by the employees of the enterprises in question. In Poland privatization began very slowly and in accordance with similar criteria to those used in Hungary. As a result, only five firms had been sold by 1991. A new strategy was then adopted: each Polish citizen received a voucher which could be invested in large holding companies set up by foreign investment funds. The holdings used these vouchers to buy shares in state-owned companies. In the Czech Republic the Klaus government adopted a similar strategy, although vouchers could only be exchanged for shares in auctions which were intended to serve as simulated markets which would fix the price of shares. Amongst the numerous works on the different models of privatization in Eastern Europe, see in particular David Stark, 'Path Dependence and Privatization Strategies in East-Central Europe', *Eastern European Politics and Society*, 6/1 (1992), 17–20.

Eastern European economies. On the other, in market economies the state still has an important role to fulfil, supplying those things that the market cannot do well, and satisfying citizens' needs. Investment in infrastructure, the provision of education and health care, social welfare, and active manpower policies are all tasks which correspond to democratic states with market economies. In this sense, Kolodko has argued that 'rather than withdrawing its commitment to the economy, the post-socialist state should reconsider its form of intervention . . . The change to market regulation of the behaviour of economic agents in no way reduces the role of the state and of economic policy, but rather modifies it.'[78]

It was also the case that the generalized support for the establishment of both democracy and the market in Eastern Europe was combined with a widespread attribution of social responsibilities to the state. These included the reduction of income inequalities, the promotion of full employment, and provision for the unemployed, the sick, and the elderly.[79] The transitory results of the reforms scarcely matched these expectations: wages fell; unemployment, poverty, and inequality increased; the education and health systems deteriorated; and the shortage of decent housing became even more acute. Although this situation was ultimately attributable to the economic failure of communism, it nevertheless constituted a serious problem for the new democratic governments. Growing discontent was both political and economic: in 1992, 87% of Hungarians were dissatisfied with the economic situation, as were 80% of Poles with their standard of living. At the same time, 72% of Hungarians and 87% of Poles declared their discontent with the domestic political situation. In 1994 only 18% of Hungarians stated that they were better off than before the reforms.[80] The enormous social costs of the Polish reforms led Wałęsa to declare that 'we made a mistake in our economic reforms, we decided to move too fast . . . The result is that we are

---

[78] Kolodko, 'Stabilisation, récession et croissance économique'.

[79] Some 74% of the population believed that the state was responsible for assuring full employment, whilst the proportion of those who considered the state responsible for income redistribution was between 15 and 30 percentage points higher than in the West: see László Bruszt and János Simon, *Political Culture, Political and Economic Orientations in Central and Eastern Europe during the Transition to Democracy* (unpublished manuscript, Hungarian Academy of Sciences, Budapest, 1991), 43–4.

[80] Michael Deis and Jill Chin, 'Round-up: Life in Poland', *RFE-RL Research Report*, 22 May 1992, pp. 62–3; Judith Pataki, 'Hungarians Dissatisfied with Political Changes', *RFE-RL Research Report*, 6 Nov. 1992, pp. 66–70; *The Economist*, 7 May 1994.

now facing terrible problems'.[81] These costs, however, were due less to the speed of the reforms than to the deficiencies of existing social policies. In the case of Poland, for example, between 1991 and 1993 the proportion of people declaring that unemployment and living standards should be the governments' main concern rose by 10 and 7 percentage points respectively.[82]

The deterioration of the material conditions of life seriously undermined governments. In Hungary the three-party coalition backing Antall became increasingly unpopular, and in the elections of May 1994 its share of the vote dropped from 43 to 22.2%. In Poland governments proved highly unstable. As can be seen in Fig. 3.1, citizens repeatedly put their confidence in new governments, yet this invariably lasted only a short time.[83] However, the disorganization of society, the very severity of the economic situation, and the absence of other alternatives, meant that the reforms did not encounter dramatic resistance. Yet whilst opposition was weakest when the situation was at its most critical, it increased as support for the governments declined: the first strikes broke out in Hungary in 1990 in response to a drastic rise in petrol prices; in Poland protests started among the Silesian miners and railway workers in January and May 1990, their example was then copied by the peasants in the autumn of that year, and a wave of labour disputes broke out in May 1991.[84] Yet rather than provoking open conflict, the social costs of the reforms gave rise to a silent reaction which showed itself at election time. In Hungary the Democratic Forum, which had won the elections in March 1990, lost partial elections held only six months later, when the participation rate fell to just 30%. In Poland the dissent was expressed in the presidential elections of September 1990, in which Stanisław Tymiński won 23% of the vote, forcing Wałęsa to a second round and relegating Mazowiecki to third place. In other words, the response to the reforms came in the ballot-box rather than

[81] *Le Monde*, 11 Sept. 1991.

[82] Centrum Badania Opinii Społecznej, *Polish Public Opinion* (Warsaw, CBOS, Oct. 1993), 2.

[83] The governments concerned were those led by Tadeusz Mazowiecki from September 1989, Jankrzysztof Bielecki after the presidential election of December 1990, Hanna Suchocka from July 1992, and Waldemar Pawlak from October 1993.

[84] For the dynamic of support, discontent, conflict, and resistance, see László Bruszt, 'Transformative Politics in East Central Europe', *East European Politics and Societies*, 6/1 (1992), 55–72; see also Adam Przeworski, 'Intertemporal Politics: The Support for Economic Reforms in Poland' (unpublished manuscript, University of Chicago, 1993).

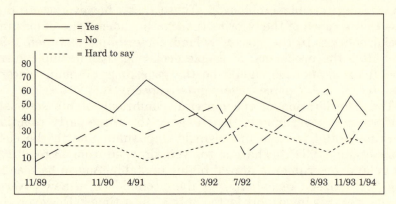

F IG. 3.1. *Opinion of the government's economic policy in Poland ('Does it serve to resolve the economic crisis?')*
Source: Centrum Badania Opinii Społecznej, *Polish Public Opinion* (Warsaw, CBOS, January 1994).

the streets, and generally took the form of abstention or a shift towards anti-party politics.

Despite the social costs involved, and the political reactions to these, there was no change of direction in the economic reforms. The level of electoral support might have varied and the governments may have become weaker, but the different political organizations shared similar economic strategies, no clear alternatives to these existed, nor did the citizens themselves believe there was any other solution. Thus, when the left won the elections in Poland in 1993 and in Hungary in 1994, the governments led by Waldemar Pawlak and Gyula Horn did not alter the basic principles of the existing economic policy. The new socialist parties adopted the typical social democratic stance of the time: that is, they accepted the market reforms and assigned to the state a role centred above all in the sphere of social policies.

Thus, after the end of the dictatorships, the new Eastern European democracies set out to reform their economies radically. Inflation fell most in those countries which held genuinely democratic elections, as was the case of Poland, Hungary, and the Czech Republic, as well as Slovenia, Estonia, and Latvia. In contrast, the economic crisis lasted longest where the elections were most suspect, as in Romania, Bulgaria, and Albania. On the one hand, political legitimacy made it easier for democratic governments to carry out reforms. On the other, these governments also benefited from a much richer flow of economic information, both from within the country and abroad, than they had received in the past, and this helped them design their economic policies. As exemplified in the Polish case, the pace of reform was much faster when the economic crisis was most acute. A legacy of market reforms under the previous regime, as in the Hungarian case, or a more balanced macroeconomic situation, as in Czechoslovakia, gave the governments greater freedom when deciding the timing of reforms. The political characteristics of the transition also had a strong influence on initial economic decisions. Thus, when the collapse of communism was more radical (as in the Czech case, or when the Mazowiecki government came to power in Poland), reforms were likewise more drastic. Weak governments or partisan fragmentation did not necessarily lead to unstable economic policies, above all as a result of the dramatic economic situation and the cross-party consensus which only broke down over the pace of reform, the preference for 'decretist' or 'pactist' strategies, and the role assigned to social policies.

3.3. Conclusions

A comparison of the experiences of Southern and Eastern Europe shows that the agenda of economic reforms was much more limited in the case of Spain, Greece, and Portugal. However, in these countries democracies were established at a time of considerable economic laxity and, initially, the character of the transitions had a strong influence on economic policy. Thus, for some time politics predominated over the economy. When economic policies became more important in the governments' agendas, they did so because of the worsening economic situation and the evolution of the intellectual maps of the politicians. Despite the persistence of major differences (particularly in the Greek case), the paradigms of economic policies converged over the course of the 1980s, due both to the new economic conditions of that decade and the growing agreement over the causes of economic failure and success. One feature of this was a less hostile attitude towards the role of markets in the organization of the economy, although, as we shall see in the next chapter, variations continued to exist in this respect.

In all three countries, the effect of the political conditions on economic strategies has been shown to be complex. On the one hand, a government's strength (measured in terms of the breadth of its mandate) facilitated political decision-making; but it was not a necessary or sufficient condition, nor did it influence the content of the decisions taken. Strength could be compensated for by opportunist strategies of the type followed by Papandreou; weakness by the existence of a wide consensus, as during Cavaco Silva's minority government. On the other hand, the timing and sequence of decisions had important consequences for political success. The earlier decisions were taken, the larger the 'window of opportunities' available. In contrast, the later they came, the more they would be dependent on strategies of concertation.

In all three Southern European countries, democratization had important economic consequences for the states. Their economic capacity increased, in terms of both fiscal revenue and expenditure. I argued in Chapter 1 that this pattern, which fits de Tocqueville's analysis of the effects of democracy, has been the predominant one in the new democracies. The change of regime modified the functions of the states, rather than simply delegating them to markets. Of these state functions, social policies were those which grew most in importance, and this affected the relations between citizens, governments, and regimes. In difficult economic conditions (such as unemployment in Spain), these policies fostered political stability and social equity.

In Eastern Europe, the economic scenario was much more dramatic, with hyperinflation in Poland and an overwhelming foreign debt burden in Hungary. In consequence, economic reforms were both more urgent and more comprehensive, and governments took initiatives much more quickly than in Southern Europe, implementing stabilization programmes and major structural changes. No attempt was made to experiment with 'third roads' (as Portugal had done in the 1970s, and Greece, in a more limited fashion, in the 1980s). Rather, there was considerable consensus among citizens and politicians regarding the termination of both the political regime and the economic system, and the economic model that should be erected in their place. The persistent discrepancies among the different political options concerned the strategies used to establish this model, and the role the state should fulfil in combination with the market.

In Hungary, Poland, and the Czech Republic, governments were both more willing to act and to opt for 'shock therapy' and 'decisionist' strategies when the economic crisis was especially severe, when they could count on wide support, and when the type of transition endowed them with considerable political autonomy from society. Thus, even though the governments were coalitions, their political capacity was strengthened by the collapse of the communist regimes and by the extensive inter-party consensus concerning the generic economic model to be followed. Although the 'valley of tears' proved long and deep, the enormous social and economic costs of the reforms had only a limited impact on democracy itself. Such costs contributed to the governments' defeat in the elections in Poland in 1993 and Hungary in 1994; the new social democratic governments placed more emphasis on social policies and stressed the role of the state, but they did not question the model of the mixed market economy nor embark on a radical change in economic policy.

Thus, the capacity of democratic governments to manage their economies in hard times was strengthened by mandates and/or consensus, that is through the complicity of the societies. And their performance was not determined by a foreordained logic that favours dictatorships but, rather, was largely the result of decisions made by governments, social groups, and citizens themselves. The new democracies in Eastern Europe, therefore, offer no support for the thesis that markets can only be established by authoritarian regimes, or that the most viable sequences are those in which economic reforms come before political reforms. Democracy did not make the path longer, the difficulties greater, or the hardship any more unbearable.

The Economic Identity of the Left

To what extent did the growing convergence of economic policies erase the differences between distinct political options? Did left-wing governments accentuate the redistributive tendencies of the new democracies? How far was social democracy able to represent a political alternative with a distinctive identity? How was this identity affected by social democracy coming to power in newly established democracies? In order to answer these questions, in this chapter I will examine the programmes and policies of the Southern European socialist parties, and compare them with the experience of European social democracy. I will study the Spanish PSOE, the Greek PASOK, the Portuguese PS, the Italian PSI, and the French PS. In the first three cases, democracy was a recent development, the result of transitions from authoritarian regimes in the 1970s. In the other two countries, democracy had been re-established at the end of the Second World War. Three of the parties—namely the PSOE, the French PS, and the PASOK—first formed governments in 1981 or 1982 with absolute parliamentary majorities and after a long period of exclusion from power. In contrast, with the exception of the short-lived period of single-party socialist rule in Portugal from the elections in 1976 to the end of the following year, the Portuguese and Italian parties formed part of coalition governments during the 1980s. Moreover, although a socialist held the post of prime minister in Italy between 1983 and 1987, the PSI was always the junior partner in these coalitions. The comparative analysis of these parties' policies, therefore, will have a *géométrie variable*. Given that the performance of coalition governments cannot easily be considered to exemplify socialist policies at work, I will focus above all on the Spanish, French, and Greek cases.

My first hypothesis is that ideology affects policies. In other words, I will argue that, despite the differences in these countries' institutional structures and economies, when the social democratic parties gained power they shared policy preferences which were clearly distinguishable from those of non-socialist governments. I will try to identify the similarities and differences that existed between the policy preferences of these parties, and to compare them with those of conservative governments. I will pay particular attention to the way in which they shaped economic and social policies, and consider the outcomes of these in terms of economic efficiency and equality. It will be argued that the principal common characteristic of these social democratic governments was the way in which, for both ideological and electoral motives, they attempted to use the state in a non-subsidiary role to redistribute material resources and life chances equally, and that they also sought to make this policy preference compatible with economic policies promoting development. Furthermore, it will be suggested that the notable shifts in these governments' strategies reflected social democracy's deep uncertainties with respect to economic policy during the 1980s. The thesis that redistributive policies constituted the essential distinctive component of the social democratic identity will be validated if we find that when faced by economic crisis, these governments proved more reluctant to renounce these policies than other elements of their programmes.

A second hypothesis is that these governments' programmes were influenced by variations in the institutional, political, and economic environment in which they operated. It will be argued that as a result of the recent authoritarian regimes and/or a long period of exclusion from power, the Southern European socialists had to address questions which did not figure in the programmes of their Northern European counterparts. It will be further maintained that the social democratic agendas became increasingly similar, and that the experience of government also inspired some convergence in their policies. Nevertheless, I will suggest that the differences in the preferences of citizens and the characteristics of the trade unions contributed to variations in the economic policies adopted in the Southern European countries.

An additional hypothesis defended here, and one which qualifies those outlined above, is that programmes and policies were also the result of choices made by parties and their leaders from among a range of available policy options. The existence of a margin for choice will be revealed if we find different policies being practised in what were essentially similar circumstances. It will further be argued that parties' policy options were influenced by the size of their mandates as well as by the intellectual visions and cognitive maps of their leaders. This study of the experience of Southern Europe may shed some light on the broader issue of the political profile of social democracy in the 1980s, by addressing the question as to what left-wing governments meant in that decade of serious social democratic dilemmas.

This analysis of the relative effect of ideology on politics is also of some significance for our interpretation of the policy alternatives available to Eastern European governments. It is certainly true that with the collapse of communism the range of economic policies considered viable narrowed significantly. Equally, in the unstable political scenarios of the post-communist countries, none of the earlier social democratic parties won sufficient seats in the first democratic elections to form their own parliamentary group. Yet, on the one hand, market reforms could be combined with a greater or lesser role for the state and social policies. That is, the consensus on economic policies had limits which reflected the existence of distinct ideological profiles. On the other, the social distribution of ideological sympathies always revealed considerable potential support for social democracy. Thus, in January 1990, only a short time after the fall of communism, the majority of Poles and Hungarians identified social democracy as their preferred political alternative, largely on the grounds of the social policies with which it was associated.[1] These factors enable us to understand the social democratic victories in the elections held in Poland in September 1993 and Hungary in May 1994. In these new political circumstances, both Aleksander Kwaśniewski, leader of the Polish SdRP, and Gyula Horn, leader of the Hungarian MSZP, expressed a keen interest in the social democratic experience in

[1] In Hungary whilst 68% of citizens had positive opinions of social democracy, in the case of communism this was true of only 15%. Liberalism and capitalism were considered favourably by 57% and 37% respectively. With respect to social policies, 40% preferred a social democratic government and 19% opted for a liberal or conservative one. A social democratic government was also considered preferable for civil rights: 28% compared to 21% for a liberal or conservative government. In Poland whilst 58% of the citizens had a positive opinion of social democracy, liberalism and capitalism were seen positively by 47% and 42% of the population respectively. In the field of social policies, 29% preferred a social democratic government, compared to only 11% who chose a liberal or conservative one. As for civil rights, 26% considered that these would be safest under a social democratic government compared to 13% who preferred a liberal or conservative one. The polls were conducted by Median in the case of Hungary, and Demoskop for Poland: see *El País*, 19 Feb. 1990, pp. 5–8.

Southern Europe, and Spain in particular.[2] This comparison raises the question of the options open to social democrats if they come to power in new democracies facing critical economic conditions.

4.1. The Changing Scenario for Social Democracy

When the Socialist parties came to power in Southern Europe the basic characteristics of the social democratic experience since the Second World War were increasingly being questioned. Social democracy had consisted of a particular mix of politics and market: a combination of political pluralism, mixed economies, Keynesian policies, and the welfare state. The latter, in particular, was the principal mechanism of income redistribution, promoting greater 'equality of conditions' (through the minimum wage, pensions, the health service, unemployment benefits and policies to combat poverty) and 'equality of opportunities' (through public education). The state's extensive responsibilities for the material conditions of the life of citizens were financed by increases in progressive taxation, and above all income tax. In contrast, nationalization of the means of production had gradually been abandoned as a means of achieving social democracy's goal of equality. This emphasis on social egalitarianism rather than economic collectivism was first defined in the 'functional socialism' practised by the Swedish Social-demokratiska Arbetartpartiet (SAP) when it came to power in 1932, during Hugh Gaitskell's leadership of the British Labour Party, and in the Bad Godesberg Congress of the German Sozialdemo-kratische Partei Deutschlands (SPD) in 1959. State intervention through social and fiscal policies was defended on the grounds of both social fairness and economic efficiency. On the one hand, it permitted the modification of the distributional outcomes of market forces. On the other, Keynesianism and the theory of public goods made these social objectives compatible with economic principles. The result was that, during the course of almost four decades, social democracy developed the welfare state far further than liberal or conservative conceptions had originally intended.

This expansion of the welfare state was to a large extent responsible for the massive increase in public expenditure seen in most of

---

[2] In an interview in *El País*, 26 Sept. 1993, pp. 8–9, Kwaśniewski affirmed that the ideology of the Polish social democrats 'despite all the differences, is a conception similar to that carried out, in other circumstances, by the Spanish socialists. . . . I have great respect for Felipe González. He knew how to be a socialist and at the same time to develop Spain'.

Western Europe. Between 1900 and 1945, this tripled as a proportion of the GDP in countries such as Germany, Great Britain, and Sweden. Over the following three decades, public expenditure continued to rise, until in 1975 it absorbed 54% of the GDP in the Netherlands, 51% in Sweden, 48% in Denmark, 47% in Norway, and 46% in the United Kingdom. Welfare policies and progressive taxation also led to a reduction in economic inequality. In countries such as Denmark or Great Britain, the share of total income belonging to the richest 5% of the population was almost halved between the end of the nineteenth century and the end of the 1960s.[3] Probably the most important effect of the welfare state was the improvement in the living conditions and life chances of the most underprivileged groups, in accordance with criteria very similar to John Rawls' 'difference principle',[4] and a specific conception of 'citizenship'.[5]

Let us consider these questions in a little more detail. What consequences did this social democratic model have for the structure

[3] Peter Flora and Jens Alber, 'Modernization, Democratization, and the Development of Welfare States in Western Europe'; Jürgen Kohl, 'Trends and Problems in Postwar Public Expenditure Development in Western Europe and North America'; Franz Kraus, 'The Historical Development of Income Inequality in Europe and the United States'. All three studies are published in Peter Flora and Arnold J. Heidenheimer (eds.), *The Development of Welfare States in Europe and America* (New Brunswick, NJ, Transaction Books, 1981), see 48–50, 194–206, 309–12.

[4] The 'difference principle' consists of a criterion for the organization of society according to which 'social and economic inequalities are to be arranged so that they are both (*a*) to the greatest benefit of the least advantaged and (*b*) attached to offices and positions open to all under conditions of fair equality of opportunity'. This equality implies a socialization of capacities; according to Rawls, 'no one deserves his greater natural capacity nor merits a more favourable starting place in society'. Thus, 'the difference principle represents, in effect, an agreement to regard the distribution of natural talents as a common asset and to share in the benefits of this distribution whatever it turns out to be'. Only those inequalities which improve the living conditions of the most disadvantaged to a greater extent than any other alternative would be justified. See John Rawls, *A Theory of Justice* (Oxford, Oxford University Press, 1971), 83, 102, 101.

[5] In T. H. Marshall's famous 1949 lecture on *Citizenship and Social Class*, which would later be very influential in social democratic thinking, citizenship was defined as 'a kind of basic human quality, associated with full community membership'. In this way 'citizenship is a status bestowed on those who are full members of a community. All who possess the status are equal with respect to the rights and duties with which the status is endowed.' See Thomas H. Marshall, *Class, Citizenship, and Social Development* (Garden City, NY, Doubleday Anchor, 1965), 128 and 92. Democracy would be a society in which there would only exist one status, that of the 'citizen', and in which the living conditions of each individual would be such that his/her rights would have the same value as those of any other citizen.

of inequality during the period from the Second World War to the 1980s? How far did it lead to the redistribution of resources and opportunities? Or to put it in another way, what empirical basis is there for the social democrats' claim that they do in practice defend the principle of equality?

Over the last two decades, 25 quantitative comparative studies have examined the redistributive consequences of social democracy. Of these, six have concluded that social democratic policies scarcely had any impact on welfare, education, and health care budgets, or income distribution. The other nineteen, however, have argued that both the size of these budgets and the number of people benefiting from them have grown under social democratic governments.[6] These studies have analysed the equality of opportunities in terms of what John Stephens has called 'mobility politics', and the equality of condition in terms of 'consumption politics'.[7] The former were essentially based on education, hence studies have tended to focus on the scope of social democratic educational reforms. Some studies[8] have argued that these reforms were confined to the introduction of meritocratic changes (that is, they permitted the educational advancement of intelligent young people from poor families), and did nothing to modify the contours of the stratification system or the selective character of the education system. However, abundant empirical evidence reveals that social democratic governments correlate with the expansion of both education budgets and enrolment rates.[9] On average, public expenditure on education rose by 1.5 points of the GDP under social democratic governments; access to higher education also became more open, and the education system as a whole was democratized. In general, the evidence suggests that social democracy did promote equality of opportunities in Western Europe. Moreover,

---

[6] See Appendix 3.

[7] John D. Stephens, *The Transition from Capitalism to Socialism* (London, Macmillan, 1979), 53–4.

[8] Frank Parkin, *Class Inequality and Political Order* (London, Paladin, 1972), 107–14; Richard Scase, *Social Democracy in Capitalist Society* (London, Croom Helm, 1977), 76–9; Christopher Hewitt, 'The Effect of Political Democracy and Social Democracy on Inequality in Industrial Societies', *American Sociological Review*, 42/3 (1977), 450–64.

[9] Francis G. Castles (ed.), *The Impact of Parties: Politics and Policies in Democratic Capitalist States* (London, Sage, 1982), 63; Stephens, *Transition from Capitalism to Socialism*, 109. Castles found a correlation of .32 between public expenditure on education and the presence of social democratic ministers in governments, whilst Stephens identified a correlation of .39 between this expenditure and years of social democratic rule.

this equality was not conceived in merely meritocratic terms, in so far as education expanded more than was required for an efficient selection to social positions and addressed the needs of disadvantaged groups.

'Consumption politics', that is, those related to equality of condition and the idea of 'citizenship', include pensions, unemployment benefits, and health care, and were largely financed through fiscal reform. They were intended both to improve the standard of living of those most in need and to reduce existing differences in income distribution. Any attempt to analyse the impact of social democracy on these welfare programmes and on the pattern of income distribution is inevitably faced by a number of difficulties. Not only are the data not always comparable over time or for different countries, but the samples and independent variables used in the studies also vary.[10] However, these studies generally show a clear association between social democratic governments and expenditure on welfare and health care.[11] Several of these studies present similar findings for long periods of time.[12]

Social democratic policies also seem to have had an effect on income distribution. Whilst some authors[13] argue that their impact was much less significant than that of the market itself, the accumulated empirical evidence in fact suggests that income inequality diminished as a result of these policies.[14] There is a negative

[10] Thus, the samples consist of more or less homogeneous series of countries and chronological periods. Studies also use different independent variables: the percentage of votes or seats obtained by social democratic parties, the number of ministerial posts held by them, or the existence of a social democratic prime minister.

[11] Castles, *Impact of Parties*, 63; Stephens, *Transition from Capitalism to Socialism*, 100; Castles argues that the correlation between social democratic ministers in the government and public expenditure on health was .45. According to Stephens, there was a correlation of .72 between years of social democratic rule and public expenditure on welfare.

[12] For example, for the period 1957–82, see Alexander Hicks, Duane H. Swank, and Martin Ambuhl, 'Welfare Expansion Revisited: Policy Routines and their Mediation by Party, Class and Crisis', *European Journal of Political Research*, 17 (1989), 401–30.

[13] Robert W. Jackman, *Politics and Social Equality: A Comparative Analysis* (New York, John Wiley, 1975); and the same author's, 'Socialist Parties and Income Inequality in Western Industrial Societies', *Journal of Politics*, 42 (1980), 135–49; and 'The Politics of Economic Growth in the Industrial Democracies, 1974–1980: Leftist Strength or North Sea Oil?', *Journal of Politics*, 49 (1987), 242–56; Parkin, *Class Inequality and Political Order*, 54–62.

[14] Hewitt, 'The Effect of Political Democracy and Social Democracy', 450–64; John Dryzek, 'Politics, Economics and Inequality: A Cross-National Analysis', *European Journal of Political Research*, 6 (1978), 399–410; Manfred G. Schmidt,

correlation between social democratic governments and the concentration of income among the richest 20% of incomes after taxes and public expenditure, and a positive correlation with redistributive taxation. The Gini coefficient and the proportion of income corresponding to the highest income bands fell due to public transfers, the provision of collective goods, and progressive taxation. In the Netherlands and Sweden these social democratic policies reduced the richest 10%'s share of the national income by 11 and 8 points respectively. Equally, taxation and transfers reduced the Gini coefficient by 36% in Sweden and 23% in Norway in the 'golden age' of social democracy, between the Second World War and the 1970s.

These policies, therefore, do seem to have had consequences for equality of opportunities, welfare expenditure, progressive taxation, and income distribution. Quite another matter is whether this impact could have been greater, or whether it would be possible to maintain or reinforce these policies and their consequences when the new economic conditions of the 1980s created serious constraints on taxation and public expenditure. However, Przeworski is right to argue that whilst the result was nothing like socialism, 'the general gist of evidence indicates that social democratic tenure in office does make a difference for efficiency and equality'.[15] Similarly, in a critical evaluation of social democratic policies, Karl Ove Moene and Michael Wallerstein have pointed out that

the elimination of severe poverty and the granting of health care, housing and a modest but decent income as a right of all citizens stands out as their most important accomplishment.... The social democrats were perhaps the first to assert that the most important economic resource of

'The Role of the Parties in Shaping Macroeconomic Policy', and Corina M. von Arnhem and Geurt J. Schotsman, 'Do Parties Affect the Distribution of Incomes? The Case of Advanced Industrial Democracies', both in Castles, *Impact of Parties*, 97–176 and 283–364; Sten G. Borg and Francis G. Castles, 'The Influence of the Political Right on Public Income Maintenance Expenditures and Equality', *Political Studies*, 29 (1981); Edward Tufte, *Political Control of the Economy* (Princeton, NJ, Princeton University Press, 1978), 88–100; Stephens, *Transition from Capitalism to Socialism*, 89–108; Alexander Hicks and Duane Swank, 'Governmental Redistribution in Rich Capitalist Democracies', *Policy Studies Journal*, 13 (1984), 265–86. Schmidt for example, shows a correlation of .46 between the months of a social democratic prime minister's tenure in office and fiscal redistribution between 1960 and 1975. Stephens found a negative correlation of –.70 between the proportion of the total income corresponding to the richest 20% of the population and years of social democratic government.

[15] Adam Przeworski, *Capitalism and Social Democracy* (Cambridge, Cambridge University Press, 1985), 241.

a country is the health and training of its workforce, and that part of their programme endures.[16]

It might, of course, be argued that even if these results were socially redistributive, they proved prejudicial for the economy. Indeed, the thesis that the social policies associated with the welfare state generate economic inefficiency is far from new.[17] Contrary to the argument that social democracy neglects redistribution for the sake of efficiency, this thesis maintains that egalitarian policies inhibit economic competitiveness and growth. Any modification in the distribution process, it is argued, would distort the signals the market gives to indicate how economic resources should best be allocated, interfere with the mechanism of incentives, and undermine the optimum adjustment of the factors of production. Thus, equality and efficiency would be incompatible and antagonistic objectives. At the beginning of the century, this argument was developed by Alfred Marshall when he considered how changes in the property structure or restrictions on the freedom of business could be justified if they only produced a reduction in aggregate wealth.[18] Sixty years later, Arthur Okun affirmed that 'any insistence on carving the pie into equal slices would shrink the size of the pie. That fact poses the trade-off between economic equality and economic efficiency'. And, he went on to argue, 'efficiency is bought at the cost of inequalities in income and wealth and in the social status and power that go along with income and wealth.'[19] Hence, the conclusion would be that social democracy sacrifices efficiency for the sake of equality. These economic theses have been complemented by a political thesis, namely that welfare social policies overload the state with responsibilities which it is incapable of fulfilling, and create passive clienteles, situations of ingovernabiliy arising from excessive demands, and 'democratic excesses'. It has also been suggested that these policies might eventually provoke a crisis of representative government itself.

[16] Karl Ove Moene and Michael Wallerstein, 'What's Wrong with Social Democracy?' (unpublished manuscript, Berkeley, University of California, 1991), 29.
[17] Thus, as early as 1961 Asa Briggs wrote that 'the ideals which inspired the achievement of the "welfare state" are no longer universally shared. Comprehensive notions of a "welfare state" based on complete "equality of citizenship" no longer receive universal assent. . . . Against a background of recurring fiscal crisis, "paying for services" has replaced "fair shares for all" as a current political slogan'. See his article, 'The Welfare State in Historical Perspective', *European Journal of Sociology*, 2 (1961).
[18] Alfred Marshall, *Principles of Economics* (London, Macmillan, 1907), 41.
[19] Arthur M. Okun, *Equality and Efficiency: The Big Trade-Off* (Washington, Brookings Institution, 1975), 91.

There can be no doubt as to the enormous cost of these social policies. Between 1950 and 1975, public expenditure in the Western European countries rose by an average of 18 points. The escalating cost of social policies was the main cause of increased public expenditure. Moreover, this continued to rise after the 1973 oil crisis. Thus the average level of public expenditure in the European Community rose from 41.2 to 49.9% of the GDP between 1975 and 1985. This tendency was maintained both by conservative and social democratic governments; under Giscard D'Estaing in France and Suárez in Spain, for example, public expenditure grew 6.4 and 6.8 points faster than the European average.[20] Nor was there a clear relationship between the level of public expenditure, or the rate at which it increased, and GDP growth during the 1980s. Comparatively high economic growth rates were registered both in countries with high levels of public expenditure (France, Italy, Luxembourg) and in those in which expenditure had increased rapidly (France, Italy, Spain, Portugal, Belgium, Denmark, the Netherlands). At first sight, higher public expenditure did not necessarily have negative consequences for economic performance.

Fourteen quantitative comparative studies have examined the effects of social democratic policies (cum neo-corporatism) on economic growth. Twelve have found that these policies proved economically efficient in relative terms.[21] Walter Korpi, for example, has shown that the economies of those countries with an egalitarian model of social policy grew, as an annual average between 1950 and the mid-1980s, one point of the GDP more than those characterized by a residual model of social policy.[22] Equally, Peter Lange and Geoffrey Garrett found that social democracies performed better in terms of inflation and employment.[23] And

[20] The data have been taken from Commission des Communautés Européennes, *Économie Européenne: Rapport économique annuel*, 50 (Brussels, Commission of the European Community, 1991), Table 55, p. 283.

[21] See Appendix 4.

[22] Walter Korpi, 'Riformare lo stato sociale con eguaglianza', *Democrazia e Diritto*, 3 (1986), 77–114.

[23] Peter Lange and Geoffrey Garrett, 'The Politics of Growth: Strategic Interaction and Economic Performance in the Advanced Industrial Democracies, 1974–1980', *Journal of Politics*, 47 (1985), 792–827, and their 'Government Partisanship and Economic Performance: When and How Does "Who Governs" Matter?', *Journal of Politics*, 51 (1989), 676–93. See also Alexander Hicks, 'Social Democratic Corporatism and Economic Growth', *Journal of Politics*, 50 (1988), 677–704; and the same author's 'The Social Democratic Corporatist Model of Economic Performance in the Short- and Medium-run Perspective', in Thomas Janoski and Alexander M. Hicks (eds.), *The Comparative Political Economy of the Welfare State* (Cambridge, Cambridge University Press, 1994), 189–217.

Przeworski concluded from his comparative analysis of 25 industrial economies between 1960 and 1980 that 'countries which combine strong unions with social democratic governments did better than those OECD countries that relied more heavily on markets in terms of several indicators of economic performance, such as inflation, unemployment, investment, and growth.'[24]

Their record was worse on productivity and wages, but better in terms of assured incomes and 'social wages' (that is, public transfers and services provided by the state). The 'virtuous circle' of social democratic growth was to a large extent grounded on the consensus created by social policies. The assurance of minimum incomes and the equality of distribution permitted inter-temporal trade-offs which kept wages under control, facilitated investment, and promoted employment. And public revenue was optimized in Paretian terms; private post-tax profits and the effective tax rate could both be high, in so far as balanced macroeconomic management, a coherent and predictable tax system, and stable politics proved compatible with high rates of returns on private investment.[25]

However, the economic scenario of the 1980s was very different to that which had existed during the previous three decades. The ever-greater globalization of the economies had a profound impact on this 'virtuous circle' of growth and redistribution. The interdependence of domestic economies, the integration of the financial markets, the elimination of restrictions on international currency flows, the constant possibility of flights of capital, trade liberalization, and the competitiveness of international product markets, all severely restricted the autonomy of national governments. They had much less room for manœuvre in the use of monetary and fiscal policies. The evolution of inflation, the public deficit, and labour costs very rapidly affected competitiveness, employment, and the viability of social policies. The 'Butskellite consensus'[26]

---

[24] Adam Przeworski, 'Economic Barriers to Income Inequality under Capitalism: A Review of Some Recent Models' (unpublished manuscript, University of Chicago, 1990), 9; Jeong-Hwa Lee and Adam Przeworski, 'Cui Bono? Una stima del benessere nei sistemi corporativisti e in quelli di mercato', *Stato e Mercato*, 3 (1992), 345–76.

[25] See e.g. the argument made by Mario Blejer and Adrienne Cheasty, 'Fiscal Policy and the Mobilization of Savings for Growth', in Mario I. Blejer and Ke-young Chu (eds.), *Fiscal Policy, Stabilization and Growth in Developing Countries* (Washington DC, International Monetary Fund, 1989), 46.

[26] This play on words combines the surnames of Rab Butler and Hugh Gaitskell, the British Conservative and Labour leaders of the 1950s and 1960s. It alludes to the supposed common denominator in the economic policies of both right and left, consisting of the acceptance of the market, on the one hand, and the welfare state, on the other.

was definitively abandoned, and replaced by a new economic orthodoxy. This advocated a greater role for markets, the reform of
the public sector, less state intervention, and greater international
integration of national economies. These new post-Keynesian principles were far less compatible with egalitarian social policies.
Monetarist doctrine maintained that public expenditure was the
principal cause of economic difficulties; that a direct relation existed between public budgets, the amount of money in circulation,
and inflation; that public deficits led to the crowding out of private
firms in relation to credits; and that state fiscal or financial intervention and control of prices and wages could not stabilize the
economies. Hence, balanced budgets and reduced state intervention were considered prerequisites for economic efficiency. In fact,
the influence of post-Keynesian ideas can be seen in the reduction
of the economic role of the state in the Western European countries from 1985 onwards. To give just one example, in the European Community as a whole public expenditure fell by an average
of one point of the GDP in the second half of the decade.[27]

To what extent did these changes undermine the identity of
social democracy as a distinct political alternative? In this new
economic context, it could no longer rely on ever-increasing public
expenditure and taxation, nor could it guarantee full employment,
or easily reach agreement with the unions. So began a new historical period of deep social democratic uncertainties;[28] Ralf Dahrendorf
rather dramatically announced the end of the 'social democratic
century'.[29] However, if Keynesian policies and neo-corporatism are
only seen as instruments to promote equality in conditions compatible with other objectives such as pluralist democracy and economic efficiency, and if economic indiscipline is not necessarily the
test of social democracy, then our approach must change. We must

[27] Commission des Communautés Européennes, *Économie Européenne*: *Rapport
économique annuel*, 50 (Brussels, 1991), Table 55, p. 283.
[28] The debate over the new problems facing social democracy in the 1980s has
generated a vast body of literature. See e.g. Przeworski, *Capitalism and Social
Democracy*; Adam Przeworski and John Sprague, *Paper Stones: A History of Electoral Socialism* (Chicago, University of Chicago Press, 1986); Claus Offe, *Contradictions of the Welfare State* (London, Hutchinson, 1984); Ralf Dahrendorf, *Life
Chances: Approaches to Social and Political Theory* (London, Weidenfeld and
Nicolson, 1980), esp. ch. 5; Gösta Esping-Andersen, *Politics Against Markets*
(Princeton, NJ, Princeton University Press, 1985); Walter Korpi, *The Democratic
Class Struggle* (London, Routledge and Kegan Paul, 1983); Fritz W. Scharpf, *Crisis
and Choice in European Social Democracy* (Ithaca, NY, Cornell University Press,
1987); Jonas Pontusson, *The Limits of Social Democracy* (Ithaca, NY, Cornell
University Press, 1992); Herbert Kitschelt, *The Transformation of European Social Democracy* (Cambridge, Cambridge University Press, 1993).
[29] Dahrendorf, *Life Chances*, 106–7.

consider whether equality persisted as the political preference of social democracy and as the core of its identity, explore the effects of the new combinations of policies, and see whether social policies made a difference between political alternatives.

The new economic scenario of the 1980s gave rise to the second great crossroads for social democracy. The first had been confronted in the 1930s, when economic collectivism had been renounced in favour of social egalitarianism. On this second occasion, the result was the adoption of new supply-side policies combined with redistributive social programmes. A number of studies have examined the way in which social democracy adjusted its egalitarian objectives to the new economic circumstances. Geoffrey Garrett and Peter Lange, for example, concluded from their comparative study of fifteen industrialized countries that although the macroeconomic policies of ideologically distinct governments to a large extent converged during the 1980s, social democratic governments nevertheless maintained some distinguishing features. The most important of these were higher rates of total public expenditure, civil consumption (health and education), public investment, total taxation, and more progressive income tax. Subsequently, Garrett has analysed the distinctive features of social democracy in more detail.[30] He found that whilst international economic competition had increasingly constrained public expenditure and that this tended to blur the differences between governments, the distinctiveness of social democratic policies could still be seen in the fields of social transfers (that is, pensions and unemployment benefits), and expenditure on civil consumption (in other words, health care and education). The evidence suggests that at this new crossroads, and in a period of major economic difficulties, although social democracy replaced its old Keynesian formulae with supply-side economic policies, it still attempted to preserve egalitarian principles through social policies.

This is the framework in which I will analyse social democratic policies in Southern Europe. It has been agreed that when the socialist parties came to power in France, Greece, and Spain 'there were high hopes that in the 1980s, the Southern European social democrats would "show the way" for their frustrated northern counterparts'.[31] It is true that the average share of the vote of

---

[30] Geoffrey Garrett and Peter Lange, 'Political Responses to Interdependence: What's "Left" for the Left?', *International Organization*, 45/4 (1991), 539–64. Geoffrey Garrett, 'Economic Internationalization and Economic Policy in Advanced Industrial Democracies' (unpublished manuscript, University of Stanford, 1993).

[31] Donald Share, *Dilemmas of Social Democracy: The Spanish Socialist Workers' Party in the 1980s* (Westport, Conn., Greenwood Press, 1989), 7.

the sixteen main social democratic parties in Europe generally remained very stable over the decade[32] when, at 31.7%, it stood at the same level as during the 'golden age' of social democracy (1945–73). Yet this aggregate figure conceals a major shift in the geography of social democratic support. On the one hand, this period was marked by the electoral defeats of the British Labour Party and the German SPD, by the end of the rule of the Danish Socialdemokratiet (SD), and by the political difficulties of the Swedish SAP and the Norwegian Det Norske Arbeiderpartiet (DNA). On the other hand, there was a major increase in socialist support in Southern Europe. Over the decade, the French PS won an average of 34.7% of the vote, the PSI 16.4%, the PSOE 45.5%, the PASOK 43.4%, and the Portuguese PS 27.2%. In Southern Europe, therefore, the socialist parties obtained an average of 33.4% of the vote, that is, nearly two points more than the average for Western Europe as a whole. In the mid-1980s, all five countries were led by socialist prime ministers. How far did their policies differ from those of European social democracy in general? To what extent did they reflect the new dilemmas and changes of course arising from the transformation of the economic environment? Finally, is it possible to define their policies using the criteria of equality?

4.2. The Southern European Syndrome

The comparative analysis of social democratic policies in Southern Europe must necessarily consider the specific context in which they were conceived and implemented. When they came to power, these parties faced a particular syndrome of economic, social, cultural, and political constraints which differed from that facing other Western European social democrats. This syndrome influenced their programmes, agendas, and strategies. In economic terms, these five countries were obviously very different. In 1981, the per capita GDP (adjusted to purchasing power parities) was only 54% of the EC average in Portugal, 58% in Greece, and 73% in Spain, whilst in Italy and France it stood at 104 and 113%, respectively. Trade and industry were more highly protected, labour markets more rigid, and social legislation more paternalistic in the three new democracies than in Italy or France. Yet despite

---

[32] See Wolfgang Merkel, 'After the Golden Age: Is Social Democracy Doomed to Decline?', in Christine Lemke and Gary Marks (eds.), *The Crisis of Socialism in Europe* (Durham, NC, Duke University Press, 1992), 136–70.

these differences, the new social democratic governments in Southern Europe shared a common problem, namely the declining competitiveness of their economies in a rapidly changing international environment. In the early 1980s, the annual GDP growth rates in all these countries were at least three times lower than they had been ten years earlier; unemployment had doubled in France and Greece and quadrupled in Spain during the same period.[33] Behaving as if the crisis was cyclical in nature, the governments of Giscard d'Estaing and Raymond Barre in France had failed to carry out any economic adjustment. Real wages and public expenditure had been allowed to rise rapidly; whilst the former increased at an annual average rate of 3.0%, the latter grew by nine percentage points, rising from 39.7 to 48.6% of the GDP. Much the same had happened in Greece. Public expenditure had risen considerably since the mid-1970s, fuelled by the transition to democracy and largely financed by budget deficits and public debt. Under Karamanlis, real wages had grown at an annual average rate of 3.7%, or twice the European average. In Spain, the transition to democracy had taken place in the midst of an economic crisis that followed two decades of expansion. As we saw in Chapters 2 and 3, in its final phase the dictatorship had been unable to adjust the economy to the new international situation, whilst in the first years of the democracy, politics had taken precedence over the economy.

Thus, in the five Southern European countries, economic 'modernization' became a key word in domestic politics during the 1980s. Moreover, in Greece, Portugal, and Spain, 'modernization' also implied 'catching up' with Western Europe. The economic constraints on governments were stronger in these three countries, not only because their economies were weaker, but also because economic inefficiency posed a more serious problem for political legitimacy. Spain constitutes a good example of the connection between the two. On the one hand, economic pessimism intensified during the early years of democracy; between 1975 and 1980, the proportion of people who believed that the economy was in a healthy state fell from 50 to 3%. On the other hand, political

---

[33] In 1975 the GDP growth rate stood at 4.2% in France, 6.4% in Greece, and 3.3% in Spain; in 1981, the rates had dropped to 1.2%, 0.1%, and 1.2%, respectively. In 1974, 2.9% of the active population in France were unemployed, 2.1% in Greece, and 3.1% in Spain. By 1981 these figures had risen to 7.6% in France and 4.0% in Greece, and the following year, 16.3% in Spain: Commission des Communautés Européennes, *Économie Européenne: Rapport économique annuel*, 50 (Brussels, 1991), Tables 10 and 3, pp. 250 and 246.

scepticism also spread: whilst in 1978, 65% believed that the system was both legitimate and efficient, two years later this figure had dropped to 40%. And despite the overwhelming support for democracy, only one out of three Spaniards thought that it would resolve the country's problems. In Portugal, four years after the 'revolution of the carnations' a majority of the population believed that democracy had a positive effect on wages but negative consequences for the economy and production.[34]

The Southern European social democratic parties also confronted specific cultural conditions which affected the range of strategic options open to them, in terms of both policies and their electoral support. As we shall see in more detail in Chapter 5, in comparative terms the combination of 'political cynicism' and extensive social demands was very widespread in these countries. In the mid-1980s, the political parties in Italy, Spain, Greece, and Portugal attracted the lowest sympathy scores of all the institutions. Throughout the decade, all three societies displayed a considerable lack of trust and disinterest in politics;[35] 73% of Italians, 68% of Spaniards, and 66% of the Portuguese expressed indifference or hostility towards politics. Attachment to parties was also low, and political participation comparatively limited.[36] These cultural traits did not seem to be affected by the passing of time, as they had been a feature of Italian society for decades and scarcely altered in Spain during the 1980s.

Expectations had soared when the new democracies were established in Southern Europe. In Portugal, the type of transition reinforced the feeling that anything was possible. Yet even in the

[34] For Spain see the polls conducted by the Centro de Investigaciones Sociológicas in Sept. 1979 and July–Sept. 1980; the data for Portugal come from Thomas Bruneau and Mario Bacalhau, *Os portugueses e a politica quatro anos depois do 25 de abril* (Lisbon, Meseta, 1978).

[35] José Ramón Montero and Mariano Torcal, 'La cultura política de los españoles: Pautas de continuidad y cambio', *Sistema*, 99 (1990), 39–74. The proportion of the population agreeing with the statements that politicians only defend their personal or partisan interests, and that nothing could be done against an unfair decision (whether at the national or local level) increased, albeit only slightly, between 1978 and 1989.

[36] For party attachment, see Hermann Schmitt, 'On Party Attachment in Western Europe and the Utility of Eurobarometer Data', *West European Politics*, 12/2 (1989). Since 1976 the proportion of the population of Western Europe identified with a party dropped by some 10 points, and stood around 60%. It was slightly higher in Greece (around 65%), lower in Portugal (around 45%), and lowest of all in Spain (around 30%). Party affiliation rates were also low: in Spain, fewer than 3% of the adult population belonged to a party, five times less than the Western European average.

case of a 'pragmatic transition' of the Spanish type, expectations rose. It was widely hoped that democracy would bring not just political, but also social goods. The 1981 European Values Study revealed the existence of very extensive social reformism in Southern Europe. Some 70% of the population considered that society ought to be transformed through reform, compared to 59% in Northern Europe.[37] The Southern European societies also ranked very high on a scale of 1 to 5 of attribution of responsibility to governments for social equality. This was particularly true of Spain, which came top: in the 1980s, the proportion of people in favour of an egalitarian distribution of income was nearly three times higher than in the United States. From the beginning of the transition very strong demands were made on the state, with more than two-thirds of the Spanish population considering it responsible for the welfare of each and every citizen, compared to only one-quarter in the United States and half in France.[39]

These extensive social demands contrasted with the comparatively under-developed welfare systems inherited by the new democracies. The dictatorships had also had social consequences: in 1976 social expenditure amounted to 9.9% of the GDP in Spain, as against 22.6% in Italy and 22.9% in France in 1977; the proportion of the Spanish social security budget financed by the state was only one-sixth of the European average, whilst public expenditure on education was only one-third; at the same time, income distribution was more unequal than in Italy or France.[40]

---

[37] See Juan J. Linz, 'Legitimacy of Democracy and the Socioeconomic System', 75–6, 79–80, 98, 109. Of thirteen Western European countries, the highest percentages were found in Spain (75%), Sweden (72%), Italy (70%), and France (68%).

[38] According to Peter McDonough, Samuel H. Barnes, and Antonio López Pina, 'Economic Policy and Public Opinion in Spain', *American Journal of Political Science*, 30/2 (1986), 453 n. 4; and Samuel H. Barnes, Max Kaase, *et al.*, *Political Action: Mass Participation in Five Western Democracies* (Beverly Hills, Calif., Sage, 1979), 409–33, 568–73.

[39] The data come from polls conducted by Demoscopia, S. A. in Oct. 1988 (see *El País*, 16 Oct. 1988) and the Centro de Investigaciones Sociológicas in May 1988.

[40] For social expenditure, see the report by the Comisión de las Comunidades Europeas, *La protección social en Europa, 1993* (Brussels, Commission of the European Community, 1994), 42. With the exception of France, social expenditure in Southern Europe was below the EC average. The highest levels in the European Community were found in the Netherlands, Denmark, and Belgium. As for income distribution, in Spain in 1970 the top decile of incomes received 40.7% of the total. See Banco de Bilbao, *Informe Económico 1984* (Madrid, Banco de Bilbao, 1985), 47 and 122; see also Julio Alcaide, 'La distribución de la renta en España', in Juan J. Linz *et al.*, *España: un presente para un futuro* (Madrid, Instituto de Estudios Económicos, 1984), 127–50.

The political conditions facing the social democrats also varied considerably. In Portugal, Greece, and Spain, democracy had only recently been established. The type of transition had also differed in the three countries. In the cases of Greece and Spain, there had been no clear break with the past, the new rules of the game were based on implicit or explicit agreements which limited the degree of the rupture, and a number of groups retained a capacity for political destabilization. Terry Karl and Philippe Schmitter have argued that these types of transition to democracy, although successful in the short term, may subsequently prove problematic if governments are unable to implement substantial reform that improves the lot of their poorest citizens. In this case, they add, the 'successful' democratic transitions of the 1980s may turn into the 'frozen' democracies of the 1990s.[41] In other words, democracy may have been established at the cost of social democracy. These constraints on reforms, however, may in time evolve if the balance of the political forces changes and if democracy is consolidated. In Greece Karamanlis managed to greatly extend the democratic political space only a short time after the start of the transition. In Spain, the persistence of anti-democratic conspiracies, terrorism, and profound political uncertainties meant that constraints remained more important for some time.

Social democratic strategies and policies were also conditioned by the strength of the opposition. On the right, there was no common pattern of support for conservative parties in Southern Europe. There was greater unity among conservative forces in Italy and Greece, whilst they were more fragmented in France and Spain, in the case of the latter partly as a consequence of the existence of nationalist and regionalist parties. The strength and cohesion of the conservative opposition were not only important for electoral reasons, but also due to their capacity to resist social democratic policies both within and outside parliament. Yet the electoral strength of the conservative parties did not always reflect the full extent of opposition to government policies. In France and Spain, conservative resistance was often very strong in society, and led by different social organizations, influential media, and occasionally by the Catholic Church (as, for example, was the case of educational reform and new legislation on abortion).

The importance of opposition on the left (and in particular the communist parties) also varied. It was particularly strong in Italy,

[41] Karl and Schmitter, 'Modes of Transition in Latin America, Southern and Eastern Europe', 281–2.

where the communist vote was 2.6 times larger than that of the PSI when Craxi was appointed prime minister in 1983. In France, Greece, and Portugal, although the socialists came to power as the largest parties on the left, they faced communist parties which enjoyed considerable electoral support. During the 1980s, Spain was the country in which the communist support was weakest and the socialist strongest; although the PCE was very influential within the CCOO, in 1982 the difference in votes was in the order of one to ten. Table 4.1 shows the distribution of electoral support in the five countries when the socialists came to power in the 1980s.

However different, the communist parties tended to win greater electoral support in Southern than Northern Europe, where they were only of any significance in Denmark and Finland. It was sometimes thought that the communist influence might force the socialists to adopt more radical political rhetoric and programmes. This was one of the reasons why Linz affirmed at the end of the 1970s that 'there are undeniable differences of outlook between southern and northern socialists'.[42] For a long time, the politics of the French PS appeared to confirm this impression. Its strategy of *esprit unitaire* included electoral pacts, common programmes (in February 1968 and June 1972), and the presence of four communist ministers in Mitterrand's government from June 1981 to July 1984. During the first stages of the transition in Spain and Portugal, competition with communist parties that had been comparatively strong under the dictatorships encouraged the socialists to espouse a radical discourse. In both countries, however, the PSOE and the PS followed an 'autonomous' (in other words, non-unitary) strategy and, given that the elections quickly confirmed their predominant position, they soon abandoned any attempt to compete in radicalism. In Greece, in contrast, the PASOK rapidly established itself as one of the two poles of the increasingly antagonistic political scene from 1974 onwards, resorting to very radical, nationalist, and populist rhetoric. The KKE's association with the Soviet Union and memories of the Civil War contributed to its comparative weakness.

These were the broad 'confining conditions'[43] within which the

[42] Juan J. Linz, 'Europe's Southern Frontier: Evolving Trends Towards What?', *Daedalus*, 108/1 (1979), 194.

[43] Otto Kirchheimer, 'Confining Conditions and Revolutionary Breakthroughs', *American Political Science Review*, 59 (1965), 964–74. The term 'confining conditions' refers to the economic and social factors which set the conditional perimeter of political choices and define the framework for political action. Confining conditions are never static and the perimeter may expand over time.

TABLE 4.1. *The socialist, communist, and conservative vote in Southern Europe*

	France (1981)	Greece (1981)	Italy (1983)	Portugal (1983)	Spain (1982)
Socialist vote	37.8	48.1	11.4	36.3	48.4
Communist vote	16.1	12.3	29.9	18.2	4.1
Conservative vote	20.9:RPR	35.9:ND	32.9:DC	27.0:PSD	26.2:CD/PP
	19.2:UDF	3.2:Others	20.2:Others	12.4:CDS	16.6:Others
	2.7:Others				

social democrats' programmes and policies must be assessed. This specific syndrome of economic problems, social demands, cultural disenchantment, and electoral competition influenced political choices. These conditions varied significantly from those facing Northern European social democracy. As a result, the political agenda of the Southern European socialists would also be somewhat atypical.

4.3. Intellectual Visions and Party Programmes

The particular strategies and policies of the Southern European social democrats were not only adopted in response to these constraints. They were also the product of choices which reflected determined 'cognitive maps'. Subjective factors, normative filters, moral visions, values, and convictions all mediated between objective circumstances and decisions.[44] They shaped the political perceptions that politicians had of the challenges they faced and the range of options open to them.

The principal intellectual references for the political choices of the PSOE leaders were European integration and Northern European social democracy. The European influence stemmed from a long tradition of Spanish reformism and regenerationism, in which Europe was associated with modernity, and national isolation with backwardness; as José Ortega y Gasset once commented, 'Spain is the problem, Europe the solution'.[45] European social democracy, in turn, played a decisive role in the PSOE's ideological redefinition from 1979 onwards. Felipe González, in particular, was very heavily influenced by his contact with Olof Palme and Willy Brandt, by the ideological debate within the SPD following the 1959 Bad Godesberg Congress, and by some of the moderate figures within the British Labour Party. The influence of Europe and social democracy was reinforced through the Spanish socialists' particular political learning from past democratic failures both in Spain and elsewhere. The experiences of the Spanish Second Republic, the Popular Front in France, Allende in Chile, the first years of democratic government in Portugal, and the British Labour Party's problems in the 1970s, were interpreted by the PSOE leaders as

[44] For a defence of this perspective see Peter A. Hall, *Governing the Economy: The Politics of State Intervention in Britain and France* (Oxford, Oxford University Press, 1986), 276–80.

[45] José Ortega y Gasset, *Obras Completas*, i (Madrid, Revista de Occidente, 1963), 521.

indications of the limits of the politically and economically feasible. Their perception of these episodes helps to account for their pragmatism and concern to avoid costly experiments, as well as the priority given to democratic consolidation and to catching up with Europe.

The PSOE had adopted a social democratic identity before coming to power, as with the return to democracy the party was obliged to adapt its ideology and strategy to the new constitutional framework. Although this process led to serious internal upheaval, the party nevertheless chose to abandon its previous radical discourse. In 1982 the PSOE stood on an explicitly reformist electoral programme: no reference was made to a 'qualitative break' with capitalism or an 'irreversible step' towards socialism. Faced with the prospect of governing in difficult political and economic circumstances, the programme also attempted to avoid making unrealistic electoral proposals. González insisted that he would not make promises which he could not keep. Nevertheless, the programme made two commitments that appeared feasible at the time but which would subsequently cause the socialists serious problems: the creation of 800,000 new jobs within four years, and a referendum on Spain's membership of NATO. The main electoral promises of the PSOE in 1982 had to do with the consolidation of democracy, including military reforms, the decentralization of power to the new Autonomous Communities, a legislative protection of civil rights (from *habeas corpus* to abortion), the expansion of the welfare state and of redistributive policies, and integration into the European Community.

The Portuguese PS won the first two elections held in the new democracy. As a result it had less breathing space in which to adjust its ideology and programme than the PSOE would have in Spain. On its creation in 1973, still under the dictatorship and facing strong competition from the Partido Comunista Português (PCP), whilst rejecting totalitarian 'bureaucratic socialism', the party had espoused 'non-dogmatic Marxism'. At the beginning of the transition to democracy, the PS still defended the nationalization of private enterprises and banks, as well as the redistribution of the large estates in the south of the country. However, social democracy had always had a strong underlying influence: the party had been founded under the patronage of the SPD, and its leader, Mario Soares, had very close ties with Western European social democratic leaders. When in power, the PS shifted to the defence of the mixed economy and parliamentary democracy against the more radical aspirations of the communists and the far left. After his second electoral victory in April 1976, Soares presented Parliament with a moderate programme of government. He initiated negotiations for Portugal's membership of the European Community in 1977, when he also attempted to secure an IMF loan, and gradually abandoned the programme of economic collectivization. In the opposition since 1978, the following year the party approved a new programme, 'Ten years to change Portugal', which was based on the standard social democratic formula of the mixed economy and redistribution. When the PS returned to power between 1983 and 1985, this time as part of the Bloco Central coalition, it implemented a programme of economic austerity far removed from the initial postulates of the 'revolution of the carnations', at the same time as it concluded the negotiation of Portugal's entry into the European Community.[46]

The cognitive maps of the French socialist leaders were shaped by a number of factors: the *enarque* origins of Laurent Fabius, Michel Rocard, and many other leaders of the party;[47] the secular republican ideology of the French left; a nationalist and statist tradition which far outweighed the appeal that ideas of workers' self-management had for one wing of the party; and, finally, the experience of a long period out of government. The leaders of the PS believed that the state should play an active role in the promotion of economic growth and redistribution, and that nationalizations would reinforce the capacity of a 'rational', developmentalist, and reformist state. The party had promised profound socioeconomic change ever since signing the *Programme Commun* with the communists in 1972. In the Metz Congresses of 1979 and 1983, the PS had affirmed its commitment to a much more radical transformation of society than that envisaged by social democracy, denounced as 'pactist' and moderate, that should lead to a definitive break with capitalism. In its 1981 electoral programme, the party promised to reform vast areas of civil legislation, decentralize the public administration, nationalize a large number of industries and banks, redistribute work, extend welfare provision and

---

[46] Thomas Bruneau, *Politics and Nationhood: Post-Revolutionary Portugal* (New York: Praeger, 1984), 89–107; Thomas Bruneau and Alex Macleod, *Politics in Contemporary Portugal: Parties and the Consolidation of Democracy* (Boulder, Colo., Reinner, 1986), 181–97.

[47] See e.g. Pierre Birnbaum (ed.), *Les Élites socialistes au pouvoir. 1981–1985* (Paris, Presses Universitaires de France, 1985), 308–11. The term *'enarque'* refers to the exclusive French post-graduate academy, the École Nationale d'Administration (ENA).

workers' rights, and promote economic growth through demand management and a stronger public sector.[48]

The PASOK, in turn, was heavily influenced by nationalist and populist ideas. It was suspicious of Europe and also very critical of social democracy. Western intervention was seen as the main cause of the failure of previous democratic regimes in Greece, at the same time as Greek society was interpreted in terms of a Manichaean division between a disadvantaged majority and a small oligarchic minority with links with foreign interests and domestic monopolies. Thus, the PASOK's intellectual vision responded to a 'logic of simplification of the political space'[49] that did much to foment the polarization of Greek politics. At the same time, one group within the party leadership defended a more social democratic line. These tendencies coexisted under the charismatic authority of Papandreou, who himself embodied the PASOK's two contradictory 'souls'. Nationalism, populism, and charismatic leadership were combined with the idea that political will was the decisive requirement to reshape the economy and society.

From the 'Declaration of Objectives and Principles' of 3 September 1974 to the party's 1981 electoral programme, PASOK declared that its goal was to surpass capitalism, proclaiming a 'third road' to socialism that was neither communism nor social democracy. This, however, was not to involve large-scale nationalizations, as the party considered that the public sector already had a significant hold on the Greek economy. In fact, the nationalizations carried out by Karamanlis after the return to democracy in 1974 had considerably enlarged the productive public sector, which now covered much of the oil industry, transport, telecommunications, the banking sector, and seaports. Rather than demanding further nationalizations, which they argued would 'not guarantee democratic control by the people', the socialists called for the 'socialization' of industries, that is, workers' participation in management. They also defended the decentralization of the state and the extension of social policies. The PASOK's programme also pledged it to

[48] For the PS's programme, see Byron Criddle and David S. Bell, *The French Socialist Party* (Oxford, Oxford University Press, 1988), 151–90; Philip G. Cerny, 'Socialism, Power and Party Politics', in Philip G. Cerny and Martin A. Schain (eds.), *Socialism, the State and Public Policy in France* (London, Frances Pinter, 1985), 13–41; Michel Beaud, *Le Mirage de la croissance: La Politique économique de la gauche* (Paris, Syros, 1983).

[49] Christos Lyrintzis, 'The Power of Populism: The Greek Case', *European Journal of Political Research*, 15/6 (1987), 667–86.

a foreign policy of non-alignment, Greek withdrawal from NATO, and the renegotiation of the terms of adhesion to the European Community.

Finally, the PSI's political vision was dominated by what Craxi called the imperative of *primum vivere*, that is, the urgent need to strengthen the party against its two major competitors on the left and right. Since the end of the 1960s, the socialists had failed to win more than 10% of the vote. After the change of leadership in 1976, when the party ousted the old guard of the *centro-sinistra*, the PSI attempted to widen its political space, defending greater governmental stability and practising a more 'decisionist' style in power. This political objective became more important than the party's policy proposals, and in what constituted a clear example of a Downsian strategy, the latter were often instrumental to the former.[50] The socialists' ideological justification for this strategy was that it accorded with the transformations which had been taking place in Italian society. Economic modernization, the evolution of the class structure, and the secularization of social values had weakened the Catholic and communist subcultures and given rise to an increasingly large 'modern' sector in need of political representation.[51] The party's deputy leader, Claudio Martelli, defined the social interests which the party ought to represent in terms of a broad and heterogeneous coalition of 'merits' and 'needs'.[52] The latter consisted of the requirements of those social groups without resources and in a precarious economic position; the 'merits' were those of a growing number of people with abilities, knowledge, and information. The PSI thought that by presenting itself as the party of 'modernity' its influence and electoral support would grow.

Thus the PSI had its own formula of 'modernization'. Whilst this did, of course, involve political and economic change, it had much less to do with social policies. The party called for institutional changes in the system of proportional representation and in the role of parliament, the executive, and the president of the Republic.

---

[50] Anthony Downs, *An Economic Theory of Democracy* (New York, Harper and Row, 1971), 28, 100–3. According to Downs's model, parties do not win elections in order to implement policies; rather, they formulate policies to win elections, and ideologies are an instrument to win power.

[51] See Gianfranco Pasquino, 'Modernity and Reforms: The PSI between Political Entrepreneurs and Gamblers', *West European Politics*, 1/9 (1986), 120–41.

[52] Claudio Martelli, *Governare il Cambiamento* (Rome, Rotostilgraf, 1983). Martelli first referred to these 'merits' and 'needs' in the *Conferenza Programmatica del PSI*, held in Rimini in 1982.

It attached great importance to civil rights, participation, and individual capabilities. It proposed the reform of a state which it considered inefficient and archaic, the transformation of the public sector, and greater trade union democracy. Much less importance was attached to the goals of social welfare and redistribution. In this way, the party hoped to win the support of voters attracted by ideas of progress, secularism, individualism, efficiency, and governability, and who were tired of governmental paralysis. It attempted to do so by making skilful use of the media, through the highly presidentialist politics of Craxi, and by stressing 'decisionism' (that is, the capacity to take rapid and effective decisions).

These different strategies and programmes reflected the distinct interpretations and 'intellectual visions' of the political actors. In consequence, the parties differed in their preference for caution or experimentation, pragmatism or voluntarism. Some leaders sought to avoid experiments which might prove costly in political or economic terms. They were more likely to make this choice if they were particularly influenced by past experiments, whether in their own country or elsewhere; if the risks of a destabilizing political opposition were seen as high; if their commitment to the European Community was strong; and if they were greatly influenced by social democracy. Others, in contrast, opted for experimentation and had more confidence in the power of political will. These leaders aspired to advance towards a different type of economic system in the belief that opportunities existed for demand-led growth, extensive social redistribution, and greater national economic independence. Thus, at the beginning of the 1980s there was no consensus among the socialists of Southern Europe as to whether it was possible to break with capitalism or as to the alternative models of society that were viable.

When the various Southern European socialist parties came to power in the 1980s they did so in very different circumstances. The Portuguese PS and the PSI came to power as part of coalition governments. Soares headed the Bloco Central alliance in the context of a major economic crisis that had been aggravated by many of the reforms introduced by the provisional Portuguese governments, the passivity of the conservative Alianza Democrática coalition between 1978 and 1983, and the political instability which had characterized the first decade of democracy. Thus, economic reforms were the main priority for this government. In Italy Craxi was appointed prime minister of a five-party coalition government in 1983 at a time of great political instability. In what had traditionally been a very stable electorate, the Partito Comunista

Italiano (PCI) had lost votes (4.5 points since 1976), whilst the electoral support of the Democrazia Cristiana (DC) dropped to 33%. A great many Italians shared the view that governments had long been inefficient and incapable of taking decisions. Governmental stability and 'decisionism' were the priorities for Craxi.

The French PS, the PASOK, and the PSOE formed single-party governments during the 1980s. Their parliamentary majorities and rise to power after a long period of political exclusion of the left encouraged what Keeler has called 'extraordinary policy-making',[53] that is, the idea that it was necessary and possible to carry out an unusually large number of reforms in what were perceived as exceptional circumstances. Keeler argues that these occasions arise when the combined effects of a political crisis and a strong mandate open a 'macro-window' for change. The size of the mandate appears to be the most important variable: a broad mandate would generate the feeling that the new government was 'authorized' by society (which would weaken resistance to its initiatives), as well as grant 'empowerment' (that is, the parliamentary support required to implement reforms). The French PS, the PASOK, and the PSOE saw their electoral victories very much in these terms, as creating an exceptional opportunity for change. However, both the way in which they interpreted the economic and political situation and their chosen 'policy formula' varied considerably, above all in their initial period in office.

4.4. The Convergence of Economic Policies

The first economic decisions taken by the new socialist governments differed radically. Rather than the result of the comparative state of their economies, this divergence reflected the intellectual visions of the party leaders which were to a large extent autonomous from economic conditions. The French PS, during its first two years in government, and the PASOK practised state interventionism, combined with traditional socialist policies (the PS) and populist tendencies (the PASOK). The contrast with the volte-face implemented particularly under Fabius and Rocard in the French case and with the policies of the PSOE and the Portuguese PS illustrates the dilemmas of social democracy in the 1980s.

If we start with the French case, after winning the elections in

---

[53] See John T. S. Keeler, 'Opening the Window for Reform: Mandates, Crises, and Extraordinary Policy Making', *Comparative Political Studies*, 25/4 (1993), 427–86.

1981 the Mauroy government rapidly put its nationalization programme into practice, buying 100% of the shares in 36 banks, two financial societies, and eleven industrial groups, at a total estimated cost of 2.6% of the GDP. In consequence, the public sector came to absorb 24% of employment and 60% of annual investment in industry and energy. The socialists also introduced major redistributive reforms. They believed that these would not only promote greater social equality but also improve the country's economic performance, since the additional demand from low income groups was expected to stimulate growth. Increases in the minimum wage (*salaire minimum interprofesionel garanti* or SMIG) and the lowest pensions cost two points of the GDP. The government also attempted to promote employment through active manpower policies and the redistribution of available work. Between 1981 and 1983, therefore, the PS government followed a strategy of Keynesianism in a single country combined with economic redistribution.[54] This expansionist and redistributive *dirigisme* had a considerable social impact; its economic consequences, however, were more negative. Imports soared, the trade balance deteriorated, and the budgetary deficit grew. International trade and integration into the European Community imposed severe constraints on this socialist strategy.

This was the turning-point of 1983, when the French socialists faced a similar dilemma to that which the Labour government in Britain had confronted in 1976.[55] One alternative at this point was to opt for economic autarky. If this path had been chosen, the French government would have been forced to drop out of the European Monetary System and establish trade barriers, probably at the cost of France's membership of the EC and reprisals by other countries. The risks of this alternative economic strategy were considered too great, the transitional costs too high, and the

[54] See Peter A. Hall's excellent analysis of French economic policies in George Ross, Stanley Hoffman, and Sylvia Malzacher (eds.), *The Mitterrand Experiment: Continuity and Change in Modern France* (Oxford, Blackwell, 1987), ch. 3. See the same author's, 'El impacto de la dinámica política y social sobre la evolución de la política económica en Gran Bretaña y Francia', in Alvaro Espina (ed.), *Concertación social, neocorporatismo y democracia* (Madrid, Ministerio de Trabajo y Seguridad Social, 1991), 119–60; and Howard Machin and Vincent Wright (eds.), *Economic Policy and Policy-Making under the Mitterrand Presidency, 1981–84* (London, Frances Pinter, 1985), 1–43; William Safran 'The Socialist Alternative in France: Mitterrand's Economic Policies', in Norman J. Vig and Steven E. Schier (eds.), *Political Economy in Western Democracies* (New York, Holmes and Meier, 1985), 200–28.

[55] On Labour's dilemma in 1976, see e.g. Martin Holmes, *The Labour Government, 1974–79* (London, Macmillan, 1985), 79–103.

final outcome too uncertain. The government opted instead for a more orthodox response: it devalued the franc, froze wages and prices, cut public expenditure, and moderated its policies of industrial interventionism, large-scale public investment, and raising the lowest incomes. Private investment was no longer encouraged by expanding aggregate demand, but by ensuring a satisfactory rate of profits. Hence labour costs were cut, the labour market flexibilized, company taxes lowered, and employers' social security contributions reduced. As a result of these measures, inflation dropped from 11.5% in 1982 to 5.8% in 1985, the budget deficit was brought down to half the EC average, there was a notable improvement in the balance of trade, and private investment increased. And the economy began to expand again in 1985. Forsaking its initial rejection of social democracy, the PS turned to greater economic discipline.[56]

Under Fabius and Rocard, the socialist governments persisted with this economic policy of *rigueur* and competitiveness, which they tried to make compatible with a social policy of *solidarité*. These would be the key concepts of the new socialist discourse. If we compare the Socialist policies after 1984 with those of the Chirac government from 1986 to 1988, the PS maintained a highly progressive income tax system, introduced the *revenu minimum d'insertion* (RMI—a guaranteed minimum income), and made company tax reductions dependent on the reinvestment of profits. In contrast, the conservative government, which maintained the same level of fiscal pressure, made taxation less progressive, reducing the top marginal rate, abolishing the tax on large fortunes, and increasing wage earners' social security contributions.[57] Whilst it has been argued that in France 'neo-liberalism has become a common political language for political actors on the right and left, which is expressed in the convergence of economic policies',[58] significant differences continued to exist between them. The search for a 'policy package' that combined economic competitiveness and

---

[56] See the analysis of this policy change in Pierre-Alain Muet and Alain Fonteneau, *Reflation and Austerity: Economic Policy under Mitterrand* (Oxford, Berg Publishers, 1990), 246–301, and Peter A. Hall, 'The State and the Market', in Peter A. Hall, Jack Hayward, and Howard Machin (eds.), *Developments in French Politics* (London, Macmillan, 1990), 171–87.

[57] Michel Delattre, 'L'Evolution de la structure et du poids de la fiscalité de 1983 à 1987', *Revue Française des Finances Publiques*, 22 (1988), 17–34; Antoine Cortière, 'Augmenter l' impôt sur le revenu: des mesures de portée inégale', *Économie et Statistique*, 158 (1983), 21–35.

[58] Bruno Théret, 'Neo-liberalisme, inégalités sociales et politiques fiscales de droite et de gauche dans la France des années 1980', *Revue Française de Science Politique*, 41/3 (1991), 343.

social equality emerged as the central concern of social democracy during the 1980s.

In Greece, the PASOK's economic policy initially had much in common with that of Mauroy's first government in France. When Papandreou won the 1981 elections, the economy was stagnating (it grew by only 1% in 1981), profits had fallen sharply, and inflation had reached 20%. As in France, the new government opted for a programme of Keynesian expansion, attempting to stimulate production by raising the lowest wages and pensions and providing incentives for investment. Although demand increased, production failed to follow suit. As a result, imports and the trade deficit spiralled, whilst the economy continued to stagnate (the annual rate of GDP growth was just 0.4% in 1982 and 1983). Inflation did not fall, unlike in the European Community, where it halved over the same period (and stood at 5.1% in 1985). The Greek economy became less competitive and unemployment more than doubled, rising from 4.3 to 9% between 1981 and 1983. Higher public spending was financed through budget deficits and foreign debt. Changes in the fiscal system were limited, and tax revenues as a percentage of the GDP were nine points below the European Community average. Tax evasion remained high, particularly among small landowners, shopkeepers, and members of the professions. To give just two examples: the average declared income of lawyers and doctors was lower than that of wage earners; and whilst landowners accounted for 27% of the population, they contributed just 0.1% of revenue from direct taxation.[59]

Papandreou, however, did not modify his policies, since he sought to avert the electoral costs of a political U-turn and economic adjustment. Only after the PASOK was re-elected in 1985 with 46% of the vote did he take steps to re-establish market confidence, reduce inflation, and increase the competitiveness of the Greek economy. The government devalued the currency, ended wage indexation, reduced labour costs, promoted exports, and tried to attract foreign investment. This change of strategy led to widespread social resistance and a major increase in labour disputes, above all in the public services and state-controlled companies; the number of hours lost through strike action rose from 3.5 million in 1981 to 16.3 million in 1987.[60] But the economy improved, as inflation fell to 13.9% in 1988, and the public sector borrowing

[59] Stathis N. Kalyvas, 'Parties, State, Society: Greek Politics Today' (unpublished manuscript, University of Chicago, 1991).

[60] Michalis Spourdalakis, 'The Greek Experience', in Ralph Miliband *et al.* (eds.), *Social Democracy and After: The Socialist Register, 1985–86* (London, Merlin Press, 1986), 252; Kalyvas, 'Parties, State, Society', 26.

requirement (PSBR) was cut by two points. However, the economic reforms were more limited and short-lived than those carried out by the Fabius and Rocard governments in France. After gaining some breathing space, in 1987 Papandreou reverted to his original economic policy. Once again the result was a deterioration of economic conditions, as inflation and the public deficit rose sharply, the latter to a large extent due to the deficit of the public pension scheme which reached 9.3% of the GDP in 1990 (compared to 2.5% ten years earlier). In this period, Greece became poorer in relative terms, as her per capita income, measured in purchasing power parities, shrunk as a proportion of the European Community average.[61] Rather than catching up with the rest of Western Europe, the Greek economy lost ground. Fifteen years after the return of democracy, many of the reforms necessary for economic competitiveness were still pending in Greece.

The Spanish socialists adopted a very different economic strategy. Their main priorities were to catch up with the European Community and consolidate the new democracy. Moreover, in ideological terms they were much closer than the French PS or the PASOK to social democracy. Thus, even before they came to power they had a more pragmatic conception of economic policy. On many occasions González declared that, although he considered 'economic efficiency' to be merely instrumental, it was nevertheless a precondition for 'social efficiency'.[62] Unlike in France and Greece, there was no period of Keynesian expansion in a single country later followed by another of austerity. Rather, the government introduced a programme of economic adjustment lasting three years, from 1982 to 1985, which combined supply- and demand-side policies. This macroeconomic adjustment and the structural reforms implemented by the PSOE were examined in Chapter 3. As a result of these policies, inflation and the budget deficit fell to half their 1982 level, and there was also a sharp improvement in investment. The volume of fixed capital formation doubled between 1985 and 1990, foreign investment rose five-fold, whilst the share of investment corresponding to EC countries doubled during the same period.[63] The GDP grew at an average rate of 4.5% between 1985 and 1990, higher than in the EC as a whole (3.1% in the same

---

[61] Bénédicte Larre and Raymond Torres, 'Is Convergence a Spontaneous Process? The Experience of Spain, Portugal and Greece', *OECD Economic Studies*, 16 (1991).

[62] See e.g. González's declarations in Pedro Calvo Hernando, *Todos me dicen Felipe* (Barcelona, Plaza y Janés, 1987), 132 and 213.

[63] Larre and Torres, 'Is Convergence a Spontaneous Process', 186–92.

period). In the light of these changes in the Spanish economy
during the 1980s, it was sometimes argued that the 'political transition' of the 1970s had been followed by an 'economic transition'
during the 1980s,[64] when the economy became much more competitive and open.[65]

As I noted in the previous chapter, the principal problem was
the very high unemployment rate, which rose from 16.2% in 1982,
to 21.9% in 1985. Larger youth cohorts, the growing incorporation
of women into the labour market, and the return of migrant workers from other European countries increasingly highlighted the
Spanish economy's inability to generate sufficient work for its citizens.[66] However, besides an increase of 600,000 people in the
active population, some two million jobs were lost in the decade
1975–85. Although the 'underground economy' and family support
undoubtedly helped to alleviate the impact of unemployment,[67] the
burden of the economic crisis and adjustment fell largely on the
shoulders of the young, the long-term unemployed, and, to a lesser
extent, women. Those in employment, in contrast, suffered much
less, as the income per earner grew in real terms.[68] Thus, labour-
market dualism intensified.[69] The government considered that it

[64] Guillermo de la Dehesa, 'Los limites de la política económica española',
Leviatán, 32 (1988), 27–37.

[65] At the end of the decade, however, the economy was still less open than in
most West European countries. Thus, combined total imports and exports amounted
to just 35% of the GDP, compared to the EC average of 55%.

[66] The number of young people (between 20 and 24 years old) increased from
1,897,000 in 1985 to 2,224,700 in 1989; the number of women in the labour
market rose from 4,100,500 to 5,098,400 over the same period; the balance of
migrant workers leaving and returning to the country was 270,000 between 1976
and 1981. See Ministerio de Trabajo y Seguridad Social, *El Empleo en España: un
cuatrienio de expansión (1985–1989)* (Madrid, Ministerio de Trabajo y Seguridad
Social, 1989), 21.

[67] 'Irregular contracts' have been estimated to account for 21.9% of 'real' employment. As for the support provided by families, 73% of the unemployed lived
in households with a wage earner: Ministerio de Economía and Hacienda, *Encuesta
sobre condiciones de vida y trabajo* (Madrid, Ministerio de Economía y Hacienda,
1985), 22–34 and 89–95. See also, Alvaro Espina, *Empleo, democracia y relaciones
industriales en España* (Madrid, Ministerio de Trabajo y Seguridad Social, 1990),
188–234.

[68] Over the whole period of adjustment (the three years between 1983 and
1985), the real income per wage earner rose 1.8%. During the subsequent period
of expansion (the next seven years, 1986–92), it grew 5.5%. Commission des
Communautés Européennes, *Économie Européenne*, 54 (1993), Table 29, p. 224.

[69] Gösta Esping-Andersen has argued that in Southern Europe unemployment
was aggravated by the configuration of welfare policies, which had been based on
jobs rather than citizenship or need. This reinforced the male breadwinner-

had very little margin to redistribute the available work through reductions in working hours or the retirement age, and that only a major increase in production, together with vocational training, could make any significant impact on unemployment.[70] Some econometric studies have shown, moreover, that a reduction of less than 15% in the working day (and the equivalent drop in wages) would have no effect on the distribution of employment because it would be compensated for by increased productivity. Stable growth, therefore, was the main goal of economic policies, in order both to catch up with Europe and to reduce unemployment.

It is true that when the economy began to expand again in 1985 large numbers of new jobs were created (1,485,800 between 1985 and 1990), and unemployment fell by 5.4 points. Yet Spain still had the highest unemployment rate in Europe. Growth could provide only part of the solution, since even after five years of expansion some 16% of the active population remained unemployed. According to some pessimistic estimates, in countries such as Spain and France, the unemployment rate would remain constant if the GDP grew 2.5% per year, and it would fall by 0.25% for every additional point of growth. In this case, a growth rate of 4.5% over a decade would only produce a six-point drop in unemployment. Structural unemployment (that is, unemployment independent of economic fluctuations) had indeed risen significantly since the mid-1970s.[71] Other measures, involving the flexibilization of the labour market and wage restraint, would have led to tension with the unions. On the other hand, the socialists were not prepared to redefine their social policies in terms of need rather than rights,

---

female caring model, made the family dependent on the male earner's income and entitlements, and contributed to labour-market rigidities. The bias of social expenditure towards cash transfers and passive income maintenance led to unfavourable population dependency ratios, heavy fixed labour costs, higher unemployment and severe insider–outsider problems in the labour market. See Gösta Esping-Andersen, 'Welfare States without Work: The Impasse of Labour Shedding and Familialism in Continental European Social Policy', *Working Paper no. 1995/ 71* (Madrid: Center for Advanced Studies in the Social Sciences, Instituto Juan March de Estudios e Investigaciones, 1995). Also 'After the Golden Age: The Future of the Welfare State in the New Global Order', *Occasional Paper no. 7* (Geneva: United Nations Research Institute for Social Development, 1994), 16–18.

[70] Working hours had already been cut significantly since 1977 (–1.7% annually), and new reductions would have required a redistribution of the aggregate income among wage-earners and the unemployed. At the same time, the budget for pensions rose by 5.2 points of the GDP between 1975 and 1989.

[71] It has been estimated that in the European Community it rose from 4% to 10% between 1974 and 1992.

a change which would also have provoked the resistance of the middle classes who already believed that they were paying more in taxes than they obtained in provision.

The Southern European social democrats faced a difficult dilemma. On the one hand, they could opt for comparatively low unemployment, but at the cost of low quality, precarious and poorly paid jobs, and cuts in the scope of social policies. On the other hand, they could choose comparatively high unemployment, but relatively secure jobs, albeit hard to get by those who had never worked or had been made redundant, with broad social policies to provide for those in need, but inefficient labour markets. To put it more crudely, more employment and more poverty, or less employment and less poverty. Whilst many countries faced this dilemma, it was particularly acute in the new democracies. In an increasingly integrated Europe, their economies still suffered from a lack of competitiveness, inflation, trade and public deficits, and technological backwardness. The industrial sector found it harder to compete than the services sector, and also bore the brunt of unemployment. Moreover, at the same time as these countries were experiencing de-industrialization, foreign capital was acquiring a much more prominent role in their economies.[72] The sudden onset of the crisis of the early 1990s hit these economies hard, provoking a sharp rise in unemployment and reinforcing the view that competitiveness, employment, and welfare policies were inextricably linked.

After a long period of economic vicissitudes, Spanish society was very sceptical about the evolution of the economy and economic policies. This can be seen from the figures given in Table 4.8. At the end of the 1980s, when Spain was still immersed in a phase of strong expansion, 35% of the population thought that the economy was in a worse state than five years earlier; only 31% considered that it had improved. Criticisms of the government's economic policies largely reflected a widespread belief that economic conditions could be modified by policies, and that difficulties

---

[72] In 1991 foreign capital had shares in 22,000 Spanish companies. Whilst these enterprises only represented some 20% of the total number, they accounted for 50% of production and 43% of employment Of these enterprises, some 10,000 were at least 50% foreign-owned. This process led to a growing debate on how a more open economy could best be combined with a stronger national industrial sector. A good example of this literature is the study by Oscar Fanjul, '¿Es necesaria la existencia de empresas industriales españolas?' (unpublished manuscript, Madrid, 1991). See the discussion of the role of Spanish industry in the European economy in the *Negocios* supplement of *El País*, 6 June 1991, pp. 3–6.

were the government's responsibility. Nevertheless, for some time economic policies benefited from the overall political support for the government. At the end of the decade, preferences for the PSOE's handling of the economy doubled those for the PP, and were ten times higher than those for the communist-led coalition Izquierda Unida (IU).[73] When this changed in the mid-1990s, this was the result of political, rather than economic circumstances. We will return to these questions in the following chapter.

In Portugal and Italy competitiveness and growth were also the main priorities of the PS and PSI. After an initial period of social-ist radicalism after the collapse of the dictatorship, the minority PS government which came to power in 1976 presented Parlia-ment with a very pragmatic modernization programme and attempted to win the IMF's backing for its planned economic adjustment. However, these reforms proved impossible due to the government's lack of solid parliamentary support. The attempt to strengthen this through the formation of a coalition with the CDS only lasted until the summer of 1978. Thus, the instability of Portuguese politics during the first decade of democracy made it difficult to maintain coherent economic policies. These had to wait until 1983, when the PS–PSD coalition led by Soares had suffi-cient parliamentary backing to launch an adjustment programme that brought down inflation and the budget deficit. The political benefits of these policies, however, were reaped by the PSD, which won the 1985 elections and went on to win a further two consecu-tive parliamentary majorities in 1987 and 1991. Cavaco Silva implemented a programme of austerity and liberalization which brought rapid economic growth from 1986 onwards that eventu-ally came to end with the onset of the European crisis of the 1990s. In Italy the Craxi government in power between 1983 and 1987 also tried to stimulate economic competitiveness and reduce the public deficit and inflation. It ended wage indexation after winning a referendum on the issue in 1985, tightened control of public expenditure, raised the age of retirement, and privatized a number of publicly owned companies.[74] Inflation fell from 15% in 1983 to 4.8% in 1987, the public sector borrowing requirement (PSBR) was cut significantly, the balance of trade redressed, and after three years of economic stagnation, the annual rate of GDP growth rose above the EC average.

---

[73] Centro de Investigaciones Sociológicas, polls of 12–16 Feb. 1988 and 20–5 April 1988.

[74] Spencer M. Di Scala, *Renewing Italian Socialism: Nenni to Craxi* (Oxford, Oxford University Press, 1988), 205–27.

Table 4.2 gives further information on the economic records of the Southern European socialist governments, and compares them with those of the non-socialist governments and the European Community as a whole. It covers fifteen periods of government in five countries, seven of which were social democratic. However, the comparison must be treated with caution. Two of the seven cases were in fact coalitions: in Portugal, Soares headed a coalition made up of the PS and PSD; in Italy, only six ministers belonged to the PSI, and the Budget and Finance ministries were in the hands of the DC and the Partito Repubblicano Italiano (PRI). Equally, the causal relationship between governments and economic performance is far from clear. Not only do the consequences of decisions taken by previous governments persist for some time, but new policies do not immediately take effect. Moreover, domestic and international economic cycles also have a decisive influence on performance, independently of the policies adopted; economic performance in the period 1974–85 was generally much worse than in 1985–90 in terms of growth, employment, and inflation. However, the variations in the performance within each period may be due to differences in economic policies. Furthermore, since the table not only gives the results of the socialist and conservative governments, but also those of the European Community as a whole for the same period, it is possible to control for the effects of the economic cycle.

The table reveals the growing discipline of economic management during the 1970s and 1980s. If we look at inflation, it can be seen that this improved over time in the fifteen governmental periods and the five countries. There were only three exceptions: Greece under the PASOK (1981–9), and Portugal under the Alianza Democrática (1978–83) and Bloco Central (1983–5) coalition governments. As for public expenditure, in France, Italy, and Spain (the three countries which provided information for every period), this grew faster down to the early 1980s than during the rest of the decade. If we compare the two periods 1974–81 and 1982–90 in the European Community as a whole, public expenditure decreased in the second period, inflation dropped, and there was a reduction in real unitary labour costs. Greater economic discipline eventually led to higher rates of growth: these doubled between the first and second period. As a result, the rate of job creation also rose. Table 4.2 shows that the economic policy paradigm consisting of greater fiscal control, lower public deficits, more open trade, increased exports, and the deregulation of the economies exercised growing influence on the Southern European governments during the 1980s.

TABLE 4.2. *Comparative economic performance of social democratic governments*

	1	2	3[a]	4[a]	5[a]	6[a]	7[a]
France							
Non-socialist							
1974–81	2.3	2.4	11.1 (12.0)	3.2 (2.3)	0.9 (0.0)	0.1 (0.1)	9.7 (3.3)
1986–8	2.1	−2.0	3.8 (4.7)	0.1 (1.0)	−1.4 (−0.6)	0.4 (1.2)	−0.9 (−1.3)
Socialist							
1981–6	1.7	−2.1	8.6 (7.5)	0.6 (0.8)	−1.5 (−1.0)	−0.3 (−0.1)	2.9 (0.2)
1988–90	3.3	−0.1	3.4 (5.4)	1.6 (1.2)	0.3 (−0.1)	1.2 (1.6)	0.9 (0.2)
Greece							
Non-socialist							
1974–81	2.7	4.5	15.7 (12.0)	5.0 (2.3)	2.1 (0.0)	1.5 (0.1)	—
Socialist							
1981–9	1.8	−3.8	18.0 (6.4)	1.3 (0.9)	−0.1 (−0.8)	0.5 (0.5)	10.4 (−1.5)
Italy							
Non-socialist							
1974–83	2.2	1.6	17.2 (11.8)	2.0 (2.1)	0.4 (−0.2)	0.7 (−0.2)	15.7 (8.9)
1987–90	3.5	0.8	5.7 (4.3)	2.3 (1.3)	−0.2 (−0.7)	1.0 (1.4)	0.4 (−2.2)
Socialist							
1983–7 (Socialist PM)	3.0	2.0	7.9 (5.1)	1.2 (0.8)	−1.2 (−1.0)	0.6 (0.7)	2.1 (−0.8)

	1	2	3	4	5	6	7
Portugal							
Non-socialist							
1978–83	2.9	2.8	20.9 (13.3)	1.9 (1.5)	−1.6 (−0.3)	−0.1 (−0.2)	—
1985–90	4.4	3.3	13.9 (5.1)	2.0 (1.1)	−0.8 (−0.6)	0.1 (1.3)	−1.3 (−1.7)
Socialist							
1976–8	6.2	1.5	16.2 (12.9)	0.4 (2.1)	−8.1 (−0.6)	−0.3 (0.1)	—
1983–5 (coalition)	0.7	−2.4	22.3 (7.1)	−1.4 (0.6)	−2.2 (−0.8)	−0.5 (−0.3)	−2.6 (0.4)
Spain							
Non-socialist							
1976–82	1.3	−7.7	16.8 (11.4)	2.8 (1.8)	−0.8 (−0.4)	−1.8 (0.0)	11.8 (5.0)
Socialist							
1982–90	3.6	3.6	8.6 (5.8)	0.2 (1.0)	−1.5 (−0.6)	1.4 (0.8)	3.9 (−1.3)
TOTAL[b]							
Non-socialist	2.6	1.0	14.1 (10.4)	2.7 (1.8)	0.1 (−0.3)	0.2 (0.3)	6.3 (1.8)
Socialist	2.8	−0.2	11.9 (6.6)	0.7 (1.0)	−1.4 (−0.7)	0.5 (0.5)	4.3 (−0.7)

Source: Figures calculated by the author from data provided by Commission des Communautés Européennes, *Économie Européenne*, 46 (1990), Tables 2, 9, 10, 23, 29, 33, and 35.

Notes:

1: Annual rate of GDP growth in real terms.

2: Variations in the differentials between national GDPs per capita (at purchasing power parities) and the EC average over the period (positive numbers: the differential is reduced).

3: Average rate of inflation.

4: Annual variations in real wages per earner (average for the period).

5: Annual variations in real unitary labour costs (average for the period).

6: Annual rate of variation in employment.

7: Evolution of public expenditure as a % of GDP.

[a] Figures in brackets are EC averages.

[b] The totals have been calculated by taking into account the years included in each of the different periods.

If we compare the different governments, the social democrats had a better record on growth, inflation, and employment. They were also more successful in lowering unitary labour costs, restraining real wages, and controlling public expenditure. However, if we compare these governments with the performance of the European Community as a whole, a rather different picture emerges. The inflation differential was slightly worse under social democratic than conservative governments. Real wages went up comparatively less under the socialists, and labour costs fell more than in the EC as a whole. Although public expenditure expanded more under non-socialist governments, it always rose faster than in the European Community. Whilst the GDP grew more rapidly under the social democrats, they generally failed to reduce the gap with the average GDP per capita in the European Community. Finally, the socialists could claim a better record on employment, as they achieved a higher rate of job creation than the conservative governments.

Generally speaking, the evolution of unitary labour costs suggests that the socialists tried hard to improve the competitiveness of their economies. They attached more importance to wage moderation than the non-socialist governments and also introduced tighter budget controls. Socialist policies, therefore, were neither populist nor monetarist.[75] However, a number of factors should be borne in mind when considering these comparisons. On the one hand, the limited number of cases considered means that a given political experience may have a disproportionate effect on the aggregate results. This is the case of the Rocard and González governments' record on job creation, and the PASOK's and UCD's performance in terms of various economic indicators. Moreover, a profound crisis may conceal the positive effects of economic policies for some time. This is clearly the case of the Soares government, as well as that of Cavaco Silva's first period in office.

The effect of the governments' ideology on the economic performance of the five Southern European countries from 1974 to 1993 is further explored in the analyses of Table 4.3. The results show that during this 20-year period the social democrats tended to control prices and wages more effectively than conservative governments, they generally raised more revenue through taxation,

---

[75] On the one hand, since social democratic governments did not opt for raising public expenditure and fiscal indiscipline, they cannot be described as 'populist'. On the other, neither did they follow monetarist policies: they tried to moderate wages in order to control inflation, at the same time as they increased the resources of the state.

TABLE 1.1. The effects of government ideology on economic performance in Southern Europe
(annual data for the period 1974–93)

	Inflation (1974–93) (1)	Increase in real wages[a] (1974–93) (2)	Job creation (1974–93) (3)	Fiscal revenue/GDP[b] (1974–93) (4)	GDP/EC[c] (1984–93) (5)
Constant	15.089*	2.778*	-.839*	35.107*	64.475*
	(1.104)	(.554)	(.273)	(1.178)	(7.972)
Strength of social democracy[d]	-.587*	-.259**	.099**	.583**	3.358**
	(.282)	(.141)	(.055)	(.301)	(1.757)
GDP growth[e]	—	—	.039*	—	—
			(.59)		
R^2	.43	.034	.229	.038	.071
Signif. F	.040	.069	.000	.055	.062
No. of observations	98	98	98	98	50

Source: Calculated by the author from the data in Commission des Communautés Européennes, *Économie Européenne*, 54 (1993), Tables 2, 9, 10, 24, 29, and 54; pp. 197, 204, 205, 219, 224, and 247.

Standard errors in parenthesis.

* Statistically significant at 5% or less.

** Statistically significant at 10% or less.

Notes:

[a] The increase of real wages is per earner for the whole economy, year by year for the two decades 1974–93.

[b] Fiscal revenue refers to the current revenues of all levels of the public administration, in annual figures for 1974–93.

[c] The dependent variable consists of the annual GDP per capita in constant prices and at purchasing power parities as a ratio of the European Community average.

[d] The independent variable has values from 0 to 6 (0: majority conservative government; 1: minority conservative government; 2: coalition government without social democrats; 3: social democrats in coalition but without prime minister; 4: social democrats in coalition with prime minister; 5: minority social democratic government; 6: majority social democratic government). In columns 1 to 4, the values are annual for 1974–93. In column 5, the values refer only to the governments in the decade 1984–93.

[e] GDP growth refers to the annual figures in constant terms for the period 1974–93, except in column 5 (which refers to the decade 1984–1993).

and they had a positive, albeit limited, impact on the rate of job creation. Data on the growth of the GDP per capita refer to the second decade, from 1984 to 1993, when Greece, Spain, and Portugal joined the European Community: the rates under the social democrats in the five countries outstripped the EC average. For every one point increase in the strength of social democracy inflation fell by .59 and wages by .26, whilst the rate of job creation, fiscal revenue, and the relative GDP per capita increased by .10, .58, and 3.36 respectively. However, the model explains only a very small fraction of the variation. The main exception is the case of job creation, where the governments' ideology and economic growth together explain 22.9% of the variation. And if we control for growth, social democracy still seems to have created more jobs.

The economic performance of the social democratic governments varied significantly. From a comparative perspective, the first period of PS rule in France produced poor results in terms of growth, inflation, labour costs, and employment. The same was true of the PASOK governments. They brought little economic growth, lost ground with respect to the EC, and allowed real wages and public expenditure to rise sharply. The opposite experience was that of Spain under González between 1985 and 1990, and Rocard in France between 1988 and 1990. Under the Rocard government, the French economy expanded fast, inflation remained low, and real wages went up. Under González, Spain experienced rapid growth during this period, the economic differential with the EC was reduced, inflation fell, the rate of job creation was high, and although real wages increased in a more moderate fashion, they did not lose purchasing power.[76] The economic policies of these two governments serve as a contrast to those of Papandreou and Mauroy, in terms of inflation, as well as growth and job creation. Similar differences existed between the non-socialist governments. Thus, Cavaco Silva achieved better results in Portugal than the UCD in Spain. Although 'objective conditions' and institutional constraints

[76] Juan Martínez-Alier and Jordi Roca are mistaken when they affirm otherwise in their article, 'Spain After Franco: From Corporatist Ideology to Corporatist Reality', *International Journal of Political Economy*, 17/1 (1987), 56–87. See n. 68 of this chapter which gives data for the periods 1983–5 and 1986–92. The real income per earner rose by 1.2% between 1983 and 1987, and by 6.9% between 1983 and 1992. Whilst employment decreased between 1983 and 1985 by −4.2% (compared to 0.1% in the European Community), between 1986 and 1992 it grew 15.9%, compared to the European Community average of 7.4%. See the monthly data compiled by the Instituto Nacional de Empleo (Ministerio de Trabajo y Seguridad Social), and the Censuses of the Active Population produced by the Instituto Nacional de Estadística.

were a crucial factor, the policy options of the politicians also had a major impact on economic performance. As Joan Nelson has argued, the variations in the economic performance of the different countries during the 1980s were to a large extent due to leadership, to 'skilful political strategy and tactics combined with leaders' courage and vision.'[77] In Southern Europe, the differences in economic policies between and within the different ideological camps were also influenced by these 'subjective factors'.

The 1980s saw a profound revaluation of social democratic economic policies. This was not confined to Southern Europe; the governments of Bob Hawke in Australia, David Lange in New Zealand, Franz Vranitzky in Austria, Ingvar Carlsson in Sweden, further illustrate the way policies were adapted to the new demands of economic competitiveness. Almost everywhere, social democracy evolved in a similar direction. Over the decade, the economic strategies of the different parties tended to converge. The new social democratic blueprint included a sound macroeconomic framework, in terms of inflation, fiscal revenue and expenditure, the exchange rate, and foreign trade, together with supply-side policies, consisting above all of public investment in fixed capital and training,[78] in order to increase the competitiveness of the economy. Moreover, not only social democratic, but all governments were affected by the new economic constraints. Thus, the conservatives also had to readjust their policies and learn from their failures, as in the case of the Union pour la Démocratie Française–Rassemblement du Peuple pour la République (UDF–RPR) coalition in France, Nea Demokratia in Greece, and the UCD in Spain. What is more, these constraints affected all economic regimes, and not just capitalism; the collapse of communism showed to devastating effect that they were not merely derived from 'the logic of capital'.[79]

---

[77] See Joan M. Nelson (ed.), *Economic Crisis and Policy Choice* (Princeton, NJ, Princeton University Press, 1990), 13.

[78] See Boix, 'Partisan Strategies and Supply-Side Policies in Advanced Nations: 1960–1990', Ph.D. thesis (Harvard University, 1994), parts 1 and 2.

[79] It should be noted that the 'cognitive map' of the PCI, and later the Partito Democratico della Sinistra (PDS) was very similar to the prevalent social democratic one. In the resolutions of its 1988 Congress in Rome, the PCI declared that 'the market is a means of assuring the efficiency. . . . of the economic system. The demands of equity impose policies that redistribute resources and power, but that do not eliminate the bases of accumulation.' The PDS's 1994 electoral programme argued that 'in the existing historical circumstances, there is no alternative to the market economy . . . In current conditions it is not possible to defend the classic formula of promoting employment through aggregate demand and consumption'.

The Southern European social democrats learned, often from negative experiences, that ever-greater international interdependence meant that all governments and economies faced strict requirements in relation to investment, production costs, and competitiveness. In these circumstances, the governments had to find ways to produce more and better, and not just to redistribute. Their intellectual visions and policies had to adapt to these conditions, to the need for economic discipline in hard times. They did so through different processes and with different results, as they were often heavily influenced by rhetorical inertias, populist ideas, or short-term electoral interests, and constrained by different objective economic conditions and institutional arrangements. The redefinition of economic policies was frequently inspired by strategic considerations, the belief that in the prevailing economic conditions they would find it hard to win majority support for populist redistributive policies, that these majorities would always prove volatile, and that they would end in defeat. However, the main reason for such a redefinition was the intellectual conviction that it was no longer possible to achieve social democratic goals through redistributive Keynesianism, and that economic efficiency was essential for the viability of egalitarian social policies. Close contact with European social democracy facilitated this process in all five Southern European countries; the experiences of the French PS in the early 1980s, and of the PASOK during the entire decade prove that the process could be painful or protracted. However, the fact that three out of the five regimes were new democracies does not appear to have had a decisive impact on their economic policy preferences.

4.5. The Crisis of Social Democratic Neo-corporatism

During the 1980s social democratic governments in Southern Europe and elsewhere found it increasingly difficult to pursue neo-corporatist policies and reach comprehensive agreements with the unions. Neo-corporatism had been a strategic model which incorporated organized interests (and more particularly, the unions) into the political process, giving them a role in the design and execution of economic policies.[80] In this model, the government

[80] See the classic works by Philippe C. Schmitter, 'Still the Century of Corporatism?' in Philippe C. Schmitter and Gerhard Lehmbruch (eds.), *Trends toward Corporatist Intermediation* (London, Sage, 1979), 7–49, and his 'Reflections on where

relinquished autonomy in return for reciprocity: that is, through the co-operation of these social agents, governments also secured that of large parts of society. In order for this strategy to work, therefore, these interlocutors had to represent a large area of the social interests in a society, to be encompassing organizations (to use Olson's term), as well as centralized and representative in character. For such organizations the incentive for negotiating government policies was that in return for their co-operation they gained compensations which generated a net benefit for the social groups which they represented. The empirical correlates of neo-corporatism were low strike rates, the absence of government-imposed incomes policies, and strong economic growth.[81]

Neo-corporatism was originally a strategy adopted by some European democratic governments in the context of the economic conditions of the Second World War and post-war reconstruction. It was closely connected with the electoral strength of social demo-cracy, with states with centralized administrative structures and considerable political legitimacy, and also with small and interna-tionally vulnerable countries.[82] It was a formula which did not seek to substitute the democratic mechanisms of territorial repre-sentation, nor circumscribe electoral competition or the constitu-tional rules. This is what distinguished it from earlier conceptions of corporatism associated with Catholic social doctrine or adopted by the fascist regimes. Nevertheless, there has been considerable debate over the extent to which neo-corporatism challenges essen-tial features of democracy: since interest groups do not present

the Theory of Corporatism has gone and where the Praxis of Neo-Corporatism may be going', in Gerhard Lehmbruch and Philippe C. Schmitter (eds.), *Patterns of Corporatist Policy-Making* (London, Sage, 1982), 259–79. Wilensky has defined neo-corporatism as 'the capacity of strongly organized centralized economic inter-est groups interacting under government auspices within a quasi-public frame-work to produce peak bargains involving social policy, fiscal and monetary policy, and incomes policies—the major interrelated issues of modern political economy', in Harold L. Wilensky, 'Leftism, Catholicism, and Democratic Corporatism: The Role of Political Parties in Recent Welfare State Developments', in Flora and Heidenheimer (eds.), *Development of Welfare States in Europe and America*, 345.

[81] Manfred Schmidt, 'The Welfare State and the Economy in Periods of Eco-nomic Crisis. A Comparative Study of 23 OECD Nations', *European Journal of Political Research*, 11 (1983); see also the refs. given in n. 23.

[82] The classic study of neo-corporatism in small countries is by Peter Katzenstein, *Small States in World Markets* (Ithaca, NY, Cornell University Press, 1988). See in particular ch. 3, which studies the similarities and variations betwen the 'lib-eral corporatism' of Switzerland, Holland, and Belgium, and the 'social corporat-ism' of Austria, Norway, and Denmark, with Sweden combining elements of both models.

candidates for election and are not responsible to parliaments, corporatist agreements may elude the majority principle, and decisions may affect the protection of minorities or prejudice those citizens who are not represented by the interest organizations.[83] Doubt has also been cast on the economic consequences of neo-corporatism, in so far as concertation and agreements interfere with the efficient functioning of markets, limit competition, and encourage the postponement of decisions which, although necessary, prove unacceptable to organized interests.[84]

Neo-corporatist strategies have been defended on the grounds of both political and economic efficiency. On the one hand, democracy as a procedure for determining the distribution of public goods may be ungovernable if distributive conflicts are resolved in accordance with the majority principle. Negotiation based on pluralist representation does not necessarily result in decisions that run counter to democratic mechanisms.[85] On the other hand, concertation may facilitate more beneficial trade-offs between wages, investment, employment, and social policies. Trade unions and employers might both benefit from negotiating lower wages than the unions would unilaterally choose, and higher employment than companies would decide if those wage rates were established. At the same time, government participation in agreements makes it more likely that these will be honoured.[86] Given that

[83] To the extent that neo-corporatism addresses special interests, it might undermine the principle of 'one man, one vote'; similarly, agreements might limit the sovereignty of the legislative power. Schmitter has argued that neo-corporatism leads to a political system in which 'votes are counted, but interests are weighed', and 'rulers may become more accountable under such arrangements, but to the wrong collectivities. . . . Governments may also be more responsive, but to the wrong needs': see Philippe C. Schmitter, 'Democratic Theory and Neo-Corporatist Practice', *Working Paper 74* (Florence, European University Institute, 1983), 55–6.

[84] For an example of this critique in the Spanish case, see Victor Pérez-Díaz, *The Return of Civil Society: The Emergence of Democratic Spain* (Cambridge, Mass., Harvard University Press, 1993), chs. 5 and 6.

[85] See the discussion of this problem in Manfred E. Streit, 'The Mirage of Neo-Corporatism', *Kyklos*, 41 (1988), 603–24.

[86] The participation of governments would also prevent employers from breaking their side of the agreement (employment), once the unions had agreed to wage moderation. For the economic behaviour of the actors, see Ian M. McDonald and Robert Solow, 'Wage Bargaining and Unemployment', *American Economic Review*, 71 (1981), 896–908; Carl Shapiro and Joseph E. Stiglitz, 'Equilibrium Unemployment as a Worker Disciplining Device', *American Economic Review*, 74 (1984), 433–44; Robert M. Solow, 'Unemployment: Getting the Question Right', in Charles R. Bean, Richard Layard, and Stephen J. Nickell (eds.), *The Rise in Unemployment* (Oxford, Oxford University Press, 1987), 23–34; Olivier Blanchard and Lawrence H. Summers, 'Fiscal Increasing Wage, Real Wages, and Unemployment', *European Economic Review*, 31 (1987).

high wage rises would reduce investment, unions may accept a transaction between present consumption and investment promising employment and future consumption, above all if it is possible to redistribute consumption and increase the 'social wage'. The incentives for the unions derive from their belief that, in comparison with the transitional costs involved and the risk that pacts might not be fulfilled, agreement would produce better medium-term results and generate public goods for the workers.[87] Certain institutional, political, and economic conditions would facilitate neo-corporatist strategies; the institutional factors include strong and undivided labour movements, as well as centralized collective bargaining arrangements; left-wing governments which could guarantee the fulfilment of agreements and compensate for their costs would also favour neo-corporatism; and this, finally, would also be more viable when growth proved difficult and the economic future seemed bleak.

However, in all the OECD countries it became harder to achieve comprehensive socio-economic agreements during the 1980s. Governments increasingly tended towards 'decisionism' and 'mandatism' rather than neo-corporatist strategies which were often considered slow and inefficient in economic terms. Doubt was also cast on the political benefits of neo-corporatism, above all in the light of the British Labour governments' experience between 1974 and 1979. At the same time, the unions gradually became convinced that the costs of neo-corporatist agreements were greater than their benefits. If economic problems were structural in nature, there was little to be gained by controlling wages and consumption. If unemployment was going to remain high, and the provision of public goods was universal, there were fewer incentives for the unions to make agreements. Governments' role as 'compensators'[88] might remain important for citizens, but it became less significant for the unions. Thus, the traditional co-operation between social democracy and the unions was increasingly questioned.

Despite these problems, the social democratic governments in Southern Europe attempted to negotiate industrial restructuring,

[87] This argument has been extensively developed in terms of rational choice in Adam Przeworski and Michael Wallerstein, 'Structural Dependence of the State on Capital', *American Political Science Review*, 82 (1988), 11–29. Peter Lange has examined neo-corporatist agreements in terms of an individually rational strategy in a Prisoner's Dilemma game repeatedly played over time, in Peter Lange, 'Unions, Workers, and Wage Regulation: The Rational Bases of Consent', in John H. Goldthorpe (ed.), *Order and Conflict in Contemporary Capitalism* (Oxford, Oxford University Press), 98–123.

[88] The term has been borrowed from Lange, 'Unions, Workers, and Wage Regulation', 109.

the distribution of wages and profits, and social policies with the unions, whilst insisting that the final decision on economic policies rested with the government alone. However, it was not easy to strike a balance between the theory of the mandate and that of democratic consent. The unions often had only a small membership, they did not always defend general interests, and their demands were often essentially corporatist rather than egalitarian in character. Yet given their considerable symbolic influence, conflict with the unions isolated governments, encouraged criticism of social policies, and contributed to the erosion of the governments' electoral support. The crisis of the traditional relations between social democracy and the unions posed two strategic dilemmas for governments: whether major reforms were viable (that is, if the resistance to them could be overcome) without the support of the unions; and whether, in contrast, reforms could be efficient (that is, if they could accomplish their objectives) if they were negotiated.

In Southern Europe, the labour movement was also both internally divided and numerically weak.[89] In Portugal the union space in the new democracy was divided between the pro-social democratic União Geral de Trabalhadores (UGT) and the pro-communist Confederaçao Geral de Trabalhadores Portugueses (CGTP). In Greece the Panellinio Agonistiko Syndikalistiko Kinima Ellados (PASKE) faced growing organizational pluralism after 1985. In Spain the UGT and CCOO had maintained a union duopoly since the beginning of the transition to democracy, winning ever larger and relatively equal shares of the vote in union elections.[90] The pattern of union affiliation changed in all three countries over the course of the 1980s. In Spain there was a sharp decline, from 30%

[89] For the structure of the labour movement, see *Trade Unions of the World 1989–1990* (London, Longman, 1990); see also, Rossetos Fakiolas, 'Interest Groups: An Overview', in Kevin Featherstone and Dimitris K. Katsoudas (eds.), *Political Change in Greece: Before and After the Colonels* (London, Croom Helm, 1987), 174–88; Uwe Optenhogel and Alan Stoleroff, 'The Logic of Politically Competing Trade Union Confederations in Portugal: 1974–1984', in Eduardo de Sousa Ferreira and Walter C. Opello (eds.), *Conflictos e Mudanças en Portugal, 1974–84* (Lisbon, CEDEP-Teorema, 1985), 179–92; Fishman, *Working Class Organisation and the Transition to Democracy in Spain*, chs. 4 and 5.

[90] The first trade union elections were held in 1978 and won by the CCOO (with 34.5% of the vote compared to the UGT's 21.7%). The results were more even in 1980 (30.9% for the CCOO as against 29.3% for the UGT). From 1982 onwards the balance shifted in favour of the UGT, which won 36.7% of the vote that year, 40.9% in 1986, and 44.4% in 1990, whilst CCOO won 33.4%, 34.5%, and 36.4% on those three occasions. The figures clearly reveal the growing duopoly of union representation.

of the active population in 1977, to 25% in 1980, 16% in 1986, and 13% in 1989. Although this was the general tendency in the OECD, the average rate in these countries was double that in Spain, and whilst Greece and Portugal had comparable levels to those in the rest of Europe, only France had such a low affiliation rate.[91] However the unions did not only derive their strength from their memberships, but also from the votes they attracted in union elections and their capacity for mobilization. In these respects, the Southern European labour movements enjoyed considerable support.

The social democratic governments of Southern Europe reformed labour legislation in order to strengthen the unions. In Greece Act 1264/82 regulated their rights and internal organization; in France the 1984 Auroux Laws reinforced workers' and unions' rights in the workplace; and in Spain the 1985 Law of Trade Union Freedom favoured the larger unions, as did the new French legislation. The Spanish unions also obtained considerable resources from the public budget, were compensated for the expropriations carried out by the Francoist regime, and were given the property of the former state unions. The governments of Fabius and Rocard in France, and González in Spain, sought to secure agreements whereby the unions would accept wage moderation and the flexibilization of what were comparatively rigid labour markets in return for organizational support and social policies. The socialists believed that this strategy would make it possible to raise the competitiveness of the economy and create jobs, at the same time as promoting stronger unions and social welfare. The unions, however, refused to accept this formula, in the belief that a commitment of this type would limit their freedom of action and that the cost of economic discipline was too great. Relations between the socialists and the unions worsened in France with the change in economic policy in 1984 and the exclusion of Communist ministers from the new

[91] See the data in OECD, *Perspectivas del Empleo* (Paris, OECD, 1991), 218–25; in the OECD countries, the average affiliation rate fell from 35% in 1975 to 28% in 1988. The only exceptions to this tendency were Sweden, Finland, and Iceland. Whilst the European Community gave different figures, they painted a similar picture, with affiliation rates of 11% in Spain, between 12% and 16% in France, around 35% in Portugal and Greece, and more than 40% in Italy. The latter figure was similar to that found in the United Kingdom and the Federal Republic of Germany. In Belgium and Denmark over 75% of the active population were union members. The average for the European Community was 42%. See Comisión de las Comunidades Europeas, *Estudio comparado de la normativa reguladora de las condiciones de trabajo en los Estados miembros* (Brussels, Commission of the European Community, 1989), 3–7.

TABLE 4.4. *Labour conflict in Southern Europe*
(days lost per 1,000 workers)

	Spain	France	Greece	Italy	Portugal
1977–81	1,410	1,135	905	206	203
1982–6	610	705	548	112	148
1987–91	677	275	939	101	65

Source: Eurostat, *Statistiques Rapides*, 2 (1993).

Fabius government. In Spain the consolidation of democracy and the onset of economic recovery in 1985 convinced the UGT that it was no longer necessary for the unions to co-operate with the government.

Thus, although neo-corporatist pacts were possible under the UCD government and in a period of economic crisis, they proved much more difficult under the PSOE government and in a period of economic growth. The socialists only managed to negotiate one comprehensive pact, the Economic and Social Agreement in force in 1985 and 1986. Spain, therefore, was characterized by a complex and changing pattern of labour relations. This ranged from extensive mobilizations at the start of the transition (in 1976 and 1977); the Moncloa Pacts, which expressed political support for a programme of economic reforms (in Autumn 1977); the Inter-Union Framework Agreement between the UGT and the employers (in 1979); the National Agreement on Employment, signed by the government, employers, the UGT, and the CCOO (in 1981); the Economic and Social Agreement between the government, the UGT, and the employers (in 1985); and the absence of comprehensive agreements after 1987. With the collapse of the neo-corporatist model, the socialist governments in Spain, Greece, and France faced considerable labour unrest. As can be seen in Table 4.4, conflict intensified in both Spain and Greece during the second half of the decade.

In Greece the number of hours lost through strike action almost doubled during the PASOK's first twelve months in office, rising from 3.5 million to 6.5 million. As a result, the government passed Act 1365/1983 regulating strikes in the public sector. There was a further wave of protest during the period of economic austerity between 1985 and 1987; in 1987, 16.3 million days were lost through strikes and the socialist-controlled union organization, the PASKE, split in two. Labour conflict was also a feature of socialist rule in

France, where the 1.5 million working days lost through strike action in 1981 rose to 2.3 million the following year. Conflict intensified in response to the economic discipline introduced by Fabius, and again in autumn 1988 under Rocard, when the nurses, postal workers, the tax service, the Peugeot workers, and public employees declared a succession of strikes. Concertation failed time and time again, and the unions accused the government of 'Jacobinism', of attempting to impose austerity measures unilaterally, of 'enlightened despotism'. In Spain, in turn, the number of days lost through strikes rose from 2.8 million in 1982, to 4.4 million in 1983, and 6.3 million in 1984, and in December 1988 the unions successfully called a one-day general strike.[92]

Conflict with the unions and the failure of socio-economic concertation posed special problems for the Spanish social democrats due to their particular relationship with the UGT. Unlike its French or Greek counterparts, the UGT had responded to the classic model of a 'fraternal' party and union. Founded by the PSOE in 1888, it had always constituted the other half of the socialist movement; both organizations shared a common history and to a large extent dual affiliation. The PSOE had also benefited from the union vote in the general elections, Thus, although union membership was comparatively low, the union's loss of confidence in the government had serious political consequences. On the one hand, it weakened the credibility of the socialists' policies. On the other, it weakened the reformist thrust of the PSOE by raising doubts as to the explicit support available for this. Generally speaking, public opinion tended to sympathize with the unions: at the time of the split between the socialists and the unions, three out of four Spaniards believed that socio-economic agreements were necessary or desirable, and a majority thought that the government was primarily to blame for their failure.[93]

The reality, however, was rather more complex. It is true that

---

[92] The strike data have been compiled from the *Boletín de Estadísticas Laborales* published by the Ministerio de Trabajo y Seguridad Social (Madrid, Mar. 1989); George Ross, 'From One Left to Another: *Le Social* in Mitterrand's France', in Ross, Hoffman, and Malzacher, *The Mitterrand Experiment*, Table 11.3 and pp. 199–216; Spourdalakis, 'The Greek Experience', 252; and Kalyvas, *Parties, State, Society*, 26.

[93] Polls carried out by the Centro de Investigaciones Sociológicas, 28 Oct.–2 Nov. 1987, and 13–15 Nov. 1988. Whilst 59% of Spaniards thought that the government should make a greater effort to reach agreement, only 17% considered that this was the responsibility of the unions and employers. Some 54% considered that the government should change its policies for the sake of good relations with the UGT.

the government operated within tight economic constraints, that its macroeconomic policy was very orthodox, and that unemployment rose dramatically. Yet conflict with the unions did not intensify during the periods of austerity (1982–6 and 1993–4) but during phases of expansion; wages did not lose purchasing power; there was, as I will argue below, a major expansion of social policies; and, as seen above, the unions had received considerable organizational support from governments. However, they considered that the development of political and economic conditions made concertation unnecessary. The instability of the transition was a thing of the past, democracy was consolidated, and the ties with the government could cost them support.[94] On the other hand, they believed that the economic growth underway from the end of 1985 permitted more radical redistributive policies, both in terms of wages and public expenditure. As the UGT General Secretary Nicolás Redondo declared during the 1986 general elections, 'the workers should now reap what they have sown'.

The union's strategy reflected a more fundamental idea, namely that the new economic conditions of capitalism left no room for the expression of alternative ideologies from governments; regardless of who was in power, things would hardly change, policies would scarcely differ. In consequence, the unions should act in accordance with a principle of 'political indifference'. Their strategy should not be determined by the colour of the government that happened to be in power, and there was no sense in sharing responsibility for the government's economic policy, establishing a list of priorities, or being drawn into discussion of what Felipe González called the 'accounts of the kingdom'.[95] When in a PSOE internal meeting González asked 'What is needed to satisfy the UGT?' Antón Saracíbar, the union's Secretary for Organization, immediately gave the following reply: 'All the unions want concertation, but above all with a government of the right. Under a socialist government, a union like the UGT has no pressing need to reach agreements.'[96] The growing strains in the relations between social democratic governments and unions were particularly evident in Spain. The incentives to make pacts shrunk, and for the unions,

[94] Thus, the UGT considered that its losses in the large companies in the 1986 union elections were mainly due to its links with the government.

[95] See Santos Juliá (ed.), *La desavenencia: partidos, sindicatos y huelga general* (Madrid, El País/Aguilar, 1990), and especially the chapter by Julio Segura, 'Concertación o conflicto', 282–91.

[96] The debate between González and Saracíbar took place during the meeting of the Federal Committee of the PSOE on 2 Oct. 1987.

the government's role as a 'compensator' appeared increasingly less attractive.

The socio-economic strategies of the Southern European social democrats did not, therefore, correspond to the neo-corporatist model. The unions were unwilling to accept that economic discipline was a prerequisite for competitiveness and employment, particularly when rapid growth resumed and profits began to rise. They demanded greater distribution of these profits; they refused to recognize that higher wages and public expenditure would lead to higher inflation, lower competitiveness, and more unemployment; they also attached more importance to wages and unemployment benefits than to the provision of collective goods such as health care and education. The strategy of the Southern European unions largely accorded with Olson's argument that when trade unions' market power is sufficient to raise wages, yet their representation is too limited to internalize the consequences, then it becomes more difficult to make pacts, the distribution of income between wages and profits is affected, and inequalities among wage earners grow.[97] Moreover, since the French and Spanish unions were strongest in the public sector, protest tended to be focused on the state rather than employers, workers' demands affecting the public budget more than profits. There was also a problem of power, one which the unions have often posed under social democratic governments, namely, as Humpty Dumpty said to Alice, 'the question is which is to be master'.

4.6. Patterns of Social Policies

The social democratic governments in Southern Europe initially generated particularly broad expectations in the field of social policies. These social demands were much stronger than in the rest of Europe, and had been a decisive factor in the electoral victories of the PS, the PASOK, and the PSOE.[98] The new social

---

[97] Mancur Olson, *The Rise and Decline of Nations* (New Haven, Conn., Yale University Press, 1982), 41–53, 146–75.

[98] For example, in the summer of 1982, just before the elections that brought the Socialists to power, between four and five times as many Spaniards preferred a PSOE to a conservative government to manage the social security system, the health service, pensions, education, or the redistribution of wealth. As can be seen in Table 4.10, at the end of the decade the socialists still had almost four times more support than the PP in these policy areas. In 1993 this enabled them to overcome the unfavourable conditions and win the general elections. In 1995 the

democratic governments found themselves in a difficult position. Whilst they considered that they had an exceptional opportunity to implement reforms, their ability to do so was severely constrained by the prevailing economic conditions. As a result, those governments that decided to introduce vast and rapid social reforms at the beginning of their mandates, were later often forced to modify or reverse them. This contradiction between demands and possibilities, and between ideology and reality, became a major political problem for these governments.

Social democrats in Southern Europe, as elsewhere, were therefore forced to strike a balance between economic efficiency and egalitarian social policies. This predicament was much harder to resolve in the 1980s than it had been for the majority of social democratic governments during the first three decades after the Second World War. Social democratic policies gradually came to consist of a particular mix of state and market, in which the former was assigned a more important role in social policies, and the latter in the economy. González frequently emphasized this particular vision of the role of the state and market:

We are not resigned to social dualism, injustice, or the blindness of the market, which we wish to correct through the finalist social policies that define democratic socialism. Nor do we accept, or are we resigned to a model that merely consists of the free market. We will use the market as an instrument to provide us with the necessary resources to implement, in a balanced way, policies with social and redistributive aims. . . . We socialists have the obligation to decide, at each moment, which is the best combination of economic efficiency and social fairness.[99]

Speaking in very similar terms, Mario Soares described the political profile of social democracy in the 1980s:

As a democratic socialist, I am in favour of the market economy and of freedom in all its forms . . . but also of the regulatory role of the state to redress inequalities between citizens and between regions. In the balance between the regulatory function of the state and the initiative of civil society lies the path to resolve inequality and ensure social justice. This

difference in percentage points between the negative and positive opinions of the government's policies among all voters was 56.4 in the case of social services, 53.8 in that of education, 47.9 in that of health, and 30.3 in that of pensions. In contrast, the balance was −45.2 in the case of the economy, −15.9 with respect to law and order, and −15.0 in relation to the judicial system: Centro de Investigaciones Sociológicas, poll 2,154 (Apr. 1995).

[99] Felipe González, 'El PSOE, un proyecto renovado en una nueva sociedad', in *Manifiesto del Programa 2.000* (Madrid, Editorial Sistema, 1991), 125.

TABLE 4.5. *Redistributive policies in Southern Europe*

	Spain	France	Greece	Italy	Portugal	EC
A. *Current expenditure on social welfare* (as % GDP)						
1970	10.0	19.2	7.6	17.4	9.1	—
1975	—	22.9	—	22.6	—	—
1980	18.1	25.4	12.2	19.4	14.7	24.4
1986	19.5	28.5	19.4	22.4	16.3	26.0
1991	21.4	28.7	20.7	24.4	19.4	26.0
B. *Level of fiscal pressure* (as % of GDP)						
1965	14.3	34.5	22.0	25.5	18.4	27.3
1975	19.4	36.9	25.5	26.2	24.7	33.4
1985	28.8	44.5	35.1	34.4	31.6	40.0
1990	34.4	43.7	36.5	39.1	34.6	40.7

Sources: Comisión de las Comunidades Europeas, *La protección social en Europa, 1993* (Brussels, Com (93) 531, 1994), p. 42; Alain Euzéby, 'La protection sociale en Europe: tendances et défis', *Futuribles*, 171 (1992), 71.

is what I call democratic socialism, and what in other countries has been called social democracy or labourism.[100]

This social democratic political profile consisted, therefore, of determined combinations of economic and social policies, wages and employment, taxation and social welfare, and the provision of social transfers and collective goods. Generally speaking, the Southern European social democrats increased social expenditure, introduced legal reforms that redefined the criteria of social policies, and raised fiscal revenues in order both to finance these policies and to reduce budget deficits.[101] Table 4.5 shows the development of social expenditure and fiscal revenue in Southern Europe during the 1980s. Social expenditure rose faster in Southern Europe than in the European Community as a whole. If we look at the three cases of single-party socialist governments in a little more detail, and only consider the years they were in power during the

[100] Mario Soares, interviewed in *El Sol*, 2 Sept. 1991, 20–1.

[101] Social democracy and other political options (notably Christian democracy), which also favoured rectifying the social outcomes of the market, differed in two aspects of their policy preferences. First, social democracy's view of the role of the state was opposed to 'the principle of subsidiarity' (a difference which was evident for example, in education policy). Secondly, it defended an egalitarian redistribution of resources not just confined to assistance in case of need (a difference that influenced fiscal policies).

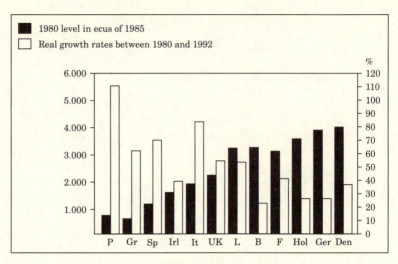

F IG. 4.1. *Social benefits per inhabitant, levels in 1980 and real growth rates*
1980–1992

Source: Eurostat, *Statistiques Rapides*, 5 (1994).

1980s (1981–9 for the PASOK, 1982–90 for the PSOE, 1981–6 and
1988–90 for the French PS) social expenditure increased in all
three cases, whilst it scarcely changed as a proportion of the
GDP in the European Community from the middle of the decade
onwards.

As a result, the differences in the proportion of resources spent
on social policies in Southern Europe and the European Community were reduced. However, they did not disappear altogether:
although social expenditure exceeded the European average in
France, in the three new democracies it remained below that level.
Nevertheless, Fig. 4.1 shows the rapid growth of social expenditure in Portugal, Greece, and Spain, whilst Fig. 4.2 highlights
the steady reduction of the gap with Europe in the Spanish case.
In 1980 public expenditure in Spain on pensions, unemployment,
health, education, and housing stood at only 65.7% of the figure
which, as a function of its income, would have been required to
match the average joint expenditure of Germany, France, Italy,
and the United Kingdom. By 1994 this proportion had risen to
87.6% of the level of these four countries.

The social democrats also raised taxes. If we examine the years
of PS rule in France, current fiscal revenues increased by 2.1
points of the GDP between 1981 and 1990. The PASOK, in turn,

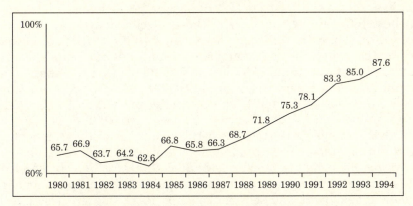

F IG. 4.2. *Spanish social expenditure as a percentage of the European level (Germany, France, Italy, United Kingdom), 1980–1994*

Source: Antoni Zabalza, 'El Estado de Bienestar: Un Pacto Social', *El País*, 8 Aug. 1994, p. 42.

raised them by 5.1 points between 1981 and 1989, and the PSOE by 9.4 points between 1982 and 1992. In all three cases taxation increased faster than in the European Community as a whole, where in these three periods, fiscal revenue only went up by an average of 0.4% (1981–90), 0.7% (1981–9), and 0.7% (1982–92). Direct taxation was also increased, from 8.6 to 9.4% of the GDP under the PS, and from 6.6 to 11.9% under the PSOE.[102] With this additional fiscal revenue the PSOE governments hoped to finance higher social expenditure and, at the same time, reduce the budget deficit; however, they were much more successful regarding the first of these two goals.[103] These changes in taxation had a redistributive impact. In Spain 52% of all income tax revenue was paid by the richest 10% of income-earners, and 20% by the top 1%.[104]

[102] Calculations based on Commission des Communautés Européennes, *Économie Européenne*, 46 (1990), and 54 (1993), Table 54. See also, Ministerio de Economía y Hacienda, *Actuación económica y financiera de las administraciones públicas* (Madrid, Ministerio de Economía y Hacienda, 1988), 47–8.

[103] Under the PSOE government, public expenditure in Spain rose by 9.3 points of the GDP between 1982 and 1992, about the same increase as that of fiscal revenue. Public expenditure grew by 2.9 points under the first PS government in France (1981–6) and by 0.9 points under the second (1988–90); this increase was slightly higher than that of fiscal revenue. Public expenditure rose by 10.4 points under the PASOK (1981–9), that is, 5.3 points of the GDP more than the fiscal revenue.

[104] José Borrell, 'Balance general de la política presupuestaria durante el período 1982–88' (unpublished paper presented at the Universidad Internacional Menéndez Pelayo, Aug. 1988).

In France the top 1% paid 27% of income tax revenue, whilst the richest 10% paid 64% in 1986.[105] These developments may usefully be contrasted with Thatcher's fiscal policy in the United Kingdom. Here the proportion of total fiscal revenue derived from direct taxation dropped from 37.9% in 1975 to 26.6% in 1990; the maximum income tax rate was reduced to 40% (when in Spain it was 56%); the income tax bill of those earning more than £50,000 fell as a proportion of their income from 64% in 1978–9 to 35% in 1992–3.[106] However, despite the fiscal reforms carried out in Southern Europe, tax evasion remained an important political problem. In Italy, for example, it was estimated that 45% of Value Added Tax was lost through fraud, which was particularly common among small shopkeepers and self-employed professionals. In Greece the evasion of direct taxes was also prevalent among members of the professions and shopkeepers, as well as among small landowning farmers. In Spain two million previously undiscovered tax-payers began to pay income tax between 1982 and 1987.

During the first phase of the PS government in France, the minimum wage and pensions were raised at a cost of 2 points of the GDP. The age of retirement was lowered, the working week shortened, and statutory paid holidays extended to a fifth week. The Auroux Laws strengthened workers' and unions' rights in the workplace. The PS's educational reforms, however, ended in failure: a new universities act, which had met considerable opposition in the Senate, was barely put into practice; and in 1984 the Savary Act, modifying the relationship between public and private education, was withdrawn in the face of massive resistance from the Catholic church and private schools' associations. The change of course of the PS's economic policy in 1983–4 had a major impact on social policies. Unemployment benefits and the health budget were cut, reforms tended to become more carefully targeted, and social expenditure grew more slowly. Perhaps the most important new social policy initiatives were the creation of a guaranteed minimum income (RMI) and the expansion of active labour-market policies, particularly for young people.[107] In this final phase of the PS government, therefore, social policies were primarily

---

[105] Delattre, 'L'Évolution de la structure et du poids de la fiscalité', 17–34.

[106] Boix, *Partisan Strategies and Supply-Side Policies in Advanced Nations*, ch. 8.

[107] Public expenditure on these policies accounted for 3.1% of the GDP in 1988 (26.4% of which was devoted to active policies). This percentage was higher than the European Community average (2.8%), but lower than in Denmark, Ireland, Belgium, the Netherlands, and Spain: see OECD, *Perspectivas del Empleo*, 222.

directed towards groups with special needs and towards promoting employment.[108]

In Greece the PASOK government implemented reforms in health care, education, and pensions. With the enactment of Act 1397/83, the socialists established a national health system which decentralized services, introduced participatory mechanisms, extended primary care, and restricted the private practice of doctors employed in the public system. This was accompanied by a sharp increase in public expenditure on health care. However, these reforms suffered from a number of shortcomings. In particular, the multiple insurance schemes were not integrated into a unified system of social security, and the incompatibility of private and public practice led many doctors to abandon the national health system. Educational reforms were concentrated on further and higher education. The university system was expanded (the number of students doubling between 1981 and 1986) and reorganized to give the departments more power and permit greater participation in their management. In practice, however, the effects of the reforms were limited by the lack of resources, the shortage of qualified teaching staff, poor research facilities, and the often inefficient administration. Papandreou's most important social reform probably consisted of the extension of the state pension scheme. The number of beneficiaries grew at an annual rate of 5.4% during the 1980s. However, the cost also rose rapidly, and the social security deficit, which had already increased from 1% of the GDP in 1970 to 2.5% in 1980, reached 9.3% in 1990.

Under the PSOE, public expenditure on pensions, health, and education rose in total by 4.1 points of the GDP between 1982 and 1992.[109] The education budget grew most, with an increase of 1.9 points of the GDP, followed by pensions, 1.3 points, and health, 0.9

---

[108] When assessing the effect that the policies of Mauroy, Fabius, and Rocard had on social inequality, opinion polls were more favourable to the latter. Some 44% of respondents considered Rocard's record on equality was positive, compared to 31% in the case of Fabius and 30% in that of Mauroy; see SOFRES, *L'État de l'opinion 1991* (Paris, Seuil, 1991), 114.

[109] When calculating public expenditure in Spain, it must be remembered that a major decentralization of resources took place during the 1980s. As a result of this process, the proportion of public expenditure administered by the regional governments increased from 2.9% in 1981 to 23.5% in 1991. Social expenditure was particularly affected, as the regional governments managed the entire budget of the guaranteed minimum income, 56.7% of the education budget, and 55.7% of the health care budget. The data in the text have been taken from the unpublished report of the Ministerio de Economía y Hacienda, *1982–1992: El trabajo de una década*.

points. At the same time, the number of beneficiaries of the public health service and pensions increased by 6.7 million and 1.6 million respectively. The number of university students expanded by 500,857, and the enrolment rate in secondary education among 16- and 17-year-olds rose by 18% of the age-group. As I noted in the previous chapter, the number of beneficiaries of social policies had begun to rise sharply from the very beginning of the transition to democracy. If we take pensions, the health service, and education jointly, an additional 14 million people were covered by these services between 1975 and 1992. However, if we compare the seven years of conservative rule (1975–82), with the first seven years of socialist governments (1982–9), the difference between the two periods becomes apparent. As can be seen in Table 4.6, whilst public expenditure on unemployment benefits, health, education, and pensions rose 39.7% in real terms in the first period, during the second it went up 57.6%. Public expenditure on each of these policies grew more during the seven years of social democratic government. This remains the case even when we control for the different rates of economic growth in the two periods: 10.7% in cumulative terms under the UCD governments; 27.7% under PSOE. The greatest difference was in education, followed, in order of importance, by pensions, health, and unemployment benefits.

New legislation also altered the model of social policies. Thus, a law on non-contributory pensions was introduced in 1991 to complement the existing public scheme. Established for those below a minimum level of income, these pensions were not linked to the recipients' past contributions but were financed directly by the public budget.[110] A law passed in 1986 reorganized the national health service, which was now mostly to be financed from general taxes.[111] Between 1982 and 1992 education reforms raised the school

---

[110] An act passed in 1985 also re-organized the pension system, introducing stricter conditions for contributory pensions, but extending them to new social groups. Over the next three years, the total number of pensioners rose by 442,096, whilst the budget was increased 53.2%. The 1991 act on non-contributory pensions extended the basic protection given to low-income groups who had not paid social security contributions. The number of these pensions went up from 27,753 in 1991 to 335,817 in 1995.

[111] At the beginning of democracy, in 1976, public health was basically financed by social security contributions which amounted to 83.9% of the health budget. In 1982, after several years of conservative governments, contributions still financed 81.1% of public expenditure on health. After the passing of the General Law on Health, contributory financing fell to 22.0% in 1989 and to 20.4% in 1994. See José Barea (ed.), *Análisis Económico de los Gastos Publicos en Sanidad y Previsión de los Recursos Necesarios a Medio Plazo* (Madrid: Instituto de Estudios Fiscales,

TABLE 4.6. *Social policies under conservative and social democratic governments in Spain*[a]

	1975–82	1982–9
1. Cumulative GDP growth in real terms	10.2	27.4
2. Evolution of expenditure on health, education, pensions, and unemployment (increase in real terms over the period)	39.7	57.6
3. Evolution of public expenditure on pensions (increase in real terms over the period)	29.3	55.5
4. Increase in the number of beneficiaries of public pensions (in millions)	1.4	1.2
5. Evolution of public expenditure on education (increase in real terms)	66.4	94.0
6. Increase in rate of enrolment in secondary education[b]	16.6	30.5
7. Evolution of public expenditure on health (increase in real terms)	8.3	30.6
8. Increase in the number of beneficiaries of the public health service (in millions)	3.7	6.3

Sources: Ministerio de Economía y Hacienda, *Gasto Público en España* (Madrid, Ministerio de Economía y Hacienda, 1989); unpublished reports of the Spanish Ministeries of Health, Education and Science, and Labour and Social Security (Madrid, 1990).

[a] The calculation of budget increases in real terms has been obtained by dividing the national and regional budgets by 3.003 and 4.892 in the respective periods in order to take into account the value of the peseta in 1975.

[b] The increases refer to the enrolment rates for the academic years 1975–6, 1982–3, and 1989–90. They include both secondary school pupils and those receiving professional training, and have been calculated for the 14–17 age-group.

leaving age by two years, increased the enrolment rate in post-compulsory education, multiplied the number of grants by 2.3 times, reorganized the relationship between private and public schools, and gave the universities an autonomy which they had previously been denied.

1992), Table 8, 469. Also Pilar Coll, 'Los Gastos Sanitarios Públicos y la Demanda de Salud en España', *Cuadernos de Actualidad* (Madrid: Instituto de Estudios Fiscales, 1991), Table 6, 247. The data on education were the following: in 1982 the enrolment rate for the age-group 16–17 was 52.0%; in 1992 it had gone up to 70.0%. In 1982 the number of students receiving grants was 313,824; ten years later it reached 706,770. See Ministerio de Economía y Haciende, *1982–1992: El Trabajo de una Década*.

Considerable differences existed, therefore, between social democratic and conservative governments in terms of both the quantitative expansion of social policies, and the criteria of provision. The social democratic governments tended to emphasize compensatory programmes. Thus, the first PS government in France raised the lowest pensions and the SMIG, later established the guaranteed minimum income (RMI), and increased the public education budget faster than subsidies for private schools. In the same way, under the PASOK new resources were also mainly spent on raising the lowest pensions and incomes. In Spain the budget for non-contributory pensions grew two-and-a-half times more than the overall pensions budget, and the lowest retirement pension was raised to the level of the minimum wage.[112] Moreover, whilst the education budget grew 25 percentage points more than the subsidies for private schools, expenditure on grants for post-compulsory education increased three-and-a-half times faster than the overall education budget. Whilst a fundamental characteristic of these governments' social policies was their quantitative expansion, above all for low-income groups,[113] less attention was paid to the qualitative improvement of programmes.[114] Poor services, the persistent shortage of resources, the limited number of qualified professionals, administrative inefficiency, and the strong corporatism of public sector employees did little to improve the efficiency and quality of welfare policies.

How did these social policies affect the structure of inequality? Their redistributive impact not only depended on the resources allocated to them and the number of citizens they covered, but also on the extent to which they benefited the lowest income groups. Considerable differences existed in the evolution of income inequalities in Spain, France, the United States, and the UK during the

---

[112] In 1982 the lowest pension amounted to only 75.7% of the minimum wage. In the decade between 1986 and 1995, the lowest retirement pension (for those with a dependent spouse) rose 13.04 percentage points more than the average.

[113] Once again, the case of Great Britain under Thatcher provides a useful comparison. The Conservative government's social policies led to cuts in means-tested benefits for the poor, child benefits, health expenditure, and personal social services; at the same time, resources were transferred from public pensions to earnings-related supplements: see Peter Taylor-Gooby, 'Current Developments in the Sociology of Welfare', *British Journal of Sociology*, 40/4 (1989), 637–56.

[114] Thus, the Secretary of State for Finance, José Borrell, declared that 'in the search for equality ... perhaps the priority should not be to improve the average quality by restricting the number of beneficiaries, but to increase the number of the latter even at the cost of reducing the average quality': José Borrell, 'Igualdad, libertad y hacienda pública', *Leviatán*, 32 (1988), 59.

1980s. As can be seen in Table 4.7, under Reagan and Thatcher, income distribution became more rather than less concentrated. In the United States the proportion of the total income in the hands of the poorest 10% of the population fell by 8.7% between 1979 and 1986, whilst the richest 10% increased their share by 6.4%. In the UK, the bottom 10% became 10.7% poorer in relative terms, whilst the top 10% became 9.5% richer over the same period. And between 1977 and 1990, the top income quintile increased its share of total post-tax income to 45%, whilst that of the bottom two quintiles was reduced from 23.4 to 16.3%.[115] In France, in contrast, there was a slight redistribution of income away from the richest decile. In the Spanish case, the redistribution of income was more marked. Between 1980 and 1990 the proportion of the total income corresponding to the poorest decile of the population rose by 17.9%, whilst that of the richest decile fell by 5.4%. The ideology of the different governments, therefore, does appear to have affected inequality. And in the Spanish case, the fact that it was a new democracy did not result in less redistributive policies.

Redistribution under these governments resulted from a combination of fiscal and social policies. If we consider the Spanish experience again, between 1982 and 1992 the proportion of total fiscal revenue paid by the poorest 25% of the population dropped from 4 to 0.3%, whilst the share paid by the 55% of middle-range incomes fell from 36.1 to 12.6%. In contrast, the contribution of the richest 20% rose from 59.9 to 87.1%. As for public expenditure, its impact on households was in inverse proportion to their level of income. Whilst in 1980 this 'indirect wage' had represented 119.1% of the monetary consumption of the poorest decile of households, by 1990 this figure had risen to 204.3%. The increase was much less significant in the case of the richest decile of households, for whom it rose from 31 to 36.6%.[116] In accordance with the compensatory criteria mentioned above, those programmes with the greatest redistributive impact developed most over the decade.[117]

[115] Boix, *Partisan Strategies and Supply-Side Policies in Advanced Nations*, ch. 8.

[116] Juan Antonio Gimeno, 'Incidencia del gasto público por niveles de renta (España 1990 vs. 1980)', in Fundación Argentaria, *Sector público y redistribución: I Symposium sobre igualdad y distribución de la renta y la riqueza*, vii (Madrid, Fundación Argentaria, 1993), 105 and 107.

[117] The most redistributive programmes were social benefits, unemployment benefits, education grants, publicly subsidized housing, social services, and health. Between 1980 and 1990 the proportion of total social expenditure devoted to these programmes increased from 26.5% to 29.8%: see Eduardo Bandrés, 'La eficacia redistributiva de los gastos sociales: una aplicación al caso español (1980–1990)', in Fundación Argentaria, *Sector público y redistribución*, vii, 124–69.

TABLE 4.7. *The evolution of income inequalities during the 1980s*

	Spain			France			United Kingdom			United States		
	1980	1990	% change	1979	1984	% change	1979	1986	% change	1979	1986	% change
Bottom decile	2.7	3.2	+17.9	3.2	3.2	0.0	3.9	3.5	−10.7	2.1	1.9	−8.7
Top decile	26.4	24.7	−5.4	24.5	24.1	−1.6	21.5	23.5	+9.5	23.2	24.7	+6.4

Source: Luis Ayala, Rosa Martínez, and Jesús Ruiz-Huerta, 'La distribución de la renta en España en los años ochenta: una perspectiva comparada', in Fundación Argentaria, *La distribución de la renta: I Symposio sobre Igualdad y Distribución de la Renta y la Riqueza*, ii (Madrid, Fundación Argentaria, 1993), 109–11.

These redistributive policies in Southern Europe accorded, in terms of both outputs and outcomes, with the social democratic model.[118]

The Southern European experience appears to confirm that economic conditions severely restricted the governments' room for manœuvre and led to the growing convergence of macroeconomic policies. The governments managed their economies on a knife-edge. As soon as they relaxed their fiscal policies or permitted excessive wage rises, the result was falling competitiveness, trade deficits, currency crises, and unemployment. However, this experience also shows that these constraints did not eliminate the differences in social policies derived from ideology. Thus, if we take the Spanish case between 1983 and 1993, the shrinking gap between the level of social expenditure in Spain and that in the European Community was scarcely affected by the annual rate of GDP growth. Over this eleven-year period, the coefficient of correlation between both variables was a mere $r = .041$. Even when the rate of GDP growth slackened off after 1990, the socialists still managed to reduce the gap in social expenditure with respect to the average of Germany, France, Italy, and the United Kingdom, which was cut by 11.7 points during the following three years. In

---

[118] As a result of economic growth, the greater role of the market in the economy, and the labour-market deregulation, the primary distribution of income became steadily more unequal in Spain during the second half of the 1980s. However, this was corrected through taxation and public expenditure, with the result that the secondary distribution of income became more egalitarian with time. Besides the references given in nn. 116 and 117, see Julio Alcaide, 'La redistribución de la renta', in García Delgado (ed.), *España: Economía*, ii, 639–67; Luis Ayala, 'Social Needs, Inequality and the Welfare State in Spain: Trends and Prospects', *Journal of European Social Policy*, 4/3 (1994), 159–79; Eduardo Bandrés, 'Análisis y evaluación del contenido redistributivo de las pensiones públicas en España' (unpublished manuscript, University of Zaragoza, 1995); Juan Antonio Gimeno, 'Incidencia del gasto público por niveles de renta: propuesta metodológica y aplicación a España en 1990' (unpublished manuscript, Universidad Nacional de Educación a Distancia, 1995); Javier Ruiz Castillo and Coral del Río, 'Intermediate Inequality and Welfare: The Case of Spain from 1980–81 to 1990–91' (unpublished manuscript, Universidad Carlos III, Madrid, 1995). Ayala, Martínez, and Ruiz-Huerta, 'La distribución de la renta en España desde una perspectiva internacional', 28–31, 52–5. This last study compares the evolution of disposable monetary incomes in eight OECD countries during the 1980s. Of these countries, the clearest trends towards greater inequality were found in Sweden, the United Kingdom, and the United States; the opposite tendency was seen in Spain. Here, Gini indices of 0.330 in 1980 and 0.305 in 1990, calculated from the *Encuestas de Presupuestos Familiares*, expressed the redistribution of the disposable monetary income by person and household over the decade. The Luxembourg Income Study (LIS) database provides a rich source of information for cross-national and longitudinal comparisons of income inequalities.

difficult economic circumstances the social democrats refused to cut the social policies that were so central to their identity. Thus, fiscal and wage discipline could give rise to very different redistributive outcomes according to the governments' ideological preferences. Nevertheless, a major question these tighter constraints posed with regard to equality was how to obtain the greatest possible effects from the limited resources available, by controlling costs and evaluating the impact of the different programmes. And in this respect, the distinctive social democratic identity becomes more evident the more we break down the aggregate figures on taxation and expenditure.

Perhaps the main problem with regard to inequality was unemployment. This was above all the case in Spain. Here, a paradoxical situation existed whereby, at the same time as income distribution became more equitable under both democracy and social democratic governments, unemployment rose dramatically over a twenty-year period. The key to this paradox lies in the role of family support and the compensatory effect of social policies. If we take the unemployed population between 1977 and 1994, in two-thirds of cases other family members contributed at least one wage to the household budget. In most other cases, one member of the family received a pension or unemployment benefit. Thus, whilst during the first decade of democracy 25% of the unemployed lived in households with no income earner, by 1994 this figure had fallen to under 10%. As a result, the mean per capita income of the household with an unemployed member was the equivalent of almost two-thirds of that of the population as a whole.[119]

However, although this policy of extending the 'social wage' reduced hardship and inequality, it did not reduce unemployment. In an attempt to reconcile equality and employment, the socialists invested heavily in human-capital formation. If we look at public expenditure both on general education and on active manpower policies, the former rose by 1.9 points of the GDP between 1982 and 1992, and the latter from 0.25 to 1.03% of the GDP between 1983 and 1991. However, these policies needed time to take effect: although the skill flows increased, the initial stocks were very low in the active population as a whole. In addition, these policies were no compensation for high interest rates, excessive wage rises, and very rigid labour markets. For this reason the socialists also introduced more flexible employment contracts; yet whilst this

[119] Luis Toharia, 'Unemployment in Spain: How can it be so High?' unpublished manuscript (Universidad de Alcalá de Henares, 1995).

increased the rate of job creation, it also led to a major increase in temporary contracts and low quality work.[120] Hence, the labour market became highly fragmented, with secure work and rising real wages existing alongside mass unemployment, large numbers of irregular contracts in the underground economy, and insecure jobs. The combination of the 'social wage', skills, and employment constituted one of the crucial dilemmas for social democratic policies.

These policies faced a number of additional problems. One was whether, regardless of the fact that they were more redistributive than conservative policies, they were sufficient to reduce inequality significantly. And, if not, what alternative policy package would be both economically and politically viable. Another problem concerned the social and electoral support available for these policies. This not only involved relations with the unions, but also the 'social democratic coalitions' which could be built around redefined programmes and policies. The social democrats did not find it easy to create new support coalitions, as their particular combination of macroeconomic, fiscal, and social policies created tensions in the middle classes and among sections of the working class.

The social democratic governments in Southern Europe faced considerable opposition to their policies. This was motivated by a number of different factors. Conflict with the unions was mainly centred around wage policies, industrial restructuring, and labour-market reform. The communist parties backed the unions on these issues, and also opposed the social democratic governments on foreign policy issues. The PCP and the KKE were hostile to European Community membership, whilst in the 1986 referendum the PCE led the campaign to take Spain out of NATO. Conservative opposition was mainly directed against fiscal and educational reform. Resistance to government policies tended to originate outside parliamentary politics, in the sense that the political parties often reacted to conflicts which had already materialized. The communist and conservative parties attempted to provide political expression for the demands or protests of the unions, the press, the Church, or corporatist groups. However, politics rather than policies did most political damage to the social democratic governments.

---

[120] A government report found that apprenticeship and part-time contracts accounted for 20.1% of new jobs in 1994: see *El empleo en 1994* (Madrid, Ministerio de Trabajo y Seguridad Social, 1994), 8. According to a report by the European Community, in 1992 temporary jobs accounted for 34.0% of all employment in Spain, compared to 15.8% in 1987: see European Commission, *European Economy: The Economic and Financial Situation in Spain*, 7 (1994), 40.

Here I am referring to their growing isolation from key social groups, the hostility of important media, the dwindling appeal of their party organizations, corruption scandals, and bitter internal disputes. I will consider some of these questions in more detail in Chapter 5.

The breadth of their mandate was a major influence on the governments' policies and strategies. The social democrats usually defended their policies in terms of the 'general interest' as opposed to particularist interests, appealed to society in general rather than just one class, and very rarely mobilized their supporters. Electoral results and opinion polls were more important than agents of intermediation in shaping government strategies. The political scenario of socialist policies was, therefore, largely unstructured; no clear correspondence existed between social groups and the parties other than the distribution of the vote. Nevertheless differences did exist between the various socialist governments. The PASOK was particularly attentive to short-term electoral considerations; the PSOE relied heavily on its electoral support when introducing conflictive reforms, and defended the 'socialist project' in terms of the general interest and a vision of its mandate infused with a sense of a mission.

The strategies of all the governments were affected in the same way by the passage of time, which weakened their initial confidence and feeling of 'authorization'. As a result, reforms tended to become more timid, and the parties modified their strategies to minimize opposition and took more account of electoral interests.[121] In France the conflict over the educational reforms envisaged in the Savary Laws marked a turning-point for the PS in terms of both its policies and strategy. In the case of the PSOE, during its first years in office the government relied heavily on its parliamentary support and 'social authorization' to implement its programme of economic adjustment, educational laws, abortion reform, or the referendum on NATO. The most notable exception in this respect was industrial restructuring, as pressure from the UGT and concern about the likely social costs led the government to modify its initial proposals. However, after their second electoral victory in 1986, the socialists gradually changed their strategy and proved more reluctant to force through policy initiatives in

---

[121] In an interview in *El País*, 14 June 1992, the Spanish Deputy Prime Minister, Narcís Serra, affirmed that 'after ten years in power, we should consider the need to revise our policy; it is necessary to dialogue, negotiate, reach agreement, to give up trying to impose policies'.

the face of serious opposition. Between 1988 and 1993 they backed down over a youth employment scheme, a revision of the property tax, and a new strike law, and substantially altered their plan for the restructuring of the Asturian mining industry. With the passage of time, the level of support and tolerance in society had diminished, and appeals to the general interest to win support and overcome opposition ran up against growing scepticism. However, even though time weakened the initial force of their mandates and strengthened the influence of partisan electoral interests, 'subjective factors' could occasionally interrupt this process. In Spain, for example, the minority PSOE government formed after the party's fourth consecutive electoral victory in 1993 introduced more initiatives than had been seen in the previous few years: the government enacted labour reforms which had previously been postponed, reformed housing legislation, and adopted greater budget discipline. It was encouraged to act by a series of economic, parliamentary, and political problems, even though politics (corruption scandals and the party's internal divisions) continued to undermine these policy initiatives.

Generally speaking, socialist voters and party members looked more favourably on the governments' social policies than their handling of the economy. At the end of the 1980s support for the government's educational policies among PSOE voters was 19 percentage points higher than that for its economic policies, despite several years of economic growth. By the mid-1990s, after a short but severe recession, the difference had grown to 48 percentage points. It was the mix of social and economic policies which made the latter acceptable to both the party and its electorate; this explains why González was frequently forced to reiterate the idea that the economic reforms were 'instrumental' for social policies. As for PS voters in France, twice as many defined the Mitterrand government in terms of social justice than economic efficiency.[122] In society as a whole, the social democratic governments' social policies provoked contradictory reactions of criticism and support. The victories of the PS, the PASOK, and the PSOE were accompanied by heightened expectations of social reform; despite the substantial increase in resources for social policies and the number of beneficiaries of these, many of these expectations

---

[122] The data for Spain comes from polls carried out by the Centro de Investigaciones Sociológicas, studies no. 1,730 (Feb. 1988); and no. 2,154 (Apr. 1995). For France, see the poll of 5–9 Mar. 1987 in SOFRES, *L'État de l'Opinion. Clés pour 1988* (Paris, Seuil, 1988), 162.

were to be disappointed. Yet at the same time, social policies remained a decisive cause of the socialist parties' electoral support.
To go back to the Spanish case, demands for social equality remained very widespread throughout the period of socialist rule,
even though a large part of the population considered that inequalities had been reduced. Thus, dissatisfaction with social policies was compatible with the belief that they had improved during
this period. Table 4.8 shows the distribution of the total electorate's opinions of different policies and inequality. In France the
most frequent criticism of the PS government was that it had done
too little to reduce inequality. This was the principal reproach of
42% of the population.[123] Yet, at the same time, when people were
asked to choose the issues that best characterized the socialists'
record in government in a positive sense, 'more social justice' came
out on top. Table 4.9 shows the different responses to this question.

Over time, however, major internal transformations took place
within the ranks of the broad coalition that had initially supported
the social democratic option. The socialist parties lost much of the
wide support which they had once enjoyed among the urban middle classes and young people. In part, this was the consequence of
economic factors, notably the concentration of social benefits among
the lower income groups and in economically backward rural
areas, and the major increase in fiscal pressure. This provoked growing discontent among tax-payers, who considered that they were
paying more than they received from the public coffers. In part,
this decline was due to political factors. From the end of the 1980s,
the socialists tried to stop their electoral decline in the cities and
among these social groups with new policy packages involving
urban infrastructure, housing, employment, and youth training
programmes; however, they were unable to prevent this shift in
their support coalition. In the early 1990s this was largely made
up of manual workers, agricultural labourers in backward rural
areas, and the dependent population.[124] Thus, the distributive

[123] SOFRES, *L'État de l'Opinion 1991*, 270.

[124] See the analysis of the change in the PSOE's electoral support in Boix,
Partisan Strategies and Supply-Side Policies in Advanced Nations, pt. 2; Arnold
J. Feldman, Jorge R. Menés, and Natalia García-Pardo, 'La estructura social y el
apoyo partidista en España', *Revista Española de Investigaciones Sociológicas*, 47
(1989), 7–72; Juan Jesús González, 'Clase apoyo electoral', *Sistema*, 112 (1993),
41–71. According to González, 54% of the socialist vote among the active population came from manual workers, and 51% of skilled workers and 63% of unskilled
workers voted for the PSOE. Between 1982 and 1993 the socialist vote dropped
from 44% to 30% in cities with more than a million inhabitants, and from 42%
to 17% among white-collar workers. These data come from the Centro de
Investigaciones Sociológicas, polls 1,327 (Nov. 1982) and 2,062 (June 1993).

TABLE 4.8. *Views on equality and policies in Spain* (%)

	1988			1989			1995		
	Has/have improved	Has/have deteriorated	Difference	Satisfaction	Dissatisfaction	Difference	Has/have improved	Has/have deteriorated	Difference
1. Pensions	46	24	+22	10	45	−35	52	22	+30
2. Education	52	17	+35	32	13	+19	68	14	+54
3. Health	41	24	+17	15	43	−28	65	17	+48
4. Economy	31	35	−4	—	—	—	20	65	−45
5. Functioning of the judicial system	19	30	−11	—	—	—	23	44	−21
6. Social inequality	42	20	+22	—	—	—	28	45	−17
7. Effect of class on inequality of opportunities	49	18	+32	—	—	—	—	—	—

Sources: Centro de Investigaciones Sociológicas, polls of 12–16 June 1988, and 4–18 Apr. 1995; Demoscopia, S.A., poll of Mar.–Apr. 1989.

TABLE 4.9. *Views on the French Socialist government (%)*

	Issues which best define the socialists' record	
	All voters	Socialist voters
More social justice	49	65
More freedom	27	39
More economic efficiency	22	32
More state	20	16
More taxes	16	9
Greater security	15	15
More employment	14	17

Source: SOFRES, *L'État de l'Opinion: Clés pour 1988* (Paris, Seuil, 1988).

TABLE 4.10. *Party considered the best option for determined policies in France and Spain (%)*

	France		Spain			
	RPR/UDF	PS	PP	CDS	IU	PSOE
1. Law and order	30	17	23	6	3	25
2. Economic performance	31	36	14	7	3	30
3. Country's position in the world	32	31	11	7	3	34
4. Reduction of social inequalities	20	41	8	7	9	32
5. Protection of civil liberties	26	39	9	7	6	33

Sources: SOFRES, *L'État de l'Opinion 1990* (Paris, Seuil, 1990), 12; Centro de Investigaciones Sociológicas, poll of 20–5 Apr. 1988.

effects of social democratic policies, despite the vast egalitarian demands in society, undermined the very bases of their majority.

At the end of the 1980s, however, the distribution of preferences on social policies in Spain had changed very little since the beginning of the decade. In France, too, this was the policy area in which the PS retained greatest electoral support. Table 4.10 shows that in both countries the socialists were considered the party most likely to reduce social inequalities. In this respect the PSOE was chosen four times more often than the PP, and three times as frequently as the IU; in France the PS had double the score of the RPR–UDF coalition. Voters, therefore, still considered that ideology mattered when it came to social policies.

Social policies were thus the core element of the identity of the Southern European social democrats. Despite the more stringent demands imposed by economic competitiveness in a global economy, social policies expanded the state's role in redistribution through taxation, social transfers, and collective goods. González repeatedly stressed this social democratic philosophy centred around social policies:

Democracy and the market economy are not one and the same thing . . . This society lives in a free market, and the state should act on this economy, taking some of the wealth it generates in order to try and further social justice and to fight for equality. . . . Education should not be subject to the market, health is not a problem of supply and demand in terms of profits. That is why, during the 1980s, Spain saw three historic developments in the provision of services: the universalization of health care, education, and pensions, and that decade will probably be remembered for this.[125]

4.7. Conclusions

During the 1980s Southern European socialism passed from opposition into power, and it did so in circumstances that varied in the different countries. In the case of the new democracies, the governments faced a particular syndrome of problems, their economies were less developed, and were suffering from a more serious crisis. But the initial differences in their economic policies were primarily the result of the distinct intellectual visions, influences, and political choices of politicians. Thus, the PASOK's policy in Greece was similar to that of the first PS government in France, but differed from that followed by the PS in Portugal and the PSOE in Spain. However, these initial differences gradually diminished under the influence of economic constraints. The parties' capacity to admit these constraints and strike a balance between economic efficiency and social redistribution varied in accordance

---

[125] Felipe González, 'Reflexiones sobre el proyecto socialista', *Leviatán*, 41 (1990), 12.

with the influence of European social democracy and their commit-ment to European integration. Thus, when the Fabius and Rocard governments reversed the PS's original economic programme, the party became a paradigmatic example of the social democracy of the 1980s. The growing difficulties of the PS after 1991 were largely political rather than programmatic: irregular party funding, inter-nal disputes, a widespread sense of uncertainty brought about by the changes in European politics at the end of the decade, the new international economic crisis, and a tired and jaded leadership which proved incapable of reacting to the situation.

As for the PASOK, its policies were still presented according to an agenda of radical rhetoric. It has been argued that 'the PASOK, in its attempt to avoid the social democratic model and to follow a third road to socialism, was lost in a pathless populist land'.[126] Whilst it is true that the Papandreou government gradually aban-doned these economic experiments with a 'third road' to social-ism,[127] its record was nevertheless characterized by high inflation, a huge public deficit, and large trade imbalances. However, the breadth of the PASOK's original mandate, the polarization of Greek politics, and the party's strong symbolic roots and extensive client networks all helped to limit the political costs of these problems. The PASOK's electoral defeat in 1989, therefore, was not so much due to its poor economic record as to political scandals and eco-nomic corruption. Yet it still won some 40% of the vote and would be returned to office in 1993.

In Spain the PSOE also initially enjoyed a broad mandate. However, its economic policies were more prudent, no radical shift took place in its overall political orientation, and its social policies developed in a more gradual and accumulative fashion. As a result, the Spanish socialists were able to win four consecutive elections despite the gradual weakening of the party's support. The growing conflict with the unions contributed to this decline, although as in Greece and France, it was primarily due to politics rather than policies. The party found itself increasingly isolated, connected only with a silent electorate, amidst accusations of sec-tarianism, major corruption scandals, and serious internal strife.

---

[126] Christos Lyrintzis, 'PASOK in Power: The Loss of the "Third Road to Social-ism"', in Tom Gallagher and Allan Williams (eds.), *Southern European Socialism: Parties, Elections, and the Challenge of Government* (Manchester, Manchester University Press, 1989), 52.

[127] Yannis Papadopoulos, 'De l'opposition au gouvernement: L'évolution idéo-logique du PASOK', *Revue Française de Science Politique*, 40/1 (1990), 98–124.

An egalitarian redistribution of resources and opportunities was a persistent preference of these governments. They pursued this objective through their fiscal and social policies, whilst their economic policies reflected the new dilemmas facing the European left. If social democracy means nationalizations, then only the first two years of the French PS government can be defined as such. Yet the principal social democratic parties have long been very wary of nationalizations. Rather than being considered necessary for their egalitarian goals, public ownership of the means of production has been seen as likely to lead to bureaucratization and inefficiency. And from the end of the 1970s, the changing conditions of competitiveness and growth gradually led to new combinations of economic and social policies. These conditions were not merely the result of the logic of capitalism: every economy faced problems of accumulation, investment, and competitiveness.

The social democratic identity was typically expressed in different combinations of competitiveness and redistribution, economic efficiency and social equality. These were the politically significant aspects which distinguished social democratic policies from conservative ones. These differences affected the distribution of the social costs and benefits of policies, rather than macroeconomic management. Thus, the social democratic governments in Southern Europe promoted equality through their fiscal policies, social expenditure, and legislative reforms in the sphere of education, health care, and pensions. The convergence of macroeconomic policy did not, therefore, lead to ideological indifference with regard to social outcomes.

....

5

....

Democracies and Democrats

This chapter analyses the subjective universes which have accompanied the political changes and economic transformations in the new democracies. It examines the political cultures of these regimes, the way these have evolved over time, and the influence which economic conditions may have had on this evolution. Hence, we shall consider the different economic and political factors relating to the legitimacy of these new regimes.

Weber defined legitimacy as the validity of an order whose mandate must be obeyed: a legitimate order is one 'which enjoys the prestige of being considered binding'.[1] Contemporary political analysis has tended to consider the validity and prestige referred to in this definition in relative terms. In this way, legitimacy is 'the belief that, in spite of shortcomings and failures, the political institutions are better than any others that might be established and therefore can demand obedience'.[2] This conception of legitimacy, therefore, is not based on a reference to a political ideal, but is above all concerned with the prospects for regime consolidation and stability. These prospects will be greater if other possible alternative regimes prove less acceptable to the citizens.

A well-established tradition of political analysis considers that the cultural bases of a democracy affect its vulnerability, and that economic conditions have a decisive influence on these bases. In other words, it has argued that the fabric of values, beliefs, ideas, and perceptions about politics, politicians, and institutions condition the perspectives for democracy and reflect economic performance. On the face of it, a number of different cases certainly suggest

[1] Max Weber, *Economy and Society*, i (Berkeley, University of California Press, 1978), 31.

[2] Juan J. Linz, 'Legitimacy of Democracy and the Socioeconomic System', in Mattei Dogan (ed.), *Comparing Pluralist Democracies* (Boulder, Colo.: Westview Press, 1988).

that economic circumstances have an influence on political culture. For example, profound dissatisfaction with the party system
and the National Assembly during the first ten years of democracy
in Portugal coincided with considerable economic inefficiency and
governmental instability. In Spain the electoral turn-about of 1982
occurred in the context of an economic crisis and profound economic and political discontent. Equally, abstention rates of 54% in
the Hungarian general elections of 1990, and of 57% in the Polish
general elections of 1991, came at a time of deepening economic
crisis in both countries. In other words, there is evidence to suggest that citizens' political perceptions vary in accordance with
economic circumstances and that these, in turn, have important
consequences for democratic politics itself. However, on close examination, the relationship between the economy, values, and
politics appears much less straightforward. First, because despite
all the information available on the distribution of values and
political attitudes in the new democracies, many questions concerning the causes of these values and attitudes have yet to be
answered. How far has the past influenced the configuration of the
political culture of democracy? To what extent were democratic
values already established under the dictatorships? To what degree may this subjective world be affected by new political and
economic experiences? Other questions concerning the effects of
values and attitudes on democracy also remain unanswered.[3] It is
not clear whether these effects are significant for democratization,
for the consolidation and stability of the new regime, or for the
'quality' of democratic political life.

[3] The thesis that political culture affects democracy has been most extensively
developed by Gabriel A. Almond and Sidney Verba in *The Civic Culture* (Princeton,
NJ, Princeton University Press, 1963), on the basis of an empirical analysis of
political values and attitudes in the United States, Great Britain, the Federal
Republic of Germany, Italy, and Mexico. Ronald Inglehart defends the same thesis
in *Culture Shift in Advanced Industrial Society* (Princeton, NJ, Princeton University Press, 1990) in which he gives data on twenty-four, mainly European countries. However, there are some problems with Inglehart's study. On the one hand,
these are related to his independent variable, as it seems doubtful that democratic
values are sufficiently operationalized in his three indicators of 'satisfaction with
life', 'interpersonal confidence', and 'rejection of revolutionary changes'. On the
other hand, it appears equally dubious that his dependent variable, defined as
the numbers of years of democracy between 1900 and 1986, coincides with democratization. Finally, there is a problem of timing in the causal relationship he
defends. The effect—the years of democracy between 1900 and 1986—pre-dates
the hypothetical cause—the values measured between 1981 and 1986. Inglehart
does not consider the opposite thesis, that values are the effect, rather than the
cause, of democratic change.

In this chapter I will focus on three aspects of this whole area of debate. The first concerns the extent to which political culture theory can explain regime change. Its capacity to do so depends on whether or not the regime change was preceded by a transformation in political values and attitudes. In other words, whether the democracies were antedated by an increase in the number of democrats. If, in contrast, it was the experience of democracy itself which transformed values and attitudes and raised the number of democrats, political culture theory will be unable to account for changes of regime.[4] As Barrington Moore observed, 'to take values as the starting point of sociological explanation makes it very difficult to understand the obvious fact that values change in response to circumstances'.[5] Similarly, Schmitter and Karl have argued that a civic culture is not a 'necessary prior condition' for democracy, but rather 'the result of the prolonged functioning of democratic institutions which generate appropriate values and beliefs'.[6] Clearly the proliferation of political transitions provides an excellent opportunity to examine these problems, for, as Brian Barry has rightly noted, regime changes constitute the *experimentum crucis* of political culture theory.[7]

The second question concerns the degree of autonomy of political legitimacy. It has often been argued that the legitimacy of democracies is to some extent independent of the performance of

[4] In contrast to Inglehart, Muller and Seligson defend the thesis that democratic values are the result of democratic experience, more than the cause of this. They add six Central American countries to those included in Inglehart's survey. However, they also use 'interpersonal confidence' (which emerges as a clear effect of democratic experience) and 'support for gradual reforms' as indicators of democratic values, whilst considering the 'level' of democracy in the period 1981–90 in comparison with the period 1972–80, which does not clearly capture the change of regime. See Edward N. Muller and Mitchell A. Seligson, 'Civic Culture and Democracy: The Question of Causal Relationships', *American Political Science Review*, 88/3 (1994), 635–52.

[5] Barrington Moore, *Social Origins of Dictatorship and Democracy* (Boston, Beacon Press, 1966), 485–7.

[6] Terry L. Karl and Philippe C. Schmitter, 'Modes of Transition in Latin America, Southern and Eastern Europe', *International Journal of Social Science*, 128 (1991).

[7] Brian Barry, *Sociologists, Economists, and Democracy* (London, Collier-Macmillan, 1970), ch. 3. In Barry's words 'the naturally-occurring "crucial experiment" is of course, a change in regime. If the "political culture" alters *afterwards* . . . this strongly supports the view that it is a more or less accurate reflection of the current political reality. If, on the other hand, it does not change, then this interpretation of the bases of "political culture" collapses; and if, some time *before* the change in regime, a change in "political culture" in the appropriate direction is observed, this would provide good evidence for the view which attributes to it causal efficacy.' (p. 52).

their political and economic institutions. For an indefinite, but prolonged period, dissatisfaction with the performance of these institutions does not undermine citizens' loyalty to the existing regime. In democracies, responsibility for unsatisfactory results may be attributed to any number of institutions: the capitalist system, the international situation, the government, employers, or the unions. And it is always possible to change a government without provoking a crisis of the democratic regime. Thus, widespread political dissatisfaction is compatible with extensive democratic legitimacy. When a democracy is legitimate it can survive profound economic crises. Between 1929 and 1932, for example, the decline of the per capita GDP and the increase in the unemployment rate in the United States, Sweden, or Holland were comparable with those of Germany,[8] yet the democracies survived, and in some cases the stability of these governments even increased during the crisis. In the same way, the survival of Indian democracy, despite the country's profound economic difficulties, has been attributed to the existence of a deep-rooted democratic political culture.[9] Thus, the principal question raised by this argument concerns what the roots of this autonomous legitimacy are.

The third question concerns the way in which political cultures are affected by the passage of time. It has often been noted that democratic values are only firmly established in a society after a prolonged period of democracy. Converse argues that a democracy only reaches maturity after at least two generations.[10] This is the time needed for the political socialization of citizens in the new regime. Until that period has elapsed, democratic stability rests on only fragile foundations. Thus, Converse notes that

[8] M. Rainer Lepsius, 'From Fragmented Party Democracy to Government by Emergency Decree and National Socialist Takeover: Germany', in Juan J. Linz and Alfred Stepan (eds.), *The Breakdown of Democratic Regimes: Europe* (Baltimore, Johns Hopkins University Press, 1978), 50–61.

[9] See e.g. Atul Kohli, 'Indian Democracy: Stress and Resilience', *Journal of Democracy*, 3 (1992), 52–64.

[10] Philip E. Converse, 'Of Time and Partisan Stability', *Comparative Political Studies*, 2 (1969). Converse focuses above all on the way in which the passing of time affects party loyalties, but he extends his reflections to the stability of the democratic system itself. Thus he writes that 'where nations have maintained democratic forms for a sufficient period of time, the implantation seems complete, and further reversals nearly inconceivable' (p. 140). He estimated that it takes two-and-a-half generations (75 years) for the system to take root. The argument that the brevity of democratic experiences weakens their cultural foundations has been applied to Southern Europe by Geoffrey Pridham, 'Comparative Perspectives on the New Mediterranean Democracies: A Model of Regime Transition?', in Geoffrey Pridham (ed.), *The New European Democracies* (London, Frank Cass, 1984), 1–29.

the threats to the survival of a new institution will be very high in its infant stages. In the degree that it can outlast these first precarious periods, it will typically have put forth roots of sufficient strength.... Newly established social and political institutions somehow accumulate a deepening stability with the passage of time ... patterns of slowly accumulating stability within new social forms reflect temporal processes of habituation or 'socialization'.... In short, they are cases of *social learning*.[11]

The obvious question this argument raises is how long do these processes take. Was Carlos Gardel right when he sang 'that twenty years is but nothing'? For after all, the brevity of Italy's democratic experience has been considered the cause of the country's political problems not just fifteen years after the end of fascism, but 25 and 50 years afterwards as well.[12] How long is it before the political experience of democracy contributes to the consolidation of these values? Attempts to answer this question have tended to distinguish between, on the one hand, cognitive, attitudinal, and evaluative elements of political culture, which would be more dependent on the regimes' performance, and on the other, deeper values, which change only slowly and which constitute an almost geological stratum with sediments from many periods and events.[13]

These questions directly affect the relationship between economies and new democracies. If democratic values pre-date the new regime, then its legitimacy will be less directly tied to instrumental considerations and to the economic performance of the new institutions. In this case, governments may have greater room for manœuvre in terms of policies, and the regime itself will be less directly implicated if these fail. The independence of the regime will be further strengthened if the responsibility for poor results is dispersed. In contrast, when legitimacy has yet to become autonomous, and while the necessary time for democratic values to become firmly established has not passed, economic crises may erode the fragile cultural 'cement' of the new regimes. However, even in this case, much remains to be explained. For it is one

[11] Converse, 'Of Time and Partisan Stability', 139–40.

[12] Norman Kogan, *The Government of Italy* (New York, Thomas Crowell, 1962), 186. Kogan argues that the weakness of Italian democracy lies in the weak legitimacy of the Republic's institutions. Robert Putnam also considers that certain characteristics of the Italian parliamentary élite's intolerance and lack of confidence can be ascribed to the country's short democratic history and the legacy of fascism. See his book, *The Beliefs of Politicians: Ideology, Conflict, and Democracy in Britain and Italy* (New Haven, Conn., Yale University Press, 1973), 84.

[13] See e.g. Harry Eckstein, 'A Culturalist Theory of Political Change', *American Political Science Review*, 82 (1988), 796.

thing to recognize that economic results affect the prospects for survival of democracies, as these may be abandoned by disaffected citizens, but quite another to argue that these results affect the consolidation of the regimes, regardless of whether democracy formally survives. Finally, it is still different to argue that economic results influence the 'quality' of the regime, which may suffer in terms of attitudes and values, participation, and political behaviour.

5.1. The Antecedents of Democratization

What are the roots of legitimacy? The incidence of cultural values which consider democracy to be the only acceptable regime largely depends on the nature of civil society. By 'civil society' I mean that space between the state and the private sphere in which individuals and their associations promote their interests autonomously and freely through spontaneous processes of voluntary transactions, whether economic or otherwise. It is a space in which parties, lobbies and interest groups, trade unions, the mass media, cultural foundations, professional bodies, academic societies, and companies implement their strategies and interact with each other and with the state. Particular traits of the political cultures of the new European democracies have been associated with the relative weakness of their civil societies in modern times. This weakness was expressed in the deficient articulation of interest organizations, the fragmentation and fragility of workers' and employers' associations, the absence of institutional mechanisms for conflict resolution, the persistence of oligarchical forms of domination, and the control of the state by autonomous political classes.[14] However, differences existed between the situation in Southern and Eastern Europe, just as they did between Central-Eastern and South-East Europe. Their civil societies had very diverse histories and developed very differently under the dictatorships. As a result, the role played by civil society in the transitions and new regimes in these countries also varied greatly.

In Southern Europe, resistance to industrialization and political liberalism limited the density of pluralism and the autonomy of

---

[14] Linz, 'A Century of Politics and Interests in Spain', 365–415. For the turbulent formation of civil societies in Eastern Europe, see George Schöpflin, 'The Political Traditions of Eastern Europe', *Daedalus*, 119/1 (1990), 55–90. See also Elemer Hankiss, *East European Alternatives* (Oxford, Clarendon Press, 1990), chs. 1, 2, and 3.

civil societies. In Spain despite early instances of development and a relatively diversified economy, important pre-capitalist elements survived for a long time. In Greece and Portugal early attempts to industrialize met with little success. As a result, their relative economic underdevelopment in comparison to Western Europe was a constant cause of concern for reformist élites in all three countries. Moreover, the relationship between political life and civil society in these countries was affected by the comparatively weak influence of the industrial bourgeoisie, the traditional oligarchies' protracted control of the state apparatus, the continued political exclusion of the subordinate classes, and frequent military intervention in politics. With the onset of industrialization and the growing strength of the rural, commercial, and industrial bourgeoisies, the first liberal governments introduced limited reforms, which were primarily intended to foment capitalism rather than transform politics. Although the political systems of these Southern European countries became less exclusive towards the end of the nineteenth century, education and property requirements remained significant obstacles to citizenship. These limitations provoked peasant revolts, labour conflicts in industrial areas, student unrest, and the political radicalization of many middle-class intellectuals. In all three countries, the dictatorships were a reaction to these social tensions and to colonial disasters such as those suffered by Spain in Cuba, the Philippines, and North Africa, by Portugal in Angola and Mozambique, and by Greece in Asia Minor. The result was these countries' prolonged experience of authoritarianism, under the regimes of Salazar (1926–74), Metaxas (1936–40), the Colonels (1967–74), Primo de Rivera (1923–31), and Franco (1939–75). In fact, Portugal had no history of mass democracy before the 'revolution of the carnations' in 1974.

In the whole of Southern Europe the organization of civil societies was seriously debilitated by the instability of the democracies and what Linz has termed the primacy of politics over the representation of interests. For whilst democratic interludes tended to promote the autonomy of interest organizations, the political oligarchies were long able to maintain their control of the state, manipulating elections and institutions. The corrupt clientele mechanisms employed by both political parties and governments meant that the exercise of power was not linked to the representation of social interests. Meanwhile, during the various democratic periods, political polarization and the simultaneous mobilization of all the cleavages scarcely left any space for civil societies to organize independently. In this way, the history of political instability, ideological tensions, and prolonged periods of dictatorship which characterized Southern Europe as a whole hindered the construction of a social fabric favourable to democracy.

Whilst the evolution of the civil societies of Southern and Eastern Europe shared several broad characteristics, they also differed in a number of important respects.[15] As a result of the periods of foreign domination, with Ottoman rule proving more destructive than that of the Habsburgs, the national institutions of Hungary, Poland, the former Czechoslovakia, Slovenia, and Croatia were particularly unstable. The tendency for governments to extend their arbitrary powers hindered the development of parliamentary sovereignty. In general terms, the state played a much more important role in the economies and societies of these countries than in the rest of Europe. There was little experience of democracy and political rights, which, in the best of cases, were limited to ritual participation in elections and very precarious social protection. Between 1900 and 1936—and with the exception of Hungary in 1905 and Bulgaria in 1932 as a consequence of divisions among the ruling élites—no Eastern European government lost an election to the opposition. Governments' control of power was based on restricted suffrage, electoral fraud, arbitrary arrests, and prohibitions. Moreover, in countries such as Poland, Hungary, Romania, Croatia, and Bosnia, the public administration was to a large extent colonized by the political oligarchies. Elsewhere, for example in Albania, it would be more accurate to speak in terms of the survival of tribal structures rather than true administration of the state. Political parties generally consisted of personal clienteles, and their commitments and political strategies tended to be unstable and opportunistic. Although the Western European countries usually served as models for the social élites, the latter proved incapable of promoting economic development. With the exception of the Czech territories, foreign ethnic groups were usually behind the limited bursts of economic development that did take place. The political integration of the states was often hindered by both

[15] See, for a contrast, the reflections on the role civil society played in political changes in Latin America included in Guillermo O'Donnell, Philippe C. Schmitter, and Laurence Whitehead (eds.), *Transitions from Authoritarian Rule: Latin America* (Baltimore, Johns Hopkins University Press, 1986), 3–18; Larry Diamond, Juan J. Linz, and Seymour M. Lipset (eds.), *Democracy in Developing Countries: Latin America* (Boulder, Colo.: Lynne Rienner, 1989), 35–44; for relations between states and civil societies see Alfred Stepan, 'State Power and the Strength of Civil Society in the Southern Cone of Latin America', in Peter B. Evans, Dietrich Rueschemeyer, and Theda Skocpol (eds.), *Bringing the State Back In* (Cambridge, Cambridge University Press, 1985), 317–43.

foreign interference and the social and ethnic heterogeneity of their inhabitants. Political élites frequently resorted to belligerent nationalism in a bid to strengthen the populations' identification with the states, and when border changes led to the creation of multi-national states, or situated significant minorities in other states, the subsequent demands for independence or annexation proved explosive.

These characteristics which were so unfavourable to the emergence of strong civil societies were much more accentuated in the countries of South-Eastern Europe, with their distinctive history of domination by the Ottoman Empire and legacy of 'sultanist' regimes. Here, democratic traditions were almost completely absent and politics were dominated by religious, ethnic, and nationalist divisions. Ethnic conflicts and movements in favour of annexation were particularly important in Bulgaria, Romania, Albania, and the former Yugoslavia. There were no organized labour movements to channel workers' interests and integrate them into the political system. The societies and states of these countries were characterized by the weakness of the intermediate associations, the limited political integration of their inhabitants, major underlying conflicts, and the fragile institutionalization of the political system.

The differences in nature of these civil societies had consequences both for the type of transition to democracy and the consolidation of the new regimes. In those countries with weaker civil societies, the dictatorships usually fell as the result of sudden popular explosions and 'palace coups'. Political change tended to be associated with economic crisis, the end of foreign hegemonic tutelage, and a brusque collapse. The roots of legitimacy were fragile, and the new democracies proved more vulnerable to problems of inefficiency. In contrast, when the organization of civil society was stronger, regime change usually followed a process of increasing social pluralism and was based on negotiations and agreements to establish democracy. Demands tended to be expressed by stable organizations and institutions rather than in sudden explosions of discontent. In these countries the foundations of democratic legitimacy were broader and the prospects of the new regimes were less closely tied to the performance of their economies.

Political change in Southern Europe must be interpreted in relation to the incidence of democratic values under the preceding authoritarian regimes. This incidence implied two things: on the one hand, that these values had survived within cultural communities notwithstanding repressive conditions; and on the other, that they had expanded after a certain point in time and as a result of certain experiences. Thus, whilst the authoritarian regimes were unable to eradicate deep-rooted democratic traditions, socio-economic transformations affected political cultures. In the case of Spain, families and certain cultural communities were to a large extent able to act as protective enclaves which shielded people from authoritarian models of indoctrination and socialization.[16] This facilitated the transmission of democratic ideological loyalties across generations and the emergence of these values with the change of regime. This could be seen, for example, in the fact that until the mid-1960s, between two-thirds and three-quarters of clandestine union and student leaders in Spain came from anti-Francoist families. With the advent of democracy, 61% of those who considered themselves to be on the left, and 83% of those who identified with the right, declared that their parents had shared the same broad ideology. Similar cultural continuities can also be found in the Greek case in relation to the three political traditions of left, centre, and right. These dated back to the conflicts between Venizelists and anti-Venizelists over the First World War, and had persisted since then.[17]

Thus, in those countries of Southern Europe with some previous experience of political pluralism, democratic values were largely able to survive: the impact of what Converse has called the 'forgetting function' was not total.[18] These values spread towards the end of the dictatorships, when the economies and societies of these countries were not entirely isolated from abroad and there was some articulation of social pluralism as an 'unintended consequence' of economic development.[19] In the case of Spain, for example, whilst in 1966 only 35% of the population supported the idea that 'important political decisions should be adopted by representatives elected by the people', this figure had risen to 60% by 1974, and to 78% by 1976, remaining fairly stable thereafter. The evolution of political principles was matched by a change in behaviour, seen in the way in which distinct sectors of society mobilized during this

[16] José María Maravall, *Dictatorship and Political Dissent* (New York: St Martin's Press, 1978), chs. 3 and 6, and the same author's *The Transition to Democracy in Spain* (New York: St Martin's Press, 1982), 24–9, 174–7.

[17] George Mavrogordatos, 'Rise of the Green Sun. The Greek Election of 1981', *Occasional Paper 1* (London, Centre of Contemporary Greek Studies, King's College, 1983), 5–19.

[18] Converse, 'Of Time and Partisan Stability', 159–60.

[19] On the cultural evolution during the last decade of Francoism, see Víctor Pérez-Díaz, *The Return of Civil Society: The Emergence of Democratic Spain* (Cambridge, Mass.: Harvard University Press, 1993), 1–53.

period. Labour disputes multiplied, the number of hours lost through strike action increasing from 1.5 million in 1966 to 14.5 million in 1975, and 150 million in 1976. Meanwhile, the proportion of political and solidarity strikes rose from a mere 4% of the total between 1963 and 1967 to 45% between 1968 and 1974.[20] Strongly influenced by the example of Europe, this period saw an implicit process of collective reflection about how to face the future and avoid the traumatic repetition of the past. This intense process of learning, both from Spain's own history as well as from that of failed democratic experiences in other countries, fostered increasing support for the democratic alternative.[21] In this way, democratic values were much more widespread than had been the case in previous episodes of democratization. The reinterpretation of political experiences reinforced the intrinsic value of political democracy. This process of collective reflection, based on the failure of earlier attempts to democratize and the terrible consequences of the dictatorships, developed first among those who could loosely be labelled the left. In Southern Europe, and above all in the Spanish case, reticence and resistance were stronger on the right.[22] Although this cultural substratum was neither a necessary nor a sufficient condition for the re-establishment of democracies, it certainly facilitated many democratization processes and, as other alternatives disintegrated, increased the prospects for the survival of the new regimes.

In some Eastern European countries, and above all in Hungary and Poland, a time came when the 'totalitarian hypothesis' ceased

---

[20] Maravall, *Dictatorship and Political Dissent*, esp. chs. 2 and 5, and *Transition to Democracy in Spain*, 5–18.

[21] The importance of 'political learning' in democratization processes has been emphasized by Nancy Bermeo in 'Democracy and the Lessons of Dictatorship', *Comparative Politics*, 24 (1992), 273–91.

[22] For a similar analysis of the growing influence of democratic values in Latin America see Angel Flisfisch, *La política como compromiso democrático* (Madrid, Centro de Investigaciones Sociológicas, 1991), 156–75. Also writing in reference to the Latin American case, Linz and Diamond have argued that 'the importance of democracy as an end in itself, and the need for political prudence and accommodation, was driven home to the citizens and politicians of Brazil, Argentina, Chile, and Uruguay by the bitter experience of economic and political stalemate, polarization, and violence, leading to democratic breakdown and repressive, bureaucratic-authoritarian rule during the 1960s, 1970s and early 1980s. The resulting "revalorization" of democracy and moderation of political behaviour is one of the most important causes for optimism about the future of democracy in these countries.' See Larry Diamond and Juan J. Linz, 'Introduction: Politics, Society, and Democracy in Latin America', in Diamond, Linz, and Lipset, *Democracy in Developing Countries: Latin America*, 12.

to correspond with reality. Many political analyses underestimated the strength of civil societies and overestimated the degree of communist domination in these countries.[23] It is certainly true that the parties and unions which had constituted civil society before or immediately after the Second World War were dismantled with the support of the police and the Red Army towards the end of the 1940s. It is also clear that until the mid-1950s the regimes attempted to penetrate the realm of the primary and secondary groups which made up the sphere of private life and domestic society, suppressing the frontiers between public and private and politicizing social relations and primary bonds. Nevertheless, domestic society was able to survive. Memory and values persisted in its midst, in small communities in which isolation and confidentiality provided protection from mechanisms of socialization imposed 'from above'. In these relatively autonomous social micro-spaces in which families played a crucial role, the 'public transcript' came to be challenged by what Scott has labelled a 'hidden transcript', underground and unofficial versions of political life which constituted the most basic form of defensive political resistance.[24] As Arato has affirmed, at this level, which precedes that of the organization of civil society, 'the potentials of resistance of traditional or inherited forms of life turned out to be astonishing'.[25]

In the wake of Stalinism, dissent slowly began to appear beyond the realm of private consciences, in a nascent public sphere. The first manifestations of this date from the 1950s in Hungary, Poland, and the German Democratic Republic, and from the 1960s in Czechoslovakia, when positive memories of the First Republic and of Tomàš Masaryk multiplied five-fold. Although this dissent was repressed, it could not be suppressed. It surfaced in Russia itself in the 1960s, in the Ukraine and Latvia in the 1970s, when dissent also re-emerged in Hungary, Poland, and Czechoslovakia. In the German Democratic Republic it would only resurface in the early 1980s. Deference and submission to the regimes were thus

[23] For an example of this over-estimation of the strength of communist cultural domination see Samuel P. Huntington and Jorge I. Domínguez, 'Political Development', in Fred I. Greenstein and Nelson W. Polsby (eds.), *Handbook of Political Science*, iii (Reading, Mass., Addison-Wesley, 1975), 31–2. See also Seweryn Bialer, *Stalin's Successors: Leadership, Stability and Change in the Soviet Union* (Cambridge, Cambridge University Press, 1980), 192–3.
[24] See the fascinating study by James C. Scott, *Domination and the Arts of Resistance* (New Haven, Conn., Yale University Press, 1990), ch. 5.
[25] Andrew Arato, 'Social Theory, Civil Society, and the Transformation of Authoritarian Socialism', in Ferenc Feher and Andrew Arato (eds.), *Crisis and Reform in Eastern Europe* (New Brunswick, Transaction Publishers, 1991), 1–26, quote from p. 8.

to a large extent instrumental, a means of survival. A culture of resistance and autonomy was maintained in arenas as diverse as the Hungarian 'Petöfi circles', the Polish 'Warped Circle clubs' which first appeared soon after the death of Stalin, *samizdat* journals, circles for the study of history, or the trade union cells which appeared twenty years later. Local traditions of resistance, popular myths, ritual acts, and political symbols endowed this autonomous culture with continuity. Thus, there existed a link between the events in Hungary in 1956 and the popular demonstrations which took place after the fall of communism and which culminated on 16 June 1989 with the immense demonstration in commemoration of Imre Nagy.[26] In Poland, the birth of Solidarność was marked by a similar connection with the past: whilst in 1977 hundreds of people met in Gdańsk to commemorate the victims of the 1970 conflicts, in 1979 the same anniversary was attended by thousands, and on 16 December 1980 the occasion attracted half a million people.[27]

Yet fear fuelled generalized passivity, a 'falsification of preferences' which took the form of apparent conformism.[28] Even so, above all after the manifestations of dissent in 1956 in Poland and Hungary and 1968 in Czechoslovakia, governments became increasingly aware that they enjoyed only limited and precarious ideological support from society. They gradually tried to obtain a degree of pragmatic consent based on the coexistence of communist regimes with private society.[29] This implicit pact consisted of the exchange of political apathy and demobilization for the toleration of private interests and a growing 'second economy'. This tacit pact, however, did not resolve the regimes' legitimacy problems. On the contrary, as the official ideological discourse collapsed, the

[26] László Bruszt and David Stark, 'Remaking the Political Field in Hungary: From the Politics of Confrontation to the Politics of Competition', *Working Papers on Transitions from State Socialism* (Ithaca, NY, Cornell University Press, 1991). See also Janos Kis, *Politics in Hungary: For a Democratic Alternative* (Highlands Lakes, NJ, Atlantic Research and Publications, 1989), 33–84.

[27] Roman Laba, *The Roots of Solidarity: A Political Sociology of Poland's Working Class Democratization* (Princeton, NJ, Princeton University Press, 1991), 126–54.

[28] For the 'falsification of preferences' due to the costs involved and the emergence of dissent as the result of variable pay-offs, see Timur Kuran, 'Now out of Never: The Element of Surprise in the East European Revolution of 1989' in Nancy Bermeo (ed.), *Liberalization and Democratization: Change in the Soviet Union and Eastern Europe* (Baltimore, Johns Hopkins University Press, 1992), 7–48.

[29] Grzegorz Ekiert, 'Democratization Processes in East Central Europe: A Theoretical Reconsideration', *British Journal of Political Science*, 21/3 (1991), 285–313.

states were gradually invaded by private interests, corruption, and clientelism.

Nevertheless, the threat of the use of force continued to deter any radical change. As a result, great pessimism surrounded the possibilities for political transformation in Eastern Europe until shortly before 1989, an attitude only reinforced by the coup d'état in Poland in 1981.[30] The consequence was that a new strategy became increasingly influential in Hungary and particularly in Poland, based on the idea that a new balance with the state could be created from within the sphere of civil society. Rather than directly questioning communist political domination, it sought to strengthen the intermediate associations so that society could become more autonomous from political power.[31] This was the essence of what Adam Michnik labelled the 'new evolutionism' in Poland, the ideas of the Danube Circle in Hungary in 1984, and the 'social contract' proposed there by the clandestine journal *Beszélö* in 1987. In Hungary, Poland, and the USSR, these ideas proved quite attractive to the reformist communists who were confronted by a deepening economic crisis. They thought that by extending the sphere of tolerated independent activity they could reduce the tension and secure a degree of social co-operation with austere economic policies. However, this was not the general response in the communist countries. In Czechoslovakia, Bulgaria, the German Democratic Republic, and Romania, the level of toleration remained minimal. Under the reformist communist governments, however, the space for the autonomous organization of civil society expanded significantly. Under Gorbachev, some 30,000 informal groups were created between 1986 and 1988, and a myriad of associations of ecologists, pacifists, war veterans, and human rights activists flourished in these countries.[32] These emergent civil societies contri-

---

[30] See e.g. the analyses by Ferenc Feher and Agnes Heller, *Eastern Left, Western Left: Totalitarianism, Freedom, and Democracy* (Atlantic Highlands, NJ, Humanities Press, 1987), 250, and Agnes Heller, 'Can Communist Regimes Be Reformed?', *Society*, 25/4 (1988), 22–4.

[31] See e.g. H. Gordon Skilling, *Samizdat and an Independent Society in Central and Eastern Europe* (Basingstoke, Macmillan, 1988); Tony Judt, 'The Dilemmas of Dissidence: The Politics of Opposition in East-Central Europe', *East European Politics and Societies*, 2 (1988), 185–241; and John Keane (ed.), *Civil Society and the State* (London, Verso, 1988), 332–80; Janina Frentzel-Zagorska, 'Civil Society in Poland and Hungary', *Soviet Studies*, 42/4 (1990), 759–77; Paul G. Lewis (ed.), *Democracy and Civil Society in Eastern Europe* (New York, St Martin's Press, 1992), 1–15, 91–112.

[32] On this dynamic see Marcia Weigle and Jim Butterfield, 'Civil Society in Reforming Communist Regimes', *Comparative Politics*, 25/1 (1992), 13. See also

buted to the revival of political societies and the formation of groups such as the Committee for Workers' Rights (KOR) and Solidarność in Poland, the People's Fronts in Estonia, Latvia, and Byelorussia, the Movement for Reconstruction in Lithuania, and alegal political parties such as those which began to operate in Hungary. In those countries in which the regimes attempted to maintain more repressive policies, governments found these impossible to sustain once Gorbachev removed the dissuasive threat and change got under way.

In this context of greater political toleration and growing autonomy of civil society, when the threshold at which citizens dared to express their opinions fell, something which Archie Brown had detected some time earlier became generally evident: namely that ideological indoctrination and planned cultural change only made a limited impact.[33] Whilst the regimes were able to impose changes in attitudes and behaviour, they had much less influence on beliefs and values. This explains how, despite 'public transcripts' and restrictions, memory of politics, and adhesion to principles and ideas, were able to survive within private spheres. In those countries in which more structured civil societies had been able to emerge and where pragmatic sectors of the communist parties were more influential, a negotiated democratization process was more probable (as in the cases of Hungary and Poland). Where this was not so, democratization began with popular mobilizations and ended with the collapse of regimes which had lost their capacity to repress. Yet, in both cases, in Eastern Europe as a whole, civil societies played a more important role in the democratization processes than either political scientists or politicians could have foreseen.

Support for Western-style democracy grew progressively during the final years of the communist regimes, above all between 1985 and 1989. Moreover, this rise accelerated towards the very end of

Christine Sadowski, 'Autonomous Groups as Agents of Democratic Change in Communist and Post-Communist Eastern Europe', in Larry Diamond (ed.), *Political Culture and Democracy in Developing Countries* (Boulder, Colo., Lynne Rienner, 1994), 155–88.

[33] Archie Brown and Jack Gray (eds.), *Political Culture and Political Change in Communist States* (New York: Holmes and Maier, 1977), e.g. 270–2; Archie Brown (ed.), *Political Culture and Communist Studies* (London, Macmillan, 1984), esp. 149–204. The following works are also of interest for political socialization under communism: Ivan Volges, 'Political Socialization in Eastern Europe', *Problems of Communism*, 23 (1974), 55; Kasimierz Wojcicki, 'The Reconstruction of Society', *Telos*, 47 (1981), 102–3; Vaclav Benda *et al.*, 'Parallel Polis or an Independent Society in Central and Eastern Europe', *Social Research*, 55 (1988), 211–46.

the regimes. In Hungary it expanded by 11 points during the brief period between the autumn of 1989 and the end of 1990. Other indicators reflecting support for party pluralism and democratic parliamentary elections confirmed this tendency. In Hungary, for example, support for party pluralism rose by 14 points during this same period. Worsening economic conditions and the political crises in Eastern Europe had enormous influence on these ideas. On the one hand, democratic loyalties resulting from processes of socialization in social micro-spaces which had withstood the regimes blossomed, whilst on the other, Western-style democracy appeared to offer a convincing solution to these countries' problems. In both Eastern Europe, under communist regimes, and in the authoritarian capitalist regimes of Southern Europe, the final years of the dictatorships saw an expansion of democratic values which became more pronounced with the onset of the transitions.[34]

In some cases, therefore, the cultural fabric of the new democracies of Southern and Eastern Europe was characterized by the survival of democratic values from the past, and by the growing social pluralism which enabled these values to spread. In other cases, the democratic option emerged 'by default' and imitation, that is, it was a consequence of the dictatorships becoming discredited and processes of diffusion and cultural contagion. As a result, the political cultures of the new democracies varied greatly, and hence so too did the roots of their legitimacy. The vulnerability of the new regimes and of their governments would also vary.

5.2. Do Democracies Produce Democrats?

What happened after the change of regime? And how far did the number of democrats increase with the passing of time? When I refer to 'democrats', I am not attributing to individuals normative

---

[34] Something similar occurred in Chile. In the final years of the Pinochet dictatorship the proportion of democrats increased from 56% to 62%, whilst the sum of 'conditional authoritarians' and 'indifferents' fell from 41% to 33%. In Brazil support for military intervention in politics decreased from 79% in 1972 to 52% in 1982 and 36% in 1990. In both cases, the democracies were preceded by a rise in the number of democrats. For Brazil, see José Alvaro Moisés, 'Democratization, Mass Political Culture, and Political Legitimacy in Brazil', *Estudio/Working Paper 1993/44* (Madrid, Center For Advanced Studies in the Social Sciences, Instituto Juan March, 1993), 41–3. The data for 1972 and 1983 only refer to the south-east of the country and some state capitals. For Chile, see Antonio Alaminos, *Chile: Transición Política y Sociedad* (Madrid: Centro de Investigaciones Sociológicas, 1991), 137–40.

commitments of a certain intensity or coherency, but simply a preference for democracy as opposed to any other type of regime. That is, I employ a common conception of legitimacy which has been adopted in numerous empirical analyses. Questions concerning the best possible form of government or preferences for democracy as opposed to other types of regime have repeatedly been asked in studies of Southern Europe and Latin America. There has been extensive unconditional support for democracy (that is, support for democracy under any circumstances) in Portugal, Greece, and Spain;[35] generally speaking, this was expressed by 75% of Spanish citizens, some 85% of the Greek population, and 65% of the Portuguese. Between 5% and 10% of the citizens of these countries were conditional supporters of authoritarianism, whilst a slightly lower proportion were indifferent towards the type of regime. This profile of democratic legitimacy in Southern Europe differed little from that found in Western Europe. Budge, for example, found that 82% of the British population were 'unconditional democrats' in 1970, whilst data compiled by Gabriel shows that this group accounted for 74% of West Germans in 1962 and 90% in 1976.[36] Table 5.1 shows the incidence of legitimacy in Southern Europe in comparison with that found in Chile, Argentina, and Brazil. In Argentina, the degree of legitimacy was similar to Southern European levels, there was greater indifference towards the regime type in Chile, whilst in Brazil the legitimacy of democracy was much more limited. As this table reveals, the proportion of 'unconditional democrats' in Brazil was half that of Spain, whilst the sum of those identifying themselves as 'conditional authoritarians' and 'indifferent' was double that found in Southern Europe. The majority of Brazilians thought that democracy was preferable from the perspective of political liberty, but not with regard to economic development or public morality, or in general terms.[37]

[35] This unconditional support for democracy as a regime has been termed 'diffuse legitimacy' by Leonardo Morlino and José Ramón Montero, 'Legitimación y Democracia en el Sur de Europa', *Revista Española de Investigaciones Sociológicas*, 64 (1993), 7–40.

[36] Ian Budge, *Agreement and the Stability of Democracy*, (Chicago, Markham, 1970), 106. Oscar W. Gabriel, *Cambio Social y Cultura Política* (Barcelona, Gedisa, 1980), ch. 2, who calculates the percentages excluding those who do not wish to respond to the question.

[37] Bolívar Lamounier (ed.), *Ouvindo o Brasil: una análise da opinão publica brasileira hoje* (Sao Paolo, Editora Sumaré, 1992). Yet six polls carried out in Brazil between 1989 and 1992 revealed a higher incidence of legitimacy. On average 'unconditional democrats' accounted for 47% of the population, whilst 'conditional authoritarians' and 'indifferents' accounted for some 39%. See José Alvaro

TABLE 5.1. *The legitimacy of democracy (Southern Europe and Latin America)*

Agreement with the following statements	Spain		Greece	Portugal	Argentina	Brazil			Chile			
	1985	1991	1985	1985	1988	1988	1991	1992	1986	1988	1990	1993
Democracy is always preferable	70	76	87	64	74	43	39	48	56	62	76	56
Authoritarianism is preferable under certain circumstances	10	10	5	11	13	21	17	24	15	10	9	18
The type of regime is immaterial	9	8	6	7	10	26	28	20	25	23	12	22
Don't know/ Don't answer	11	6	2	18	3	10	16	8	4	5	3	4

Sources: Centro de Investigaciones Sociológicas, polls 1,461 (May-June 1985) for Spain, Greece and Portugal, and 1,984 (Dec. 1991) for Spain; José Alvaro Moisés, 'Democratization, Mass Political Culture and Political Legitimacy in Brazil', *Working Paper 1993/44* (Madrid, Center for Advanced Study in the Social Sciences, Instituto Juan March de Estudios e Investigaciones, 1993), Table 3; Bolívar Lamounier, *Ouvindo o Brasil: una análise da opinão publica brasileira hoje* (Sao Paulo, Editora Sumaré, 1992); Marta Lagos, 'Cultura Política y Transición a la Democracia en Chile' (unpublished manuscript, Santigo, CERC, 1993), 22.

Although the question is phrased in a very abstract way, it none the less enables us to detect variations in the legitimacy profile of the new democracies. These variations have been interpreted as *prima facie* evidence of the greater or lesser consolidation of the regimes.

The incidence of legitimacy in Eastern Europe can be seen from the responses to a number of questions relating to elections, parliaments, and the best type of development for the country. Combining the different indicators in a single index, we find that democratic legitimacy was expressed by at least three-quarters of the populations of Hungary and Poland in 1990 and 1991. In Czechoslovakia the proportion was somewhat lower (70%), possibly as a result of the country's particular political experience, the more intransigent and repressive communist regime, and the less dramatic economic crisis. These results are shown in Table 5.2.

The extensive legitimacy attributed to democracy in Southern Europe was well established among the different social groups. In none of these three countries was support for democracy linked to education, income, age, occupation, or religious beliefs. According to a large number of studies, however, it was related to ideology. Fig. 5.1 shows that a decade after the return to democracy, the level of unconditional support for the regime varied by some 30 points between the left and right in Greece and Portugal. In Spain in 1991, unconditional support for democracy was also twice as high on the left (89%) and the centre-left (90%) than on the right (40%).

However, data referring to Spain in 1993 questions these variations.[38] In the regression analysis presented in Table 5.3 in which democratic legitimacy is examined as a function of ideology (measured on a scale of one to ten), the further to the right individuals consider themselves, the less they will agree with the statement that 'democracy is the best possible system'. Yet ideology accounts for only 2.6% of the variation, and one point to the right only increases disagreement with this statement by .04. And the political sympathies of the family, which were so relevant for the survival of democratic values under the dictatorship, were statistically

Moisés, 'Eleições, participação e cultura política: mudanças e continuidades', *Lua Nova*, 22 (1990), 153–70; and by the same author, 'Democratization, Mass Political Culture and Political Legitimacy in Brazil', 15–18, 42–3.

[38] These data have been taken from a poll carried out by DATA S.A. in May–June 1993 using a representative national panel of 1,448 adults. The poll was conducted for the Spanish component of the Comparative National Election Project.

TABLE 5.2. *The legitimacy of democracy (Eastern Europe)*

Agreement with the following statements	Czechoslovakia	Hungary	Poland
Elections are the best way to choose a government	70	88	—
Parliament is necessary for democracy	72	89	—
Parties are necessary for democracy	75	83	68
A multi-party system is the most suitable for the country	75	77	67
The country needs Western-type development	60	86	90
Index of democratic legitimacy	70.4	84.6	75.0

Source: László Bruszt and János Simon, *Political Culture, Political and Economic Orientations in Central and Eastern Europe during the Transition to Democracy* (Budapest, Institute for Political Science, Hungarian Academy of Sciences, 1992), 98, 99, 110, 119, 175.

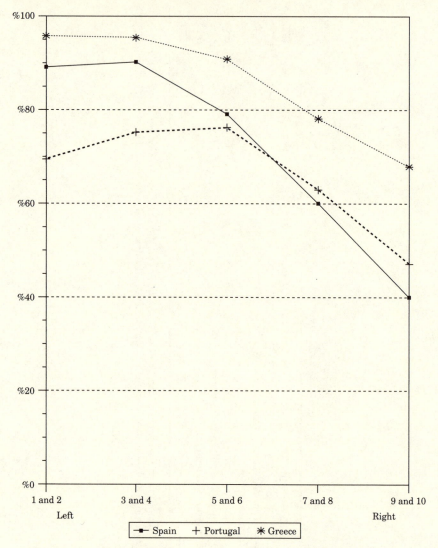

Note: Ideology is measured on a ten-point scale (1 = extreme left, 10 = extreme right).

Fɪɢ. 5.1. *Unconditional support for democracy according to ideology in Southern Europe*

Source: Centro de Investigaciones Sociológicas, polls 1,461 (May–June 1985) for Greece and Portugal, and 1,984 (Dec. 1991) for Spain.

TABLE 5.3. *The ideological bases of legitimacy (Spain)*

	Legitimacy of democracy
Constant	1.076*
	(.063)
Left–right ideological position	.039*
	(.009)
Political sympathies of family	.034
	.(.049)
R^2	.026
Signif. F	.000
No. of observations	731

Note: Standard errors in parenthesis.

  * Statistically significant at 5% or less.

insignificant for the legitimacy of the new regime. In the 1990s, therefore, democratic legitimacy was spread fairly evenly through-out society, a pattern which reflects the consolidation of the regime in terms of its social support.

How far was this pattern affected by the passing of time? According to criteria of the type proposed by Converse, Southern Europe still had only limited experience of democracy. Yet fifteen years after the re-establishment of democracy in Spain, the legit-imacy of the new regime, measured by agreement with the state-ment that 'important political decisions should be taken by representatives elected by the people', was similar to that in 1976. It appears that democratic legitimacy had largely been established some time in the past, indicating a historic change in the country's political culture. However, these aggregate data referring to the beginning and end of the period hide some important variations. On the one hand, legitimacy fell in the early days of the new regime during a period of political and economic uncertainties. Fig. 5.2 shows the evolution of the responses in Spain to the state-ment that 'democracy is the best political system for a country like ours'.[39] The erosion took place between 1979 and 1980, whilst

---

[39] Since the question used as an indicator of legitimacy is different from that in Table 5.1, the percentages obtained also vary. The introduction of 'depends' as a possible response had a notable effect on the distribution of responses, above all on the proportion of 'noes'.

'Democracy is the best possible system for a country like ours'

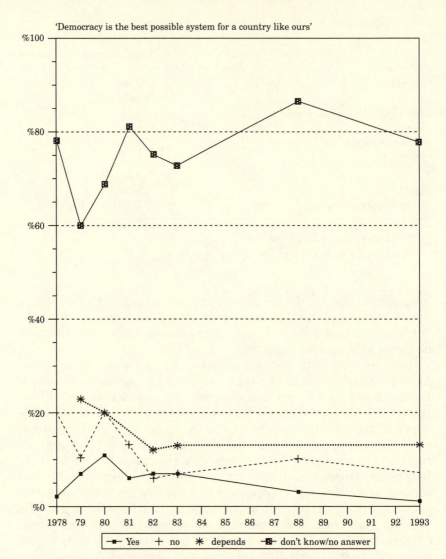

F IG. 5.2. *Time and democratic legitimacy in Spain*

Source: DATA, SA. The dates of the polls are: June–July 1978, April 1979, June 1980, March 1981, Oct.–Nov. 1982, May 1983, Sept.–Oct. 1988, June–July 1993.

positive responses subsequently rose again and remained fairly stable thereafter.[40] On the other hand, support for democracy seems to have increased among those on the right of the political spectrum.

Following the return to democracy, in Southern Europe legitimacy became increasingly autonomous from the level of discontent with economic performance and politics. Thus, despite the economic difficulties of the 1980s, unconditional support for democracy did not decline. In Spain the correlation between general support for democracy and satisfaction with concrete results progressively weakened, falling from .81 in 1978 to .68 in 1980 and .57 in 1984.[41] Nevertheless, it is true that there was no linear evolution of legitimacy after the return of democracy and that concepts such as 'consolidation' and 'stability' are always relative. Hence, Almond stated the obvious when he noted that there is always a potential for crisis within any political regime.[42] Moreover, an analysis of the factors which influenced democratic legitimacy in the case of Spain shows that, nearly two decades after the regime change, the economy still had some, albeit limited, influence on the level of democratic legitimacy.

Table 5.4 shows the results of regressions of legitimacy as a dependent variable and of twelve independent variables in Spain, based on survey data for 1993.[43] The fact that, taken together,

---

[40] The legitimacy of democracy also diminished during the first few years of the new regime in Chile: whilst 87% of those polled agreed with the statement that 'democracy is the best political system for a country like ours' in 1991, this figure dropped to 79% in 1992 and 78% in 1993. See Marta Lagos, 'Cultura política y transición a la democracia en Chile' (unpublished manuscript, Santiago, CERC, 1993), 24.

[41] Peter McDonough, Samuel H. Barnes, and Antonio López Pina, 'The Growth of Democratic Legitimacy in Spain', *American Political Science Review*, 80/3 (1986), 751–2. The evolution of legitimacy in Latin America during the 1980s was largely unrelated to the economic situation. In Chile the erosion of legitimacy took place in the context of strong economic growth.

[42] Gabriel A. Almond and Robert J. Mundt, 'Crisis, Choice and Change: Some Tentative Conclusions', in Gabriel A. Almond, Scott C. Flanagan, and Robert J. Mundt, *Crisis, Choice and Change: Historical Studies in Political Development* (Boston, Little, Brown & Co., 1973), 621.

[43] The dependent variable (democratic legitimacy) was 'democracy is the best political system for a country like ours'. The following independent variables were included:

1. General economic   'How would you judge the present economic
   situation   situation in Spain?'
2. Personal economic   'How would you judge your own economic
   situation   situation?'

these variables account for only 11% of the variations in legitimacy reveals the extent to which legitimacy had become autonomous from respondents' opinions on the economy, politics, and policies, as well as their social position. Of all these variables, only the respondents' personal economic situation proved statistically significant. In contrast, the influence of ideology disappeared. Each one point increase in the negative evaluation of respondents' personal economic situation produced a rise of .12 in the opinion that democracy was not the best political system for the country. The worse their material situation appeared to be, the greater their reservations with respect to democracy. Thus, although legitimacy may have acquired greater autonomy, it was not immune to the influence of the economy.

Even if the abstract legitimacy of democracy could give governments greater room for manoeuvre and political systems some kind of safety 'cushion', it was impossible to know when the severity of a prolonged political and economic crisis would eventually begin to erode the cultural foundations of democracy. However much values reflected a non-instrumental conception of democracy, there was nothing to guarantee that they were immune to the influence of political experiences and material conditions of life.

The impact of economic and political experiences can be seen more clearly if, rather than examining legitimacy, we consider citizens' satisfaction with the functioning of their democracies. In the case of Southern Europe, fluctuations in this initially seem to

3. Economic policies	'Do you think that the government has performed well or badly in terms of economic development?'
4. Educational policies	'Do you think the government has performed well or badly in terms of education?'
5. Educational level	'What education have you had?'
6. Occupational position	'Are you employed or self-employed?'
7. Political sympathies of family	'With which of the sides of our civil war did your family sympathize with most?'
8. Left–right ideological position	'In what position on the scale would you place yourself?'
9. Personal political efficacy:	'People like me have no influence on what the government does.'
10. Perceptions of political corruption	'Do you consider that there is a lot, quite a lot, little, or very little corruption in public life in Spain?'
11. View of politics as too complicated	'Generally, politics appears to be so complicated that people like me cannot understand what happens.'
12. View of politicians as uncaring	'Politicians do not care very much about what people like me think.'

TABLE 5.4. *Conditions of democratic legitimacy (Spain)*

		Legitimacy of democracy
	Constant	.089
		(.304)
(i)	General economic situation	.006
		(.040)
(ii)	Personal economic situation	.122*
		(.042)
(iii)	Economic policies	.102
		(.074)
(iv)	Education policies	.094
		(.068)
(v)	Educational level	−.007
		(.007)
(vi)	Occupational position	−.068
		(.042)
(vii)	Political sympathies of family	.053
		(.064)
(viii)	Left–right ideological position	.007
		(.013)
(ix)	Personal political inefficacy	.053
		(.036)
(x)	Perceptions of political corruption	.036
		(.046)
(xi)	View of politics as too complicated	.051
		(.035)
(xii)	View of politicians as uncaring	.052
		(.043)
	R^2	.105
	Signif. F	.003
	No. of observations	273

* Statistically significant at 5% or less.

Note: Standard errors in parenthesis.

have been very closely tied to economic results. Thus, satisfaction with democracy increased considerably in Portugal and Spain during the 1980s. In Portugal it rose by 30 percentage points between 1985 and 1990, a period of political stability and economic growth under the Cavaco Silva government. In the Spanish case it increased by 20 points between 1978 and 1990, above all during the period of greatest political stability and economic efficiency in the 1980s. At the end of the decade, satisfaction with democracy in both countries equalled or surpassed that in the European Community as a whole. In Spain it declined again after 1990 in a period of economic problems and corruption. The pattern in Greece was rather different. An initially very high level of satisfaction with democracy plummeted between 1985 and 1990 as the country was hit by economic crisis and financial scandals. Fifteen years after the return to democracy, two out of every three Greek citizens were dissatisfied with the regime's performance, that is, 20 percentage points more than the average for Europe as a whole (only in Italy could similar levels of dissatisfaction be found). Table 5.5 gives data for the three Southern European countries, Czechoslovakia, and Hungary, and compares these with the Eurobarometer results for the European Community as a whole. Satisfaction with the new regime was much lower in Eastern than Southern Europe. Even where it was most widespread, namely in the former Czechoslovakia, it was still lower than in Greece. In Hungary it was less than half the Greek level, as only 14% of citizens expressed any degree of satisfaction with democracy in 1991.[44]

In all cases, however, the relationship between the economy and citizens' political interpretations was more complex than might at first seem. Non-economic factors had a significant influence on this relationship. If we consider the Spanish case, it becomes apparent that evaluations of both economic conditions and economic policies were influenced by political factors. The impact of the economy on subjective appreciations was paradoxical; negative evaluations of economic conditions were much more frequent during periods of greater economic growth and rising employment than during the earlier period of austerity. Appreciation of economic policies was never very great and was generally lower than that of economic conditions. However, negative assessments of these policies were least widespread during the period of economic crisis which lasted until spring 1985. In contrast, during the subsequent period of growth more people opposed the government's economic policies, except during a brief period between July and October 1988. Whilst disapproval fluctuated, this was not a direct consequence of the evolution of economic conditions. The most negative opinions of economic policies referred to employment; wage policies

---

[44] In Chile initially there was considerable satisfaction with the new regime: in 1990, 75% of those interviewed declared that they were 'very' or 'fairly' satisfied. Subsequently, satisfaction fell significantly, as in 1993 these answers were given by only 44% of respondents. This decline took place during a period of significant economic growth under president Patricio Aylwin. See Lagos, 'Cultura política y transición a la democracia en Chile', 24–8.

TABLE 5.5. *Satisfaction with the functioning of democracy*

	Spain			Greece		Portugal		Czecho-slovakia	Hungary	European Community as a whole	
	1985	1990	1993	1985	1990	1985	1990	1991	1991	1985	1990
Very satisfied	14	14	6	19	7	—	5	3	2	7	9
Quite satisfied	37	42	39	32	27	34	62	29	12	42	47
Quite dissatisfied	27	29	41	26	25	34	19	52	63	31	28
Totally dissatisfied	12	11	13	16	38	19	8	13	17	14	12
Don't know/Don't answer	10	4	1	7	3	13	6	3	6	6	4

Sources: Eurobarometers (Oct.–Nov. 1985 and June 1990); DATA, S.A. May 1993 poll (*Comparative National Election Project*); László Bruszt and János Simon, *Political Culture, Political and Economic Orientations in Central and Eastern Europe during the Transition to Democracy* (Budapest, Institute for Political Science, Hungarian Academy of Sciences, 1992).

generated less hostility; and social policies attracted the most favourable responses. Fig. 5.3 traces the evolution of assessments of these policies during the period of economic expansion between 1985 and 1990.

Based on data from 1993,[45] Table 5.6 shows that satisfaction with democracy varied more than the legitimacy attributed to this type of regime. Thus, the twelve independent variables taken together account for only 11% of the variation in legitimacy, but for 33% of the variation in satisfaction.[46] The table also shows that political factors had as much influence as economic ones on the level of satisfaction with democracy. Five independent variables are statistically significant and these referred to economic conditions, government policies, and the evaluation of politics. A change of one point in the assessment of the country's economic situation modified satisfaction with democracy by .23 points. A change of one point in the assessment of the government's economic and education policies led to a variation of .32 and .29 points, respectively, in the degree of satisfaction with democracy. And changes of one point in the opinions that politicians do not care about citizens and that there is a great deal of corruption in public life produced variations of .19 and .18 in satisfaction with democracy.

As noted above, Eastern Europe was characterized by widespread dissatisfaction with democracy. This was greatest in Hungary, somewhat less pronounced in Poland, and lower still in Czechoslovakia. Dissatisfaction with the new regime was always high in Hungary, where as early as 1990, 70% of the population thought that the economic situation was worse than it had been during the last five years of communist rule. In contrast, at that time only 9% of Poles shared the same opinion. Accordingly, when the Balcerowicz Plan was put into operation in January 1990 it had three times as many supporters as opponents. A large majority accepted that the sacrifices it entailed were necessary in order to assure a brighter future. However, support for, and confidence in the plan fell very rapidly. A year and a half later the initial situation had been reversed, as 71% of the population thought that the sacrifices were worthless and opposition to the reforms tripled support for them.[47] Satisfaction with the results of democracy was closely associated

---

[45] Data taken from the poll cited in n. 38.

[46] The variables are the same as those given in n. 43.

[47] Luiz Carlos Bresser Pereira, José María Maravall, and Adam Przeworski, *Economic Reforms in New Democracies* (Cambridge: Cambridge University Press, 1993), ch. 3; Przeworski, 'Intertemporal Politics: The Support for Economic Reforms in Poland' (unpublished manuscript, University of Chicago, March 1993).

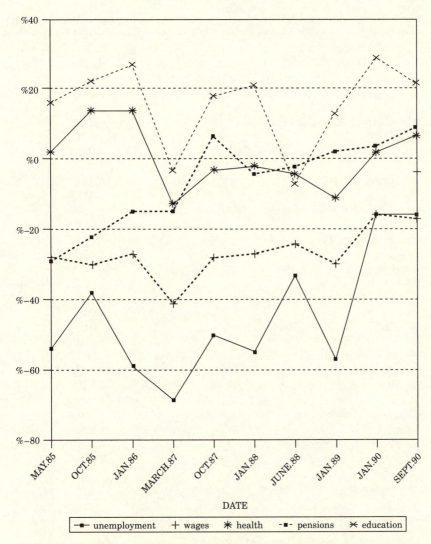

DATE

| -■- unemployment   + wages   ✳ health   -■- pensions   ✕ education |

* Difference between 'very good' and 'good', and 'very bad' and 'bad', excluding 'average'.

F IG. 5.3. *Evaluation of government policies in Spain*

Source: Centro de Investigaciones Sociológicas, polls 1,460, 1,478, 1,504, 1,614, 1,707, 1,725, 1,751, 1,785, 1,789, 1,858, and 1,884–1,889.

TABLE 5.6. *Conditions of satisfaction with democracy (Spain)*

		Satisfaction with democracy
	Constant	1.150*
		(.438)
(i)	General economic situation	.233*
		(.057)
(ii)	Personal economic situation	−.032
		(.060)
(iii)	Economic policies	.323*
		(.017)
(iv)	Education policies	.288*
		(.098)
(v)	Educational level	−.003
		(.010)
(vi)	Occupational position	−.108**
		(.060)
(vii)	Political sympathies of family	(.002
		(.092)
(viii)	Left–right ideological position	−.017
		(.019)
(ix)	Personal political inefficacy	−.006
		(.052)
(x)	Perceptions of political corruption	−.181*
		(.066)
(xi)	View of politics as too complicated	.010
		(.050)
(xii)	View of politicians as uncaring	−.185*
		(.062)
	R^2	.325
	Signif. F	.000
	No. of observations	273

* Statistically significant at 5% or less.
** Statistically significant at 10% or less.

Note: Standard errors in parenthesis.

with satisfaction with governments. This was the principal explanatory variable in Hungary, Poland, and Czechoslovakia; with a total effect reflected in a correlation coefficient of .52 and a direct effect shown by a beta regression coefficient of .35.[48] Equally, fear

[48] These figures were calculated by Araceli García del Soto and José Ignacio Torreblanca in a study carried out at the Center for Advanced Studies in the Social Sciences of the Instituto Juan March, Madrid, spring 1993. The samples of the three countries were brought together for the calculations.

of unemployment was the factor which had most impact on dissatisfaction with governments.

In Southern and Eastern Europe, therefore, whilst the legitimacy of democracy had its own roots and was largely independent of economic and political factors, government policies and the economic situation certainly did influence satisfaction with the new regimes. On the other hand, this does not resolve the question of the relationship which may exist over time between satisfaction and the legitimacy which democracies inspired.

What did citizens expect from their new political systems? If we consider Eastern Europe first, their support for democracy and for the market was accompanied by the widespread expectation that governments would reduce income inequalities, promote full employment, and provide for the needs of the unemployed, the sick, and the elderly. Accordingly, more than half the population considered that the government was responsible for assuring full employment, whilst two out of every three citizens wanted the state to guarantee a dignified life for the elderly and health care for all.[49] The proportion of citizens who thought that the state should reduce the inequalities between the rich and the poor was substantially higher than in Western European countries.[50] This high level of social demands goes a long way towards explaining the election results in Poland in 1993 and Hungary in 1994. Table 5.7 compares the responsibilities attributed to governments in Eastern and Southern Europe.

In Southern Europe, too, extensive legitimacy of democracy existed alongside pronounced social reformism, even if both constituted basically watertight compartments and a large majority saw democracy in strictly political terms. The breadth of social demands reflected a combination of Catholic protectionism and social democratic values, addressed above all to the state. Demands for improved health provision, more education, pensions for the elderly, and acceptable housing were generally articulated

[49] There were significant variations among the new democracies of Eastern Europe: 45% of Czechs, 53% of Poles, and 66% of Hungarians replied that democracy was associated with higher employment; 67% of Czechs, 71% of Poles, and 75% of Hungarians related the new regime to improved economic conditions; and 58% of Czechs, 77% of Poles, and 70% of Hungarians associated it with greater equality. See Bruszt and Simon, *Political Culture, Political and Economic Orientations in Central and Eastern Europe*, 25, 26, 28, 33, and 35.

[50] This redistributive role of the state was strongly supported ('definitely yes') by 55% of Hungarians, 47% of UK citizens, 46% of Italians, 41% of Austrians, and 27% of West Germans. See János Simon and László Bruszt, 'The Development of Party Preferences in Hungary', in *Demokratikus Átmenetek* (Evkönyv Magyar Politikatudományi Társaság, Budapest, 1991), 174–6.

TABLE 5.7. *Assignment of responsibility to government*

[To what extent do you think the following are the responsibility of the government?]	Spain		Czechoslovakia		Hungary		Poland	
	To a great extent	To some extent	Definitely	Probably	Definitely	Probably	Definitely	Probably
To provide work for all those who want it	60	33	55	31	70	19	62	26
To provide health care	62	32	77	20	87	11	65	29
To assure a decent standard of living for the elderly	59	34	79	18	89	9	64	32
To assure a decent standard of living for the unemployed	55	36	42	40	58	24	18	36
To reduce the differences between the rich and poor	50	34	37	27	56	24	25	36

Sources: Centro de Investigaciones Sociológicas, poll 1,730 (1988); László Bruszt and János Simon, *Political Culture, Political and Economic Orientations in Central and Eastern Europe during the Transition to Democracy* (Budapest, Institute of Political Science, Hungarian Academy of Sciences, 1992), 101–5.

in terms of citizens' rights, that is, in universalist terms. The incidence of these demands also explains to a large extent the electoral support for the PASOK in Greece and the PSOE in Spain during the 1980s.

To what extent did this social reformism evolve over time? Fifteen years after the return to democracy, egalitarianism and reformism were still widely instilled in Southern European societies. In Spain a large majority rejected the idea that inequalities were an inevitable product of human nature. On the contrary, four out of five Spaniards believed that inequalities could be reduced through the implementation of appropriate policies, whilst some 70% considered that the government was responsible for ensuring the welfare of each and every citizen. In comparative terms this statist-reformist profile was very striking. In France in 1985, for example, only 44% of the population assigned responsibility for these issues to the government.[51] It is clear that these types of demands may generate serious complications for governments, especially when large inequalities exist and in the context of major economic difficulties.

Large inequalities certainly existed when the democracies were re-established in Southern Europe. In previous chapters I have discussed the distributive consequences of the authoritarian regimes and the extension of social policies under democracy. The development of these policies was largely a consequence of the strong electoral support given to the left in all three countries and of a combination of 'pressure from below' and 'reforms from above' during the Spanish transition. The result was that governments understood that citizenship comprised not just political, but also social rights. This was a very important aspect of the political consensus at the beginning of the transition in Spain which was articulated for the first time in the Moncloa Pacts of 1977. The new regimes used both taxation and public spending to substantially intensify their redistributive policies, so reducing inequalities in the territorial and individual distribution of income.

However, social demands remained extensive. In general, many believed that governments did too little in relation to inequality and that they benefited the wealthy more than was desirable. Nevertheless, this opinion was accompanied by a certain amount of optimism. Thus, in Spain at the end of the 1980s, those who thought that social inequality had been reduced in recent years outnumbered those who believed the opposite by two to one, whilst

---

[51] This figure has been taken from Sondages BVA, *Expansion*, 1985.

the majority of people also expected inequality to continue to decline.[52] And although the urgency of these demands, as well as the fact that social expectations were not matched by economic resources, always constituted major problems for the governments of Southern Europe, provoking conflicts with the unions, they were not the principal difficulty facing these governments. For this was much more closely related to the hostility generated by economic policies and, above all, to politics rather than policies.

The variations in the subjective foundations of democracy were not only a consequence of the economic situation, but also of political factors. The legitimacy of democracy and above all satisfaction with its effects were dependent on a complex combination of interpretations of politics and the economy. In all three Southern European countries, the democratic experience was characterized by both considerable legitimacy and extensive political disaffection. The latter was expressed in determined visions of politics and politicians, of individuals' ability to influence politics, and of institutions and parties.

In general terms, there was a considerable lack of interest in politics, mistrust was widespread, and scepticism and apathy were shared by a large number of citizens. During the 1980s, democratic politics provoked the indifference, boredom, or distrust of a majority of the Portuguese and Spaniards. As can be seen in Table 5.8, only about one in four people conformed to the democratic ideal of the interested and active citizen. In comparative terms, the very high levels of politicization, interest, and participation in Greece were something of an exception. However, the Greeks, Portuguese, and Spaniards shared extensive suspicion of politicians. Table 5.9 reveals that between two-thirds and three-quarters of all citizens thought that politicians did not care about people like them, and that those in power always pursued their own interests. It will be remembered that in Tables 5.4 and 5.6 four of the twelve independent variables reflected political disaffection. And, whilst they did not affect the legitimacy of democracy, two of these variables had statistically significant consequences for satisfaction with democracy.

Mistrust of politics and politicians was also very widespread in Eastern Europe. In Hungary and Poland, some two-thirds of the population agreed with the statement that 'whilst things go well,

---

[52] These data have been obtained from polls carried out by the Centro de Investigaciones Sociológicas in Feb. and June 1988 and by Demoscopia S. A. in Mar.–Apr. 1989.

TABLE 5.8. *Sentiments towards politics (Southern Europe)*

	Spain			Greece	Portugal
	1980	1985	1991	1985	1985
Positive sentiments (interest, enthusiasm, passion).	27	29	23	64	20
Active negative sentiments (irritation, hostility, disgust).	4	10	12	8	16
Passive negative sentiments (indifference, boredom, mistrust).	64	55	58	27	52
Don't know/Didn't answer.	5	6	7	1	12

Source: Centro de Investigaciones Sociológicas, polls 1,237, 1,461, and 1,984.

I do not care who is in power'. And some three-quarters of citizens thought that it was unwise to trust politicians. This political disaffection was accompanied by considerable pessimism among the citizens of the new European democracies as to their capacity to influence political decisions, a characteristic which was particularly pronounced in the post-communist societies. Only 5% of Poles and 20% of Hungarians thought they could do anything if their governments took an unjust decision. Although political pessimism was less prevalent in Hungary than in Poland, even there the proportion of those who felt they could influence politics was three times lower than in Britain, half of that of Italy, and comparable only to that of Spain.[53]

It is true that disaffection exists in all democracies, that it has been on the increase since the 1970s,[54] and also that this tendency cannot be explained in terms of the evolution of the economy alone. It is also the case that the anti-party politics and protest vote seen in many countries are rooted in that tendency. Yet the level of disaffection, mistrust and alienation is lower in the old democracies. If we understand 'political cynicism' as the idea that the

[53] Distrust of politics and politicians was also high in Brazil, Argentina, Peru, and Uruguay. In Chile, for example, and depending on how the question was phrased, these sentiments were expressed by between two-thirds and three-quarters of the population. See the data in the studies by Moisés and Lagos cited in n. 37, p. 165, and n. 40, p. 35.

[54] Russell Dalton, *Citizen Politics in Western Democracies: Public Opinion and Political Parties in the United States, Great Britain, West Germany and France* (Chatham, NJ, Chatham House, 1988), e.g. 226.

TABLE 5.9. *Opinions of politics and politicians*

Agreement with the following statements about politics and politicians	Spain	Greece	Portugal	Czecho-slovakia	Hungary	Poland
Politics is too complicated for people like me to understand it.	65	62	67	—	—	—
It is better not to get involved in politics because you will get your fingers burnt.	—	—	—	54	41	70
Ordinary people are always excluded from power.	—	—	—	74	78	86
It is better not to trust politicians.	—	—	—	57	80	71
Regardless of who is in power, politicians always defend their own interests.	63	64	78	—	—	—
Politicians do not care about people like me.	64	49	77	—	—	—

Sources: Centro de Investigaciones Sociológicas, polls 1,461 and 1,788; László Bruszt and János Simon, *Political Culture, Political and Economic Orientations in Central and Eastern Europe during the Transition to Democracy* (Budapest, Institute of Political Science, Hungarian Academy of Sciences, 1992), 107.

realities of political life diverge from ideals which supposedly drive politics, that these ideals are hypocritical, and that politicians' words do not reflect their real intentions,[55] then the difference between old and new democracies oscillates between 15 and 25 points.[56]

The passage of time does not appear to have had any effect in this respect. As can be seen in Table 5.8, interest in politics in Spain did not increase between 1980 and 1991. Nor did mistrust of politicians vary significantly. Only the feeling of personal political inefficacy seems to have declined a little. This syndrome of disinterest, mistrust and impotence was, therefore, both more pronounced than in the old democracies and very stable over time. Moreover, it existed alongside the extensive legitimacy of democracy, a varying degree of satisfaction with its results which was not solely influenced by the economic situation, limited support for economic policies, and a more positive evaluation of social policies.

What were the causes of this syndrome in the political cultures of the new democracies in Southern and Eastern Europe? It is quite possible that it reflected those factors we noted at the beginning of this chapter, namely a long experience of dictatorships and pseudo-democracies, a history of political turbulence and discontinuities, manipulated elections over long periods, and a prolonged negative socialization into politics. In this sense, citizens' evaluations of politics and their personal influence may be considered simply a rational response, the result of a historical experience which would hardly have encouraged trust in politics. If this was indeed the case, it could also be argued that as time passed perceptions of politics would change and the cultural roots of democracy would grow stronger. In this way, the weakness of civil societies, of organizational networks, and of interest representation, which had failed to adequately channel the latent demands of different social groups and undermined feelings of personal political efficacy in the past, could gradually be overcome. The multiplication of expectations, which is so typical of the early stages of new democracies, would also be contained. Thus, after

[55] Putnam, *Beliefs of Politicians*, 89, 90, 232.

[56] Thus, only 40% of British citizens believed that, regardless of who is in power, politicians always further their own interests. This percentage rose to 54% in the United States, where 59% and 52% of the population believed, respectively, that politicians should not be trusted and that they do not care about people. See Budge, *Agreement and the Stability of Democracy*, 124; Seymour Martin Lipset and William Schneider, *The Confidence Gap* (New York, Free Press, 1983), 17 and 22.

the inevitable periods of disenchantment of the type witnessed in Southern and Eastern Europe, the links between the legitimacy and the results of the new democracies would be weakened.

However, this line of argument is debatable. The citizens' views of politics do not necessarily improve with time. In Southern Europe the intermediate associations (including the unions) became weaker rather than stronger during the 1980s. As seen above, in Spain the passage of time also failed to alter citizens' perception of politics.[57] Moreover, many of the new democracies can scarcely guarantee economic development and administrative efficiency in the immediate future. A complacent and passive vision of the positive effects of the passage of time not only ignores the political risks which might arise as a result of profound and prolonged economic or political crises, but also the obvious fact that the subjective foundations of democracies may be affected by citizens' immediate experience of politics.

There are at least three fields in which this is so. The first is that of symbolic politics. The impact of the symbolic example of political leaders is especially significant in periods of major change, profound economic and political transformations, modifications in normative worlds, weakly structured civil societies, and tendencies for what O'Donnell has called 'delegative politics'.[58] Diamond has emphasized the influence which certain political leaders have had on the political culture of their countries, citing the cases of Kemal Atatürk, Mahatma Gandhi, and Sun Yat-sen.[59] Here, however, I am referring to a much wider group of politicians. Questions relating to the recruitment of politicians and the political rules of the game are particularly important if the quality of politicians is not irrelevant in the new democracies. The idea that politics is a fraud and that politicians are all the same may be reinforced by the behaviour of politicians themselves and not just residues of past experiences. When this happens, the spiral of deterioration of democratic politics makes the regime very vulnerable to those elements of the mass media and economic and political circles which repudiate the regime as a whole and flourish in

[57] Additional and exhaustive evidence on the stability of perceptions of politics over time is provided in Mariano Torcal, *Actitudes políticas y participación política en España: Pautas de cambio y continuidad* (Ph.D. thesis, Universidad Autónoma de Madrid, 1995), 177–98.

[58] Guillermo O'Donnell, 'Delegative Democracy?', *Working Paper 172* (University of Notre Dame, Kellogg Institute, 1992).

[59] Larry Diamond, 'Causes and Effects', in Diamond (ed.), *Political Culture and Democracy in Developing Countries*, 229–49.

cultures of political cynicism. In all democracies, but above all in the new ones, there are moral and pedagogical aspects of politics which politicians should not ignore. For political disaffection may be the result of their negligence in this respect, and not just of bad policies or adverse objective conditions. Numerous examples testify to the way in which a combination of negative symbolic politics and economic conditions produce explosive results. This can lead to a serious erosion of legitimacy and a tendency towards demagogic economic policies. Evidently corruption has a particularly corrosive effect on citizens' perceptions of politics and politicians. And corruption in relation to both the illegal funding of parties and personal enrichment was an important political issue in Southern and Eastern Europe. As noted above, the belief that corruption was widespread and that politicians did not care about people had a statistically significant impact on satisfaction with, if not the legitimacy of, democracy in Spain.

The second field is that of economic and educational inequalities. The impact which both of these have on democratic values is a well-established subject of political analysis for which there is abundant empirical evidence.[60] Everywhere these inequalities are linked to political scepticism, pessimism regarding personal capacity to influence events, and political participation (even if not always on electoral turn-out). This relation is found in a large number of Western countries, in India, Nigeria, Japan, Israel, and Bangladesh, in the new democracies of Southern and Eastern Europe as well as in those of Latin America. Five years after the re-establishment of democracy in Spain, the influence of educational inequalities on the feeling of political efficacy could be seen in the fact that the proportion of university graduates who felt politically effective was four times higher than that of those with less than primary education. Fifteen years after the change of regime, interest in politics was three times greater among the former.[61] In Greece and Portugal the differences in level of interest among

[60] Alex Inkeles and David H. Smith, *Becoming Modern: Individual Change in Six Developing Countries* (Cambridge, Mass., Harvard University Press, 1974), 133–43, 240–3; Sidney Verba, Norman H. Nie, and Jae-on Kim, *Participation and Political Equality* (Cambridge, Cambridge University Press, 1978); 157–71, 173–214, 286–309; Ronald Inglehart, *The Silent Revolution: Changing Values and Political Styles Among Western Publics* (Princeton, NJ, Princeton University Press, 1977), 72–98, 195–215; Samuel Barnes, Max Kaase *et al.*, *Political Action: Mass Participation in Five Western Democracies* (Beverly Hills, Calif.: Sage, 1979), 120–8, 148–9; Almond and Verba, *Civil Culture*, 162–73.

[61] Maravall, *Transition to Democracy in Spain*, 80–3; Centro de Investigaciones Sociológicas, poll 1,993, Feb.–Mar., 1992.

people with these educational levels were of 29 and 45 percentage points respectively.[62] Fig. 5.4 shows the impact of educational inequalities in Southern Europe. Whilst these inequalities did not affect legitimacy, they did influence political alienation. Moreover, the evaluation of egalitarian policies also had an important influence on the level of satisfaction with democracy. As can be seen in Table 5.6, a positive evaluation of education policies had a statistically significant impact on the level of satisfaction with democracy in Spain. As for economic inequalities, in Hungary these produced a 37-point variation in the preference for democracy as opposed to dictatorship. In other words, in this case they did affect legitimacy.[63] A non-minimalist conception of democracy cannot ignore the fact that social inequalities lead to political inequalities, nor that the exercise of political rights is affected by differences in social position. The reduction of poverty and inequality and the expansion of education foment democratic values, facilitate political participation, and, in countries with adverse economic circumstances, help democracy to survive.

The third and final field is that of institutions and political parties. Little is known about the political effects of distinct partisan structures. Yet the parties are certainly the principal actors in the democratic game and hence constitute a crucial nexus between politics and civil society. Years ago Huntington argued that those societies with weak parties have a greater propensity to military intervention and to states which manipulate the pluralism of interest representation.[64] In Southern, but especially Eastern Europe, political parties enjoyed extensive legitimacy which correlated very closely to the legitimacy of democracy itself. However, this legitimacy was also accompanied by deep disaffection. In Spain, Portugal, Greece, Hungary, and Poland, parties were the institution which attracted least support. A sizeable proportion of citizens thought that there were no differences between the parties and that they merely served to create divisions among people.

How did the passing of time affect these views? The legitimacy of the parties did not decline, but the level of disaffection increased. Growing numbers of people believed that politics were increasingly controlled by bureaucratic oligarchies, that those elected had

[62] Centro de Investigaciones Sociológicas, poll 1,461, May–June 1985.

[63] In a country like Brazil, education produced a difference of 28 points in support for democracy and 39 points in interest in politics: see Moisés, 'Eleições, participação e cultura política', 160–70.

[64] Samuel P. Huntington, *Political Order in Changing Societies* (New Haven, Yale University Press, 1968), 192–264.

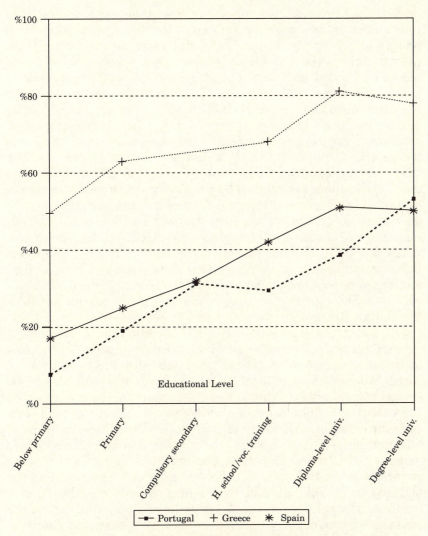

F IG. 5.4. *Interest in politics and educational levels in Southern Europe*
(% positive sentiments)

Source: Centro de Investigaciones Sociológicas, polls 1,461 and 1,993 for
May–June 1985 and Feb.–Mar. 1992.

come to depend more heavily on the party machines than on voters, that political clientelism had become firmly established, that
ideas and principles had been replaced by power and intrigue, and
that parties lacked internal democracy. As a result, important
problems emerged with regard to the parties' role as mediators

between politics and civil society. In Spain, for example, the idea that all the parties were the same rose by 50 points between 1980 and 1992, whilst there was a 17-point increase in the idea that parties only served to divide people. Opposition to closed and blocked electoral lists was considerable.[65] In fact, the control of politics by party leaders was an important feature of the three Southern European democracies. This was originally a consequence of the low levels of party affiliation and participation, the inexperience of democratic politics, and an overriding concern to avoid political instability. However, it had a number of consequences: the rigid control of the parliamentary groups by the party bureaucracies, a tendency reinforced by the electoral systems; strict party discipline, at the cost of internal democracy; and the politicization of institutions, as a consequence of the distribution of appointments by party quotas. Although the experience of democracy was much shorter in Eastern Europe, here too the divisions and internal splits, the manipulation of sentiments such as nationalism and religion, populist tendencies, and the vague political identities of the parties scarcely encouraged societies to see parties as fulfilling the ideal role that they ascribed to them.

The connection between parties and society and the question of internal party democracy became important political issues in many of the new democracies. These are fields of political analysis in which much remains to be done, since after the Second World War democratic theory has tended to neglect them on the grounds that the essential condition for democracy was genuine electoral competition between a plurality of parties. However, neither the disaffection of the citizens nor the type of politicians which democracies generate are trivial problems. For whilst it is likely that they generally affect the quality of the new democracies more than the stability or consolidation of the regimes themselves, during economic and/or political crises they may have a major impact on the prospects for democracy itself. Even if it were true that democracies could survive indefinitely without ever becoming consolidated, the quality of political life could be the exact opposite of the democratic ideal. And if excessive expectations and over-mobilized participation might in certain circumstances undermine democratic stability, there is no reason why this should lead to the conclusion that the predominant attitude among citizens should consist of political impotence, mistrust, alienation, and apathy towards democratic politics.

[65] Demoscopia, *Barómetro de Primavera*, 1992. See *El País*, 5 Apr. 1992.

TABLE 5.10. *Opinions of political parties (Southern and Eastern Europe)*

Agreement with the following statements	Spain			Greece	Portugal	Czecho-slovakia	Hungary	Poland
	1980	1985	1992	1985	1985	1991	1991	1991
There is no democracy without parties.	61	62	65	64	60	86	90	83
Political participation is possible thanks to the parties.	53	62	60	78	58	84	87	89
Parties only serve to divide people.	24	38	41	64	59	—	—	—
Parties only serve the interests of their leaders.	—	—	—	—	—	38	48	53
All the parties are the same.	13	49	63	45	63	28	32	46

Sources: Centro de Investigaciones Sociológicas, polls 1,237 (July 1980), 1,461 (May–June 1985), and 1,993 (Feb. 1992); László Bruszt and János Simon, *Political Culture, Political and Economic Orientations in Central and Eastern Europe during the Transition to Democracy* (Budapest, Institute for Political Science, Hungarian Academy of Sciences, 1992), 119–22.

However, these subjective universes of the new democracies are sometimes regarded with resignation or cynicism. After many citizens have become sceptical about their politicians, many politicians (with the support of many social scientists) have become sceptical about their citizens. Diamond is right when he affirms that

the erosion of democracy then becomes a matter not just of socio-economic change producing social mobilization in the context of stagnant and inadequate political institutions. It may also involve subtle and not-so-subtle cultural decay, in which politicians' commitments to democracy revert to an instrumental form and democrats lose the energizing force of deep conviction in the innate value of democracy itself.[66]

When this happens, the result is political conservatism and democratic impoverishment. If people express indifference or hostility towards politics, this becomes an additional argument in favour of keeping them at a distance. If politicians are not respected, this is attributed to a 'natural state' of things. However, there is no reason why this 'natural state' should be accepted as given, if in fact symbolic behaviour, social inequalities, and institutional arrangements all influence visions of politics. Nor is there any good reason to think that the passage of time alone is sufficient to strengthen the links between citizens and democratic politics. Equally, if democracies face difficult material conditions, disaffection may prove politically disastrous.

[66] Diamond, 'Causes and Effects', 243.

....

Appendix 1

....

The Impact of Economies on Regimes: A Chronology of Comparative Quantitative Studies

Seymour Martin Lipset, 'Some Social Requisites of Democracy: Economic Development and Political Legitimacy', *American Political Science Review*, 53 (1959). Study of 46 European, English-speaking, and Latin American countries. Conclusion: positive effect of thirteen indices of development on democracy.

James S. Coleman, 'Conclusion: The Political Systems of Developing Areas', in Gabriel A. Almond and James S. Coleman (eds.), *The Politics of Developing Areas* (Princeton, NJ, Princeton University Press, 1960). Study of 75 countries. Conclusion: positive effect of development on democracy.

Phillips Cutright, 'National Political Development: Measurement and Analysis', *American Sociological Review*, 28 (1963). Study of 77 countries between 1940 and 1961. Conclusion: positive effect of development on democracy.

Bruce M. Russett, *Trends in World Politics* (New York, Macmillan, 1965). Study of 89 countries. Conclusion: positive effect of development on democracy.

Deane E. Neubauer, 'Some Conditions of Democracy', *American Political Science Review*, 61 (1967). Study of 23 countries. Conclusion: weak effect of development (through the expansion of communications).

Donald J. McCrone and Charles F. Cnudde, 'Toward A Communications Theory of Democratic Political Development: A Causal Model', *American Political Science Review*, 61 (1967). Re-examination of Cutright's data for 77 countries. Conclusion: positive effect of development on democracy, through the spread of communications due to education and urbanization.

Marvin E. Olsen, 'Multivariate Analysis of National Political Development', *American Sociological Review*, 33 (1968). Study of 115 countries. Conclusion: positive effect of development on democracy.

Phillips Cutright and James A. Wiley, 'Modernization and Political Representation: 1927–1966', *Studies in Comparative International Development*, 5 (1969). Study of 40 countries between 1927 and 1966. Conclusion: positive effect, albeit mediated by the level of literacy and social security provision.

Arthur K. Smith, 'Socioeconomic Development and Political Democracy: A Causal Analysis', *Midwest Journal of Political Science*, 13 (1969). Study of 110 countries between 1946 and 1955. Conclusion: positive effect of development on democracy, except in sub-Saharan Africa.

Gilbert R. Winham, 'Political Development and Lerner's Theory: Further Test of a Causal Model', *American Political Science Review*, 64 (1970). Longitudinal study of the United States. Conclusion: positive effect of development on democracy, above all through education and communications.

Arthur S. Banks, 'Modernization and Political Change: The Latin American and Amer-European Nations', *Comparative Political Studies*, 2 (1970). Study of 36 countries between 1868 and 1963. Conclusion: positive effect of development on democracy.

Robert A. Dahl, *Polyarchy* (New Haven, Conn., Yale University Press, 1971). Study of 144 countries around 1969. Conclusion: positive effect of development on democracy.

William Flanigan and Edwin Fogelman, 'Patterns of Political Development and Democratization: A Quantitative Analysis', in John V. Gillespie and Betty A. Nesvold (eds.), *Macro-Quantitative Analysis: Conflict, Development and Democratization* (Beverly Hills, Calif., Sage, 1971). Study of 29 countries between 1800 and 1960. Conclusion: positive effect, in terms of both stability and persistence, of development on democracy.

Robert W. Jackman, 'On the Relation of Economic Development to Democratic Performance', *American Journal of Political Science*, 17 (1973). Study of 60 countries. Conclusion: positive effect, but in a curvilinear relation.

Philip Coulter, *Social Mobilization and Liberal Democracy* (Lexington, Mass., Lexington Books, 1975). Study of 85 countries. Conclusion: positive effect of development on democracy.

Kenneth A. Bollen, 'Political Democracy and the Timing of Development', *American Sociological Review*, 44 (1979). Study of 99 countries. Conclusion: positive effect of development on democracy.

George M. Thomas, Francisco O. Ramirez, John W. Meyer, and Jeanne G. Gobalet, 'Maintaining National Boundaries in the World System: The Rise of Centralist Regimes', in John W. Meyer and Michael T. Hannan (eds.), *National Development and the World System* (Chicago, University of Chicago Press, 1979). Study of 102 countries between 1950 and 1965 and between 1960 and 1975. Conclusion: positive effect of development on democracy.

Kenneth A. Bollen, 'Issues in the Comparative Measurement of Political Democracy', *American Sociological Review*, 45/3 (1980). Data on 113 countries in 1960 and 123 in 1965. Conclusion: positive effect of development on democracy.

Larry Diamond, 'The Social Foundations of Democracy: The Case of Nigeria', Ph.D. thesis (Stanford University, 1980). Calculations referring to 123 countries. Conclusion: positive effect of development on democracy.

Michael T. Hannan and Glenn R. Carroll, 'Dynamics of Formal Political

Structure: An Event-History Analysis', *American Sociological Review*, 46 (1981). Study of 90 countries between 1950 and 1975. Conclusion: development stabilizes dictatorships.

G. Bingham Powell Jr., *Contemporary Democracies: Participation, Stability and Violence* (Cambridge, Mass., Harvard University Press, 1982). Data for 29 countries between 1965 and 1972. Conclusion: positive effect of development on democracy.

Kenneth A. Bollen and Robert W. Jackman, 'World System Position, Dependency and Democracy: The Cross-National Evidence', *American Sociological Review*, 48 (1983). Conclusion: if countries are situated on the periphery or semi-periphery of the world economy, the effect of development on democracy is less probable.

Samuel P. Huntington, 'Will More Countries Become Democratic?', *Political Science Quarterly*, 99/2 (1984). Study of 120 countries in 1981. Conclusion: development promotes democratization.

Kenneth A. Bollen and Robert W. Jackman, 'Economic and Non-Economic Determinants of Political Democracy in the 1960s', *Research in Political Sociology*, 1 (1985). Study of 109 countries between 1960 and 1965. Conclusion: positive effect of development on democracy, but in a curvilinear relation.

Glaucio A. D. Soares, 'Desenvolvimento econômico e democracia na America Latina', *Dados*, 30 (1987). Study of countries in Western Europe, the English-speaking world, and Latin America. Conclusion: development has effects on democracy in the first two regions, but not in the third.

Zehra F. Arat, 'Democracy and Economic Development: Modernization Theory Revisited', *Comparative Politics*, 21/1 (1988). Study of 130 countries between 1948 and 1977. Conclusion: the level of development is not a sufficient condition for democratization.

John F. Helliwell, 'Empirical Linkages between Democracy and Economic Growth', NBER Working Paper no. 4066 (Cambridge, Mass., National Bureau of Economic Research, 1992). Study of 90 countries between 1960 and 1985. Conclusion: positive effect of development on democracy.

Larry Diamond, 'Economic Development and Democracy Reconsidered', in Gary Marks and Larry Diamond (eds.), *Reexamining Democracy* (Newbury Park, Calif., Sage Publications, 1992). Study of 142 countries between 1989 and 1990. Conclusion: positive effect of development on democracy.

Seymour M. Lipset, Kyoung-Ryung Seong, and John C. Torres, 'A Comparative Analysis of the Social Requisites of Democracy', *International Social Science Journal*, 136 (1993). Study of 104 countries in 1960, 1965, 1975, 1980, and 1985. Conclusion: positive effect of development on democracy.

Adam Przeworski and Fernando Limongi, 'Modernization: Theories and Facts' (unpublished manuscript, 1994). Study of 139 countries between 1950 and 1990. Conclusion: development is irrelevant for the establishment of democracies, but the growth rate is crucial for the survival of regimes.

Ross E. Burkhart and Michael S. Lewis-Beck, 'Comparative Democracy: The Economic Development Thesis', *American Political Science Review*, 88/4 (1994). Study of 131 countries between 1972 and 1989. Conclusion: the level of economic development improves the prospects for democracy.

....

Appendix 2

....

The Impact of Regimes on Economies: A Chronology of Comparative Quantitative Studies

Adam Przeworski, 'Party Systems and Economic Development', Ph.D. thesis (Northwestern University, 1966). Study of 57 countries between 1949 and 1963. Conclusion: mobilizing dictatorships in middle levels of development, followed by democracies, promote development most.

Irma Adelman and Cynthia F. Morris, *Society, Politics, and Economic Development* (Baltimore, Johns Hopkins University Press, 1967). Study of 74 countries between 1950 and 1964. Conclusion: dictatorships have some positive effects at low or middle levels of development, but not at higher levels.

Ivo K. Feierabend and Rosalind L. Feierabend, 'Coerciveness and Change: Cross-National Trends', *American Behavioral Scientist*, 15 (1972). Study of 84 countries before 1965. Conclusion: there is no difference.

William G. Dick, 'Authoritarian versus Nonauthoritarian Approaches to Economic Development', *Journal of Political Economy*, 82 (1974). Study of 59 under-developed countries between 1959 and 1968. Conclusion: democracies generate more growth.

Samuel P. Huntington and Jorge I. Domínguez, 'Political Development', in Fred I. Greenstein and Nelson W. Polsby (eds.), *Handbook of Political Science*, iii (Reading, Mass., Addison-Wesley, 1975). Study of 35 under-developed countries during the 1950s. Conclusion: dictatorships generate more growth.

Bruce M. Russett and R. Joseph Monsen, 'Bureaucracy and Polyarchy as Predictors of Performance: A Cross-National Examination', *Comparative Political Studies*, 8 (1975). Study of 80 countries down to 1965. Conclusion: there is no difference.

Robert M. Marsh, 'Does Democracy Hinder Economic Development in the Latecomer Developing Nations?', *Comparative Social Research*, 2 (1979). Study of 98 countries between 1955 and 1970. Conclusion: dictatorships generate more growth.

John W. Meyer, Michael T. Hannan, Richard Rubinson, and George M. Thomas, 'National Economic Development, 1950–70: Social and Political Factors', in John W. Meyer and Michael T. Hannan (eds.), *National Development and the World System* (Chicago, University of Chicago

Press, 1979). Study of 50 countries down to 1970. Conclusion: there is no difference.

Erich Weede, 'The Impact of Democracy on Economic Growth: Some Evidence from Cross-National Analysis', *Kiklos*, 36 (1983). Study of 124 countries between 1960 and 1974. Conclusion: dictatorships generate more growth.

Dirk Berg-Schlosser, 'African Political Systems: Typology and Performance', *Comparative Political Studies*, 17 (1984). Study of 38 African countries until the early 1980s. Conclusion: in certain conditions, authoritarianism generates more growth.

Roger C. Kormendi and Philip G. Meguire, 'Macroeconomic Determinants of Growth', *Journal of Monetary Economics*, 16 (1985). Study of 47 countries between 1950 and 1977. Conclusion: democracies generate more growth.

Atul Kohli, 'Democracy and Development', in John P. Lewis and Valeriana Kallab (eds.), *Development Strategies Reconsidered* (New Brunswick, NJ., Transaction Publishers, 1986). Study of ten under-developed countries between 1960 and 1982. Conclusion: there was no difference during the 1960s, but a slight difference in favour of the dictatorships in the 1970s.

Daniel Landau, 'Government and Economic Growth in the Less-Developed Countries: An Empirical Study for 1960–1980', *Economic Development and Cultural Change*, 35 (1986). Study of 65 countries between 1960 and 1980. Conclusion: dictatorships generate more growth.

John P. Sloan and Kent L. Tedin, 'The Consequences of Regime Type for Public Policy Outputs', *Comparative Political Studies*, 20 (1987). Study of twenty Latin American countries between 1960 and 1979. Conclusion: growth is greatest under bureaucratic authoritarian regimes, followed by democracies and traditional military dictatorships, in that order.

Abbas Pourgerami, 'The Political Economy of Development: A Cross-National Causality Test of Development-Democracy-Growth Hypothesis', *Public Choice*, 58 (1988). Study of 92 countries between 1965 and 1984. Conclusion: democracies generate greater growth.

Robert M. Marsh, 'Sociological Explanations of Economic Growth', *Studies in Comparative International Research*, 13 (1988). Study of 47 countries between 1965 and 1984. Conclusion: there are no differences.

Frank Vorhies and Fred Glahe, 'Political Liberty and Social Development: An Empirical Investigation', *Public Choice*, 58 (1988). Study of 150 countries between 1973 and 1984. Conclusion: democracies generate more growth.

Gerald W. Scully, 'The Institutional Framework and Economic Development', *Journal of Political Economy*, 96 (1988). Study of 115 countries between 1960 and 1980. Conclusion: democracies generate more growth.

Robert J. Barro, 'A Cross-Country Study of Growth, Saving, and Government', NBER Working Paper no. 2855 (Cambridge, Mass., National Bureau of Economic Research, 1989). Study of 72 countries between 1960 and 1985. Conclusion: democracies generate more growth.

Kevin B. Grier and Gordon Tullock, 'An Empirical Analysis of Cross-National Economic Growth, 1951–80', *Journal of Monetary Economics*, 24 (1989). Study of 59 countries between 1961 and 1980. Conclusion: democracies in Latin America and Africa generate more growth, whilst there is no difference in East Asia.

Karen L. Remmer, 'Democracy and Economic Crisis: The Latin-American Experience', *World Politics*, 62 (1990). Study of eleven Latin American countries between 1982 and 1988. Conclusion: slight difference in favour of the democracies.

Larry Sirowy and Alex Inkeles, 'The Effects of Democracy on Economic Growth and Inequality: A Review', in Alex Inkeles (ed.), *On Measuring Democracy* (New Brunswick, NJ., Transaction Publishers, 1991). Re-evaluation of thirteen studies carried out before 1988. Conclusion: there is no difference.

Abbas Pourgerami, 'The Political Economy of Development: An Empirical Investigation of the Wealth Theory of Democracy', *Journal of Theoretical Politics*, 3 (1991). Study of 106 under-developed countries in 1986. Conclusion: democracies generate more growth.

John F. Helliwell, 'Empirical Linkages between Democracy and Economic Growth', NBER Working Paper no. 4066 (Cambridge, Mass., National Bureau of Economic Research, 1992). Study of 98 countries between 1960 and 1985. Conclusion: there is no difference.

Gerald W. Scully, *Constitutional Environments and Economic Growth* (Princeton, NJ, Princeton University Press, 1992). Study of 115 countries between 1960 and 1985. Conclusion: democracies generate more growth.

Marc Lindenberg and Shantayanan Devarajan, 'Prescribing Strong Economic Medicine: Revisiting the Myths about Structural Adjustment, Democracy, and Economic Performance in Developing Countries', *Comparative Politics*, 25/2 (1993). Study of 69 dictatorships and 23 democracies during the period 1973–81, and 59 dictatorships and 33 democracies during the period 1982–8. Conclusion: democracies promote growth more than the dictatorships do (but the established democratic regimes more than the new ones).

Fernando Limongi and Adam Przeworski, 'Democracy and Development in South America, 1945–1988', Working Paper no. 1994/55 (Madrid, Center for Advanced Studies in the Social Sciences, Instituto Juan March de Estudios e Investigaciones, 1994). Study of ten Latin American countries between 1946 and 1988. Conclusion: there are no differences in the rate of growth, but democracies are more capable of surviving.

Surjit S. Bhalla, 'Freedom and Economic Growth: A Virtuous Circle?' (unpublished manuscript presented at the I Symposium on Democracy, Nobel Foundation/University of Uppsala, 1994). Study of 90 countries between 1973 and 1990. Conclusion: democracies generate more growth.

········

Appendix 3

········

The Redistributive Effects of Social Democracy:
A Chronology of Comparative Quantitative Studies

Frank Parkin, *Class Inequality and Political Order* (London, Palladin, 1972). Greater social mobility and meritocratic education policies under social democratic governments, but not greater equality of condition.

Robert W. Jackman, *Politics and Social Equality: A Comparative Analysis* (New York, John Wiley, 1975). The egalitarian tendencies in the distribution of resources are due to economic growth and its consequences on market forces, and are not derived from politics.

Richard Scase, *Social Democracy in Capitalist Society* (London, Croom Helm, 1977). Neither greater mobility nor income equality, but greater educational opportunities under social democratic governments.

Christopher Hewitt, 'The Effect of Political Democracy and Social Democracy on Equality in Industrial Societies', *American Sociological Review*, 42 (1977). Not greater educational opportunities, but greater income redistribution under social democracy.

Douglas A. Hibbs, 'Political Parties and Macroeconomic Policy', *American Political Science Review*, 71 (1977). Less unemployment under social democratic governments.

Francis G. Castles, *The Social Democratic Image of Society* (London, Routledge, 1978). Higher fiscal revenues and greater expenditure on education under social democratic governments.

John Dryzeck, 'Politics, Economics, and Inequality: A Cross-National Analysis', *European Journal of Political Research*, 6 (1978). Lesser income concentration in the case of social democratic governments.

Edward Tufte, *Political Control of the Economy* (Princeton, NJ, Princeton University Press, 1978). Greater redistribution through social democratic fiscal policies.

David R. Cameron, 'The Expansion of the Public Economy: A Comparative Analysis', *American Political Science Review*, 72 (1978). Greater public expenditure under social democratic governments.

Francis G. Castles and Robert D. Mackinlay, 'Does Politics Matter? An Analysis of the Public Welfare Commitment in Advanced Democratic States', *European Journal of Political Research*, 7 (1979). Greater welfare expenditure under social democracy.

Redistributive Effects of Social Democracy 253

John D. Stephens, *The Transition from Capitalism to Socialism* (London, Macmillan, 1979). Less income concentration under social democratic governments due to more redistributive taxation and greater public expenditure on welfare, education, and health care.

Robert W. Jackman, 'Socialist Parties and Income Inequality in Western Industrial Societies', *Journal of Politics*, 42 (1980). No relation between the parliamentary strength of social democratic parties and egalitarian income distribution.

Sten G. Borg and Francis G. Castles, 'The Influence of the Political Right on Public Income Maintenance Expenditures and Equality', *Political Studies*, 29 (1981). Less income equality under conservative governments.

Francis G. Castles, 'The Impact of Parties on Public Expenditure', in Francis G. Castles (ed.), *The Impact of Parties* (London, Sage, 1982). Greater public expenditure on welfare under social democratic governments.

Manfred Schmidt, 'The Role of the Parties in Shaping Macroeconomic Policy', in Francis G. Castles (ed.), *The Impact of Parties* (London, Sage, 1982). Differences in employment are due more to the neo-corporatist formula rather than social democratic governments.

Corina Van Arnhem and Geurt J. Schotsman, 'Do Parties Affect the Distribution of Income?', in Francis G. Castles (ed.), *The Impact of Parties* (London, Sage, 1982). Income distribution is more equitable under social democratic governments.

Alexander Hicks and Duane Swank, 'Governmental Redistribution in Capitalist Democracies', *Political Studies Journal*, 13 (1984). Social democratic governments are associated with a reduction in income inequalities and higher welfare expenditure.

Alexander Hicks and Duane Swank, 'On the Political Economy of Welfare Expansion', *Comparative Political Studies*, 17 (1984). Reduction of income inequality and greater welfare expenditure under social democratic governments.

Robert W. Jackman, 'The Politics of Economic Growth in the Industrial Democracies, 1974–1980: Leftist Strength or North Sea Oil?', *Journal of Politics*, 49 (1987). Ideological differences between governments are not reflected in their performance.

Alexander Hicks, 'Social Democratic Corporatism and Economic Growth', *Journal of Politics*, 50 (1988). Income distribution is more equal under social democratic governments.

Alexander Hicks, Duane Swank, and Martin Ambuhl, 'Welfare Expansion Revisited: Policy Routines and their Mediation by Party, Class, and Crisis, 1957–1982', *European Journal of Political Research*, 17 (1989). Greater welfare expenditure under social democratic governments.

Geoffrey Garrett and Peter Lange, 'Political Responses to Interdependence: What's "Left" for the Left?', *International Organization*, 45 (1991). Social democracy generates greater public and welfare expenditure.

Karl Ove Moene and Michael Wallerstein, 'What's Wrong with Social Democracy?' (Unpublished manuscript, University of California, Berkeley,

1991). Social democratic governments are associated with the reduction of poverty, greater health care expenditure, and greater income redistribution.

Jeong-Hwa Lee and Adam Przeworski, 'Cui bono? Una stima del benessere nei sistemi corporativisti e in quelli di mercato', *Stato e Mercato*, 3 (1992). Lower incomes and higher taxation under social democratic governments, but a higher social wage and less unemployment.

Geoffrey Garrett, 'Economic Internationalization and Economic Policy in the Advanced Industrial Democracies' (unpublished manuscript, University of Stanford, n.d.). Greater social expenditure, both in transfers and services, under social democratic governments.

....

Appendix 4

....

The Economic Record of Social Democracy and Neo-corporatism: A Chronology of Comparative Quantitative Studies

Douglas A. Hibbs, 'Political Parties and Macroeconomic Policy', *American Political Science Review*, 71 (1977). Better trade-offs between inflation and employment under social democratic governments.

Manfred G. Schmidt, 'Does Corporatism Matter? Economic Crisis, Politics, and Rates of Unemployment in Capitalist Democracies in the 1970s', in Gerhard Lehmbruch and Philippe C. Schmitter (eds.), *Patterns of Corporatist Policy Making* (London, Sage, 1982). Better performance in terms of employment under neo-corporatist arrangements.

David R. Cameron, 'Social Democracy, Corporatism, Labor Quiescence and the Representation of Economic Interests in Advanced Capitalist Society', in John H. Goldthorpe (ed.), *Order and Conflict in Contemporary Capitalism* (Oxford, Oxford University Press, 1984). Wage restraint has positive effects on inflation and employment under social democratic governments.

Peter Lange and Geoffrey Garrett, 'The Politics of Growth: Strategic Interaction and Economic Performance in the Advanced Industrial Democracies, 1974–1980', *Journal of Politics*, 47 (1985). Greater growth under social democratic governments.

John MacCallum, 'Unemployment in OECD Countries in the 1980s', *Economic Journal*, 96 (1986). Better combination of inflation and unemployment.

Walter Korpi, 'Riformare lo stato sociale con eguaglianza', *Democracia e Diritto*, 3 (1986). Greater economic growth under social democratic governments with universalistic welfare systems.

Robert W. Jackman, 'The Politics of Economic Growth in the Industrial Democracies, 1974–1980. Leftist Strength or North Sea Oil?', *Journal of Politics*, 49 (1987). No greater growth under social democratic governments.

Peter Lange and Geoffrey Garrett, 'The Politics of Growth Reconsidered', *Journal of Politics*, 49 (1987). Better performance in terms of growth under social democratic governments.

Andrew Newell and James S. V. Symons, 'Corporatism, Laissez-Faire, and the Rise in Unemployment', *European Economic Review*, 31 (1987).

Neo-corporatist policies reduce unemployment at the expense of salaries.

Alexander Hicks, 'Social Democratic Corporatism and Economic Growth', *Journal of Politics*, 50 (1988). Greater growth with neo-corporatist policies under social democratic governments.

Robert W. Jackman, 'The Politics of Growth, Once Again', *Journal of Politics*, 51 (1989). Governments' ideologies do not affect economic growth rates.

Peter Lange and Geoffrey Garrett, 'Government Partisanship and Economic Performance: When and How does "Who Governs" Matter?', *Journal of Politics*, 51 (1989). Social democratic governments achieve a better transaction between inflation, unemployment, and growth.

Alexander Hicks and William D. Patterson, 'On the Robustness of the Left Corporatist Model of Economic Growth', *Journal of Politics*, 51 (1989). Social democratic governments and strong unions generate greater economic growth.

Adam Przeworski, 'Economic Barriers to Income Inequality under Capitalism: A Review of Some Recent Models' (unpublished manuscript, University of Chicago, 1989). Neo-corporatist policies practised by social democratic governments perform better in terms of inflation, unemployment, and economic growth.

Alexander Hicks, 'The Social Democratic Corporatist Model of Economic Performance in the Short- and Medium-run Perspective', in Thomas Janoski and Alexander Hicks (eds.), *The Comparative Political Economy of the Welfare State* (Cambridge, Cambridge University Press, 1994). The social democratic and corporatist formula fosters development and growth in the short run, less clearly in the long run.

Index

Index   263

Kohli, Atul 203 n.
Kolodko, Grzegorz 107, 112, 120
Kommounistiko Komma Ellados, see
  KKE: Greece
Kopits, George 118 n.
KOR: Poland 214
Korea, South:
  democratization 1, 7–8, 21
  economic policies 16, 20
Kornai, János 62, 64 n., 66 n., 106–7
Korpi, Walter 135, 137 n.
Kovács, Béla 58 n.
Kovács, János Mátyás 60 n.
Kraus, Franz 130 n.
Krugman, Paul 108 n.
Krushchev, Nikita 60
Kupa, Mihaly 111
Kuran, Timur 212 n.
Kuron, Jacek 70
Kwasniewski, Aleksander 104, 128–9

Laba, Roman 212 n.
labour: Southern Europe 46, 47–9
  legislation 173
  see also employment; trade unions;
    unemployment
labour disputes:
  Eastern Europe 121
  Southern Europe 48, 174–7
  Spain 210
Labour Party: Britain 129, 139, 146,
    153, 171
Lagos, Marta 217, 223 n., 226 n., 235 n.
Lamounier, Bolívar 216 n., 217
Lane, David 58 n.
Lange, Oskar 57, 60
Lange, Peter 135, 138, 171 n.
Larre, Bénédicte 75 n., 156 n.
Latin America 18
  democracy 8–9, 216, 217
  economic crises 6, 12, 28
  economic policies 13, 19, 22, 32
  inequalities 239
  see also specific countries
Latvia 122, 211, 214
Layard, Richard 108 n., 170 n.
leaders and leadership, political 36
  and economic performance 167
  symbolic example of 238–9
League of Young Democrats, see
  FIDESZ: Hungary
Lee, Jeong-Hwa 136 n.
legislation, labour: Southern Europe 173
legitimacy: of democracies 200, 202–3,
    204–5, 215–44
legitimation crises 6
Lehmbruch, Gerhard 168–9 n.

Lemke, Christine 139 n.
Lenin 3, 57
Lenski, Gerhard 25 n.
Lepsius, M. Rainer 203 n.
Lewis, Paul G. 213 n.
Liberman, Evsey 60
Limongi, Fernando 8–9, 23, 28
Linz, Juan J. 28, 42 n., 47, 142 n., 144,
    200 n., 203 n., 205 n., 206, 207 n.,
    210 n.
Lipset, Seymour Martin 2, 3 n., 4 n.,
    207 n., 210 n., 237 n.
Lipton, David 105 n.
Lithuania 214
Lockwood, David 48 n.
Logan, John R. 48 n.
Longworth, Philip 67
López Pina, Antonio 142 n., 223 n.
Lukauskas, Arvid 52 n., 87 n.
Luxemburg, Rosa 57
Lyrintzis, Christos 149 n., 198 n.

McDonald, Ian M. 170 n.
McDonough, Peter 142 n., 223 n.
Machin, Howard 153 n., 154 n.
Macleod, Alex 148 n.
Mahathir Bin Mohammed 16
Malefakis, Edward 47 n.
Mali 31
Malzacher, Sylvia 153 n., 175 n.
Maravall, Fernando 52 n.
Maravall, José María 26 n., 35 n., 42 n.,
    48 n., 75 n., 77 n., 107 n., 209 n.,
    210 n., 228 n., 239 n.
market socialism 60
markets 13, 15
  political: competitiveness of 29–30
Marks, Gary 5 n., 139 n.
Marshall, Alfred 134
Marshall, Thomas H. 130 n.
Marshall Plan 43
Martelli, Claudio 150
Martínez, Rosa 98 n., 100, 189 n.
Martínez-Alier, Juan 166 n.
Marx, Karl 48 n.
Masaryk, Tomàs 211
Mavrogordatos, George 209 n.
Maxwell, Kenneth 75 n.
Mazowiecki, Tadeusz 102
Meciar, Vladimir 112
Menés, Jorge R. 95 n., 194 n.
Merkel, Wolfgang 139 n.
Merton, Robert K. 48 n.
Metz Congresses 148
  see also PS: France
Mexico 33
  economic policies 16, 19

Šik, Ota 60
Simon, János 18 n., 120 n., 231 n., 219
Singapore 7
  economic policies 20
Sirowy, Larry 26 n.
Skilling, H. Gordon 213 n.
Skocpol, Theda 207 n.
Slovakia 104, 117
Slovenia 122, 207
Smallholders' Party, *see* FKgp:
  Hungary
SMIG: France 153, 186
Smith, David H. 239 n.
Soares, Mario 80, 147–8, 151, 178–9
social democracy:
  comparative quantitative studies
    252–6
  convergence of economic policies
    152–68
  neo-corporatism 36, 168–77
  party programmes 146–52
  social policies 129–39, 177–97
  Southern Europe 126–8, 139–46
  supply-side policies 88
Social Democracy of the Polish Republic,
  see SdRP: Poland
Socialdemokratiet, *see* SD: Denmark
social expenditure:
  and degree of democracy 24–8
  social democracy 189–90
  Southern Europe 179–80
social policies:
  and democratization 5–6, 141–2,
    231–4
  Eastern Europe 67–70, 107–8, 120–3,
    125
  social democracy 129–39, 177–97
  Southern Europe 47, 54–6, 98–101,
    124, 177–97
SOFRES 183 n., 194 n., 196
Solchaga, Carlos 93 n.
Solidarność 63, 64, 102, 212, 214
Solimano, Andrés 86 n.
Solow, Robert 170 n.
Somalia 31
Soviet Union 1, 144
  democratic values 213
  dictatorship 73
  economic policies 16, 21, 33
  equality 69–70
  influence of 40, 102
  political reforms 20
  poverty 68
Sozialdemokratische Partei
  Deutschlands, *see* SPD: Germany
Sozialdemokratiska Arbetartpartiet, *see*
  SAP: Sweden

Spain:
  attitudes to democracy 216, 217,
    218–21, 221–7, 230
  attitudes to politics 234, 235, 239, 240
  civil societies 206
  democratic values 209–10
  democratization 1, 7, 17, 21, 74–101
  economic crises 13, 32, 33
  economic effects of dictatorship 40–57
  economy 20, 38, 39, 41
  elections 201
  equality 233–4
  political parties 241–2
  public expenditure 135
  see also PSOE; social democracy
SPD: Germany 129, 139
Spourdalakis, Michalis 155 n., 175 n.
Sprague, John 137 n.
Sri Lanka 20
Stalinism: end of 60
Stallings, Barbara 19, 113
Stark, David 119 n., 212 n.
state, role of 119–20, 125, 207
state ownership: Eastern Europe 57
Stepan, Alfred 75–7 n., 203 n., 207 n.
Stephens, Evelyne H. 7 n.
Stephens, John D. 7 n., 131, 132 n.,
    133 n.
Stiglitz, Joseph E. 170 n.
Stoleroff, Alan 172 n.
Streit, Manfred E. 170 n.
strength: political regimes 16–19, 123–4
  and democratic capacity 33–4
strikes, *see* labour disputes
Strimska, Zdenek 69 n.
Strougal, Lumobir 71
studies:
  economic efficiency of regimes 249–51
  economic record of social democracy
    and neo-corporatism 255–6
  impact of economies on regimes
    245–8
  redistributive consequences of social
    democracy 252–4
Suárez, Adolfo 79, 80, 84
Suchocka, Hanna 114
Sudan 31
Sudrià, Carles 41 n., 45 n., 84 n.
Summers, Lawrence 108 n., 117 n., 170 n.
Sunkel, Oswaldo 86 n.
supply-side politics
  social democracy 138
  Spain 88
Swank, Duane H. 132 n., 133 n.
Sweden 69
  public expenditure 130
  social democracy 133, 167

DATE DUE

GAYLORD			PRINTED IN U.S.A